DIGGING FOR GOLD IN YOUR OWN BACKYARD

THE COMPLETE HOMEOWNERS GUIDE TO LOWERING YOUR REAL ESTATE TAXES

By Gary Whalen

R.E.I. PRESS

Published by:

R.E.I. PRESS
36 S. Washington
Hinsdale, Il. 60521

This publication is designed to provide accurate and authoritative information, regarding the subject matter covered. This book is sold with the understanding the publisher and author aren't engaged in rendering legal, accounting or other professional advice. If legal aid or other professional assistance is required, the services of a competent person should be sought.

Every effort has been made to make this book as thorough and as accurate as possible. However, there may be mistakes both typographical and in content. Real estate tax laws and procedures are constantly changing. We strongly recommemd you use this book as a reference guide. Verify any changes with your local government authorities. Furthermore, this book contains current information only up to the printing date.

Copyright © 1990 by Gary Whalen
First printing 1991
Printed in the United States of America

Library of Congress Cataloging in Publication Data
CIP 90-091764
ISBN 0-962682-90-X

Dedication

To my wife Lynn, my children Sean, Katie and Alison, my father Charles and to the rest of my family for their love, support and encouragement.

ACKNOWLEDGEMENT

I would like to thank all the people who contributed in the production of this book. To Robert "Les" Arling for his valuable assessment information and consultation throughout this book. To John S. Rieve of Vertex, Inc. To Dr. Andrew Linick for his valuable marketing consultation. To Dan Poynter, author of *The Self-Publishing Manual.* To Jan Fox, Mary Anthony, Debra Biela and Tammy Albanos for their assistance in the production of this book. To the many employees of each state that assisted me in the research of this book.

Set in "News Serif Type" by Lane Place Associates, Downers Grove, IL.

Cover by Greg Johannes.

Table of Contents

PART I
HOW TO LOWER YOUR REAL ESTATE TAXES

PART II
STATE BY STATE SUMMARY

PART I

HOW TO
LOWER YOUR
REAL ESTATE TAXES

INTRODUCTION

You don't need a book to tell you real estate taxes are up. If you're like most homeowners, you have seen property taxes escalate to the point where they now constitute a major part of household expenses. But what can you, an average homeowner, do? There are over 80,000 taxing jurisdictions in the United States, collecting over $90 billion annually in property taxes.

There are also 51 sets of laws -- one for each state, plus the District of Columbia. These 51 areas are subdivided into more than 13,000 separate property tax districts, but the tax laws aren't applied uniformly from one district to another. At this point, you begin to see what a headache it can be to sort them all out.

Prudent management of your finances means keeping household costs down and that includes your real estate taxes. This book is designed to help you cut through thousands of tax laws to pinpoint those that not only pertain to *your* property, but can be applied to your advantage.

You should believe in paying your fair share of taxes, but there's no reason you should pay more.

If your property taxes are higher than you think they should be, it may be because the assessment is too high or the tax rates are too high. In this book we are going to concentrate on lowering the assessment. Why? For one reason, this approach will be easier for the average homeowner who's not familiar with tax laws. For another, it produces quicker results.

As a real estate tax consultant, I see instances every day where homeowners could lower the assessments of their residences, if they knew how to do so. Like most other consultants, I charge a fee based on how much tax I reduce (typically, that would amount to one half of the first year's tax savings). An attorney, if he specialized in tax reduction, could represent you also. This book is written for those of you who won't mind putting some of your own time into determining if you're overassessed, and take action on your behalf. By doing the legwork and follow through yourself, you won't have to pay a professional any fee. What savings you realize will most likely repeat every year you remain in that home.

The principles of assessment reduction are the same whether we're talking about a $50,000 house or a $500,000 house. The most likely way you're going to reduce your assessment is through finding errors, claiming exemptions, showing inequity and overassessments. In my investigations, for example, I found one property owner was paying tax on more land than he actually owned. Another had not claimed a four-year exemption for $30,000 worth of improvements on his property. In another instance, I proved that one homeowner's property had been assessed higher than comparable properties (his neighbors'), and so lowered his taxes approximately $1,000 a year.

It has been reported in Cook County, Illinois, over 50 percent of the homeowners who appeal are successful -- with an average tax savings between $300 and $400. Yet fewer than one percent of all homeowners appeal their assessments. And those who were not successful, I would say most were merely complaining, without showing evidence they were overassessed.

Below is a checklist of what this book will help you do:

- Look up your property identification number.
- Understand your equalization rate and tax rate.
- Know your assessment.
- Understand how your property is assessed.
- Find out if your assessment is legal.
- Detect errors in assessment.
- Know your entitled exemptions.
- Know your property's market value.
- Find how your assessment compares to your neighbor's.
- Gather evidence to show you are overassessed.
- Learn how to work with the assessor's office.
- Know when to file an appeal.
- Know how to file an appeal.
- Know how to be successful.

HOW ARE YOU GOING TO TELL IF YOUR ASSESSMENT SHOULD BE CHALLENGED?

There are five general areas of possible problems. You will want to find answers to the following questions. This book will show you the way.

1. ARE THERE ERRORS IN MY ASSESSMENT?

This is the most obvious and easily detectable example of an over assessment. The assessor's office may have made errors describing the building size, construction and amenities -- among other items. They may have used the wrong cost figures from the assessment manual or made simple arithmetic mistakes. Even the most efficient assessors make errors of this type because of the volume of properties and lack of time.

It commonly happens, in the listing of land parcels, that size and location are misstated. Usually, those responsible for describing the boundaries of a parcel of land are mapping officials, not tax officials. The assessor will accept the legal description given by the mapping offices and calculate land value accordingly.

2. IS THE ASSESSMENT LEGAL?

In most states, there are properties that enjoy partial or full tax-exempt status. One example would be housing for disabled veterans. And in many jurisdictions, there are properties that are granted a minimal "special use" valuation. Recreational properties often qualify for special treatment. A special section in the state statutes is devoted to a listing of tax-exempt properties; be aware of them. Check your state's exemptions at the back of this book and double-check with your state or local assessor's office.

3. IS MY PROPERTY VALUED HIGHER THAN MARKET VALUE?

In most any jurisdiction, the best evidence of value is the recent sale of that property, provided the sale is an arm's-length transaction (explained in chapter four) that can be verified by a recorded sales declaration. If you have evidence of such a transaction, it's almost irrefutable. Or you might find evidence by comparing recent sales with their published assessments.

4. IS MY ASSESSMENT EQUITABLE WITH THAT OF COMPARABLE PROPERTIES?

To test equity, look at properties you consider comparable, based on your knowledge of the area. But compare apples to apples; if yours is a two-story house, use two-story houses for comparison, and so forth.

Presentation of this type of evidence at a higher appeal level can be embarrassing to the assessor. Assessments should be figured in a uniform fashion, regardless of their relationship to market value, and assessors are concerned about discrimination charges. The two-story house in our example may be worth twice the indicated assessment value. That's not the issue. Your contention is that it may not have been assessed fairly relative to comparable properties.

5. DID THE ASSESSOR USE PRESCRIBED GUIDELINES?

Know the guidelines. In this book you'll learn how to obtain, review and understand the assessment manual. You will also learn what questions to ask assessment officials. In many instances, *each* local assessor's office will use its own unique guidelines for valuing property. Determine the state appeal board guidelines for assessing property. The state method may differ from the local method -- to your benefit. You should know this.

WHY SO FEW APPEALS?

If you were to ask how many appeals were filed relative to total number of parcels in your district, you would be surprised to learn that it is a small percentage. Most homeowners aren't aware they can do something about their assessments. Or, even though they know there's an appeal process, many homeowners feel it won't do any good.

Since the burden is on the homeowner to show/prove overassessment, some are often discouraged before they begin for fear they won't be successful. Another misconception homeowners have is that an appeal may get the assessor angry for "rocking the boat" -- with a subsequent increase in assessment.

If you do the research specified in this book, that won't happen. Studies show, on the average, the homeowner wins half the time, and many who weren't successful did not properly present evidence. . .or weren't overassessed. Obviously, if after doing the research you find there are errors in your favor, or you're underassessed compared to your neighbor, you need not challenge your assessment.

I hope, after reading this book, you will see that you can -- successfully!

CHAPTER 1

UNDERSTANDING YOUR TAX BILL

HOW YOUR TAX BILL IS DETERMINED

Before you can challenge your property tax, you need to know how it was determined. Let's use Illinois as an example.

In Illinois, each township or county assessor lists all taxable property in his district -- adding listings as new properties are built, changing listings as properties change through additions or demolition. At the beginning of the assessment year, he assesses all such properties, issuing assessment valuations in a complete tax roll. This roll, usually tentative, is published or posted for public announcement and review. After the announcement, a grievance period goes into effect. At that time, taxpayers can formally complain by asking for changes or reductions to assessments before the roll becomes final.

Your own area should have a similar grievance or appeal period. You can learn the dates, as well as media for public notice, from your assessor. That information is also included in the state-by-state summary at the book's end. Changes, corrections, additions and deletions to property assessments are made only once each year -- when the tax roll is established. This is why you must file your appeal before the grievance period ends. After the grievance period the roll becomes final, the tax rate is set, and your tax bill is sent out.

HOW THE TAX RATE INFLUENCES YOUR TAX BILL

How is the tax rate calculated? Each district determines how much it will need to operate during the next tax period. This amount is divided into the total amount of assessment for the district. For example:

$10,000,000.00	the one year operating budget for the tax district divided into...
$100,000,000.00	worth of total assessment in the district gives you a tax rate of...
10.0000	which may be carried to fourth decimal point and then multiplied per $100.00 of assessed value...

In this case, a home assessed at $50,000.00 times a tax rate of 10.0000 per $100.00 assessed ($50,000 divided by $100 equals $500 X 10.0000), will be taxed $5,000.00.

This tax rate will be used uniformly on every parcel assessment in the district. The assessment is often broken into two parts -- one for land, and the other for improvements (usually the building). Together, these comprise the total assessment.

FACTORS AFFECTING ASSESSMENT

Your assessment is based on what's called the *fair cash value* or *market value* for your property, and it is either 100 percent or some fraction of the fair cash value. In Illinois, for example, (excepting Cook County) the assessment rate is 33.33 percent of fair cash value. Your state's current assessment rate is listed in the state-by-state summary at the back of this book. The fair cash value or market value, as determined by the assessor, is his opinion of what your property's worth. This is the assessor's idea of the highest price the property would bring in a normal sales transaction between a willing seller and buyer. As you might imagine, this is a very broad and subjective definition.

The assessor usually bases his determination on the most current sales information, but some states base it on cost data provided by the state manual.

(Check your state summary to see how your state determines market value.). The market value and/or the assessment is going to be the basis for most appeals. We will go into greater detail in later chapters.

The assessment is further adjusted by equalization factors determined either locally or by the state. If properties in the district as a whole were assessed at a level lower than is mandated by the state, the assessment will usually be multiplied by a factor greater than 1.00. If properties were assessed higher than mandated, assessments will be multiplied by a factor less than 1.00.

After the assessment is adjusted by equalization, exemptions are subtracted, resulting in a *net equalized assessment*. This amount is multiplied by the tax rate to give you your total tax. In some states, the exemptions are taken off after the bill has been determined. Taxes are paid in one or more installments.

An equalization factor may be imposed at the local level. If so, notice of equalization is sent to the property owner (figure 1-1), and the resulting assessment can be appealed -- particularly when a factor greater than 1.00 is used.

BE AWARE OF THESE POINTS OF YOUR TAX BILL

The most important point to be aware is the property identification number for your property. If it isn't correct, you may be paying someone else's taxes! You can check by looking at your closing papers from when you bought your house or by looking it up in the assessor's book.

If you're in a state or county that has multiple classifications for properties, look for your classification code. Make sure: (a) it applies to your property and (b) the correct factor is used on your assessment. This is a common mistake that can be easily corrected to save you money.

Exemptions are another way to save money. Yet many people do not take advantage of them. In the tax bill example (figure 1-2), only two are listed -- the residential and the seniors' exemptions. Yet in Illinois alone, there are many more that can be used but aren't shown on the bill. For example:

- Home improvement
- Disabled veterans' specially-adapted housing
- Assessment freeze for historic residences
- Solar energy systems
- Senior citizen tax deferral
- "Circuit breaker" senior citizens' and disabled persons' tax relief

DATE 01/21/88   PARCEL NUMBER 09-37-200-001

NOTICE TO TAXPAYER
CHANGE OF REAL ESTATE ASSESSMENT
****

SUPERVISOR OF ASSESSMENTS ASSESSMENT EQUALIZATION NOTICE ACCORDING TO SECTIONS 95A AND 103 OF THE REVENUE ACT OF 1939 AS AMENDED.
****

09-37-200-001
TAXPAYER, JOHN & MARY   PARCEL NUMBER
411 ELM ST.   09-37-2500-001
GROVE, ILL. 60001

	1986 BOARD OF REVIEW AS EQUALIZED	1987 BY TOWNSHIP ASSESSOR	1987 BY SUPERVISOR OF ASSESSMENTS
LAND	7,130	5,580	7,060
BUILDING	23,910	18,720	23,700
PRO RATE	0	0	0
TOTAL	31,040	24,300	30,760

THE 1987 ASSESSED VALUATION, (TAXES PAYABLE IN 1988), OF THIS PARCEL 09-32-200-001 HAS BEEN CHANGED DUE TO: ERROR IN EQUALIZATION.

STATUTES REQUIRE THAT ASSESSMENT OF REAL PROPERTY, OTHER THAN FARMLAND, BE PLACED AT 33.33 PERCENT OF MARKET VALUE. THE SUPERVISOR OF ASSESSMENTS OFFICE HAS PLACED AN EQUAL-IZATION FACTOR OF 1.26582 ON ALL RESIDENTIAL CLASS, IMPROVED PROPERTIES, LAND AND BUILDING, IN DOWNERS GROVE TOWNSHIP IN ORDER TO PLACE ALL ASSESSMENTS AT THE STATUTORY 33.33 PERCENT OF FAIR MARKET VALUE.

THE MEDIAN LEVEL OF ASSESSMENT IN DOWNERS GROVE TOWNSHIP AS DETERMINED BY THE MOST RECENT SINGLE YEAR ASSESSMENT TO SALES RATIO STUDY, AS ADJUSTED FOR 1987 ASSESSMENT YEAR CHANGES IS 33.33 PERCENT (ESTIMATED).

YOUR PROPERTY IS TO BE ASSESSED AT THE MEDIAN LEVEL OF ASSESSMENT FOR YOUR ASSESSMENT DISTRICT. YOU MAY CHECK THE ACCURACY OF YOUR ASSESSMENT BY THE FOLLOWING PROCEDURE: DIVIDE YOUR ASSESSMENT BY THE MEDIAN LEVEL OF ASSESSMENT FOR YOUR ASSESSMENT DISTRICT. IF THE RESULTING VALUE IS GREATER THAN THE ESTIMATED FAIR CASH VALUE OF YOUR PROPERTY, YOU MAY BE OVER-ASSESSED. IF THE RESULTING VALUE IS LESS THAN THE ESTIMATED VALUE OF YOUR PROPERTY, YOU MAY BE UNDER-ASSESSED. YOU MAY APPEAL YOUR ASSESSMENT TO THE BOARD OF REVIEW IN THE MANNER DESCRIBED ELSEWHERE IN THIS NOTICE.

THE EQUALIZED ASSESSMENT IS SUBJECT TO THE TAX RATE WHICH IS DETERMINED BY THE AMOUNT OF THE LEVIES SUBMITTED BY THE SCHOOLS AND VARIOUS UNITS OF LOCAL GOVERNMENT PROVIDING SERVICES TO YOUR PROPERTY.

ASSESSMENTS VALUATION COMPLAINTS MAY BE FILED WITH THE DU PAGE COUNTY BOARD OF REVIEW FROM NOW UNTIL 30 DAYS AFTER PUBLICATION OF THE EQUALIZATION FACTOR IN THE FOLLOWING NEWSPAPERS: DOWNERS GROVE REPORTER, HINSDALE DOINGS, AND DU PAGE PROGRESS.

IF YOU HAVE ANY QUESTIONS REGARDING THIS ASSESSMENT OR NOTICE PLEASE CONTACT ME AT THE ADDRESS LISTED BELOW.

SUPERVISOR OF ASSESSMENTS
421 NORTH COUNTY FARM ROAD
WHEATON, ILLINOIS 60187

Figure 1-1

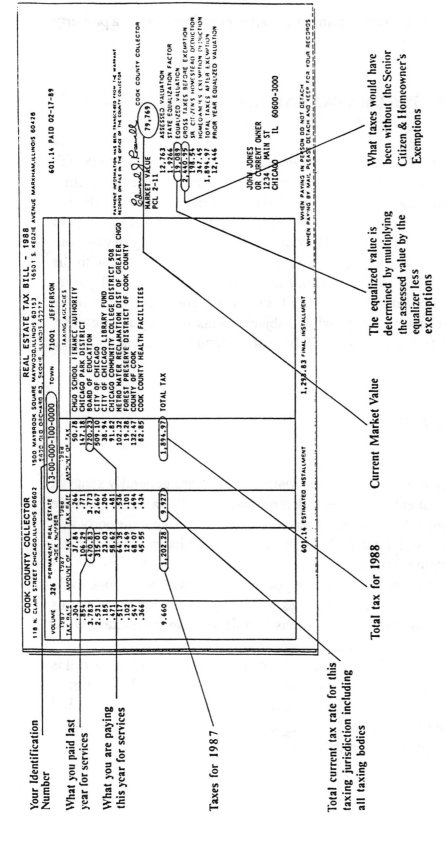

1988 Real Estate Tax Bill

Figure 1-2

Cook County Assessor's Office Graphic

Included in each state-by-state summary are all exemptions you, as a property owner, can claim in your state.

PAY YOUR TAX BILL: WHO, WHERE AND WHEN

Most homeowners who have a mortgage don't actually pay their tax bill. Rather, the mortgagee (lender) pays the bill when due from the tax escrow account.

The person, department or office to which the bill is payable is typically not responsible for determining your assessment. Their responsibility is to send your property tax bill and receive payment. They cash your check when you pay your taxes. They also impose a penalty when you don't. If you don't agree with the assessment, do not complain to the collector or withhold payment until you're satisfied. Unless it's allowed in your state, it will do no good and you will be penalized with interest charges...and possibly subject to a tax sale of your property. Pay your bill in a timely fashion and you will be sent a refund if there was a mistake or oversight.

TIMING IS EVERYTHING

Pay attention to notices you get in the mail! Tax bills are generally sent out the year after the assessments have been determined. As the tax bill example (figure 1-2) shows for the tax year 1988, the assessor determined that property was worth a certain amount as of January 1, 1988. Some states have different basis dates (check state-by-state summary).

Unfortunately, by the time you receive your tax bill it will be too late to do anything about that assessment. In some states, you can pay under protest but this seldom results in a reduction. However, you may be able to claim some exemptions and this can help significantly. Check your state requirements.

The time to challenge your assessment if you disagree is when the tax roll is announced and you receive your assessment notice (figure 1-3). Many times, homeowners disregard this notice and are shocked when they receive their tax bill the following year. The time to appeal has long expired, and they will have to wait for the next notice and appeal period to arrive.

DATE 12/16/87   PARCEL NUMBER 09-37-200-001

NOTICE TO TAXPAYER
CHANGE OF REAL ESTATE ASSESSMENT
****

THE 1987 ASSESSED VALUATION (TAXES PAYABLE IN 1988) OF THE PARCEL DESCRIBED AS
09-37-200-001 HAS BEEN CHANGED DUE TO QUADRENNIAL REASSESSMENT.

09-37-200-001
TAXPAYER, JOHN & MARY
411 ELM ST.
GROVE, ILL. 60001

	1986 BOARD OF REVIEW EQUALIZED VALUE	31,040
	1987 ASSESSED VALUE	24,300

THE MEDIAN LEVEL OF ASSESSMENT IN DOWNERS GROVE TOWNSHIP AS DETERMINED BY THE
MOST RECENT SINGLE YEAR ASSESSMENT TO SALES RATIO STUDY, AS ADJUSTED FOR 1987 ASSESS-
MENT YEAR CHANGES IS 33.33 PERCENT (ESTIMATED).

YOUR PROPERTY IS TO BE ASSESSED AT THE MEDIAN LEVEL OF ASSESSMENT FOR YOUR ASSESS-
MENT DISTRICT. YOU MAY CHECK THE ACCURACY OF YOUR ASSESSMENT BY THE FOLLOWING
PROCEDURE: DIVIDE YOUR ASSESSMENT BY THE MEDIAN LEVEL OF ASSESSMENT FOR YOU ASSESS-
MENT DISTRICT. IF THE RESULTING VALUE IS GREATER THAN THE ESTIMATED FAIR CASH VALUE
OF YOUR PROPERTY, YOU MAY BE OVER ASSESSED. IF THE RESULTING VALUE IS LESS THAN THE
ESTIMATED VALUE OF YOUR PROPERTY, YOU MAY BE UNDER-ASSESSED. YOU MAY APPEAL YOUR
ASSESSMENT TO THE BOARD OF REVIEW IN THE MANNER DESCRIBED ELSEWHERE IN THIS NOTICE.

STATUTES REQUIRE THAT ASSESSMENT OF REAL PROPERTY, OTHER THAN FARMLAND, BE PLACED
AT 33.33 PERCENT OF MARKET VALUE. ASSESSMENTS NOT AT THAT LEVEL WILL BE SUBJECT TO
BOARD OF REVIEW EQUALIZATION AS WELL AS EQUALIZATION BY THE STATE OF ILLINOIS.

THE EQUALIZED ASSESSMENT IS SUBJECT TO THE TAX RATE WHICH IS DETERMINED BY THE
AMOUNT OF THE LEVIES SUBMITTED BY THE SCHOOLS AND VARIOUS UNITS OF LOCAL GOVERN-
MENT PROVIDING SERVICES TO YOUR PROPERTY.

ASSESSMENT VALUATION COMPLAINTS MAY BE FILED WITH THE DU PAGE COUNTY BOARD OF
REVIEW FROM NOW UNTIL 30 THIRTY DAYS AFTER PUBLICATION OF THE ASSESSMENT LIST OF
YOUR AREA IN THE FOLLOWING NEWSPAPER.
DOWNERS GROVE REPORTER $.50 PER COPY AT NEWSSTAND $5.00 PER COPY BY MAIL.

IF YOU HAVE ANY QUESTIONS REGARDING THIS ASSESSMENT OR NOTICE PLEASE CONTACT ME AT
THE ADDRESS LISTED BELOW.

DOWNERS GROVE TOWNSHIP ASSESSOR
4340 PRINCE STREET
DOWNERS GROVE, ILLINOIS 60515

PTAB 228 REV 9/84
REV 9/84 SA

Figure 1-3

CLASSIFICATION OF REAL ESTATE FOR ASSESSMENT PURPOSES

Modern assessment technique requires a breakdown and classification of real estate which conforms generally to zoning or use classifications. Property may be classified as follows:

❑ *Residential Property*

Single-family
Duplex
Triplex
Multi-family
Mobile home park
Recreational

❑ *Commercial Properties*

Retail
Wholesale
Shopping center
Office building
Parking lot

❑ *Industrial Properties*

Light
Medium
Heavy
Warehouse
Industrial park

❑ *Agricultural and Rural Properties*

❑ *Recreational Properties*

❑ *Institutional or Exempt properties*

❑ *Public Properties*

❏ *Public Utility Properties*

❏ *Unimproved Properties*

❏ *Miscellaneous Properties*
(mines, pipelines, etc.)

Structures are generally classified not only as to use, but as to type and quality of construction. Further classification of the structures is part of the administration of the assessor's office.

Nonconforming and nontaxable properties are also classified separately. *Nonconforming properties* are those located on land restricted by zoning to a lesser use, such as a service station on land zoned for residences. The land is generally valued according to the benefit derived from the property, regardless of zoning. *Nontaxable property* is appraised the same as taxable property, but entered on the assessor's records as nontaxable.

Your tax bill will probably have codes that relate to the classification the assessor has assigned to you. Make sure the classification is correct since in most states this will affect your assessment and corresponding tax bill.

CHAPTER 2

HOW TO TELL IF YOUR ASSESSMENT SHOULD BE CHALLENGED

TAX ASSESSMENT: IS IT FAIR?

The assessment method described in the previous chapter is commonly known as *ad valorem*, meaning "according to value." Ad valorem tax appraisal or assessment, when made on a mass basis, is highly prone to error. And the more errors you can catch, the better position you'll be in to challenge your assessment.

Ad valorem tax appraisal is usually made at market value or a percentage of market value on every parcel of real estate -- including all parcels within a city, county or other tax district in a state. It's the basis for levying the ad valorem real estate or property tax. It's also the basis for evaluating all real estate within a tax district for municipal bonding purposes.

Used in taxation, the term "value" has many definitions and varies considerably in laws of different states (refer to Valuation Standards in the state-by-state summary). Such terms as *market value*, *fair market value*, *fair cash value* and *sales value* are common. Since market value or a percentage of market value is the basis for assessments, you'd expect to see a reasonable consistency in the definition of market value. Indeed, the International Association of Assessing Officers offers the following definition:

"Market value may be defined as the highest price estimated in terms of money which a property will bring if exposed for sale in the open market allowing a reasonable time to find a purchaser who buys with knowledge of all the uses to which it's adapted and for which it's capable of being used."

The assessor presumably considers all factors which would be given consideration by able, willing and reasonably well-informed buyers and sellers. Because we have seen a number of contradictory court decisions throughout the nation, assessors are starting to come up with variations of market value definitions to suit their local situation. This is why you must try to learn as much as you can about how market value is defined in *your* locality.

IS COST THE SAME AS VALUE?

Although the willing seller/willing buyer concept generally prevails, the courts are inclined to give less weight to the seller's position in decisions affecting assessments. Many "special use" properties have a value to the owner of approximately their cost, less physical depreciation. That same property would have less value to the average buyer. In a majority of cases concerning the properties assessment, the courts have held that the value to the buyer is the measure for assessment purposes. They clearly disregarded the price at which the owner would become a willing seller and look only at what a willing buyer would pay.

What does this mean to you as a homeowner? If you have a unique home that's not comparable to any home in your area, such as an alternative-style dome house or a 2,000 square foot home with only one bedroom, it may not have much in the way of market value to the general public. The assessment should reflect that lessened demand even though the home's cost is greater.

FREQUENCY OF ASSESSMENT AND HOW IT AFFECTS YOU

Laws and practice differ when it comes to frequency of assessments. Some assessments are reviewed yearly, some never. In some thinly-populated areas, assessments may remain unchanged for a decade or more. Changes in the assessment rolls only reflect transfers in ownership, addition of new buildings and similar changes. In more progressive and densely-populated areas, assessment is an ongoing process. But even under the best administrations, the entire assessment is reviewed only sporadically.

Yet frequency of assessment is just as important as the quality of the work done. Since the assessment becomes the official basis for the ad valorem tax, the most equitable assessments should result from annual review. But an annual review is sometimes impossible.

When the value of real estate is changing rapidly, as during periods of rapid inflation, the longer the period between assessments; the more inequitable the underlying value base becomes when computing annual tax bills. Even without inflationary pressures, real estate values are never static. They're constantly changing, as the underlying economic forces affecting value also change.

Where assessment is infrequent, the assessor's job becomes more difficult since the assessed value remains fixed for a longer period. For example, to accommodate a rapidly increasing population, an area of property assessed as residential lots may, in a comparatively short time be rezoned for business. The land's value can quickly increase to ten, even twenty times its assessed value. Conversely, development may create a competitive situation that causes a quick decline in value of another area. If the assessment is fixed for a long period, inequities are compounded annually by normal economic changes. It's the assessor's legal and moral responsibility to correct these inequities as they occur. But it's impossible for the assessor to do so unless budgetary and statutory provision is made for annual re-assessment.

To be fully effective, the assessor's office should have a fairly large staff of professionals with the expertise needed to conduct an annual re-assessment program. This may not be economically possible in smaller assessment areas.

FUNCTION OF THE ASSESSOR AND HOW IT AFFECTS YOU

The assessor is responsible for the appraisal of all real estate within their jurisdiction.

Specifically, the assessor's function is to appraise each parcel of taxable real estate within his jurisdiction at its market value or a percentage of market value as stipulated by law. If this function is performed, the result will be a reasonably fair ad valorem distribution of the total tax burden.

The assessor's responsibility may range from a small rural community with several hundred parcels of real estate, to a principal metropolitan area with hundreds of thousands of parcels -- from a vacant residential lot or slum tenement, to a skyscraper or complicated modern industrial plant.

In a small community, assessment is usually handled by one part-time assessor who may have comparatively little training. A large metropolitan area; however, requires a top-level administrator who devotes his entire time to ad valorem tax appraisal. He or she is aided by a staff of hundreds of individuals ranging from file clerk to assessor.

Assessors may be required to have a certification and several years of practical experience in real estate appraisal, and they have to pass a comprehensive examination. With the growing use of computers in large urban areas, a knowledge of computer applications is becoming essential for both the administrator and the appraiser.

Along with the ability to understand and apply computer technology to the appraisal of real estate, the assessor must have a working knowledge of title examination, surveying, architecture, cost estimating, accounting, aerial photography, mapping and other related functions. Besides being a top-level administrator and a professional appraiser, the highly qualified assessor must also be well-versed in public relations.

The assessor is an employee of some political division of the local government or the state. His compensation ranges from a small per-diem payment for the part-time rural assessor to a salary appropriate for a top-level city administrator.

THE BASIC TOOL OF THE ASSESSOR

The base for assessing each parcel of property is established by an Assessment or Appraisal Manual. The manual is designed to meet the legal requirements, construction characteristics and economic conditions that prevail in the area. Building cost estimators and research analysts compile data information and study factors such as:

- building codes
- material prices
- trade wage rates
- work policies
- rental income
- depreciation
- vacancies

· land absorption rate

These, and other complex data, are combined by the appraisal staff into tables, charts and methods employed in evaluating of real property assessment.

The manual is more a suggested guideline than hard-and-fast rules although it outlines in detail the procedures to be followed in evaluating each parcel of property. It enables the user to apply equitably the various building costs tables, depreciation charts, depth tables, etc. to each parcel of property.

Ask the local assessor or your state office referred to in the state-by-state summary for a copy of the manual. You can find the exact name under the heading "State-issued Manuals" in the state-by-state summary. Once you have it, it will serve as a valuable tool for helping to look for errors in assessments. You can review the exact procedures and figures used to determine your assessment.

OTHER FACTORS AFFECTING ASSESSMENT

In the real world, you will not find many assessor's offices that live up to the ideal situation described here. Many assessors are in over their heads or otherwise ill-equipped to keep up with the assessment responsibilities. As a result, the assessment process can be replete with error.

For example...

When elected or appointed, the assessor usually inherits property records that haven't been reviewed for years. They may contain countless errors that have gone undetected.

The assessor is often too understaffed to do a thorough job on each parcel's assessment. If the assessor cannot keep up with each sale of property, he will use average annual increases to determine current market value. This contributes to inequity of value -- either too high or too low.

The assessor whose office is understaffed is often forced to use an outside appraisal service, which may not be highly accurate -- or uses averages, rather than individuality.

When an assessor's job is politically motivated, the assessor may show favoritism to individuals or areas of his jurisdiction.

Many assessors who are elected or appointed may not have the proper education or experience to do the job correctly.

You need to be aware when any of these considerations exist, in order to determine the proper course of action to take when researching and contesting your own assessment. The better you understand the circumstances under which your assessment was made, the better position you will be in to affect changes. We will discuss exactly what steps to take in the next chapter.

CHAPTER 3
GOING TO THE ASSESSOR'S OFFICE

WHAT TO EXPECT

When you go to the assessor's office to do research, be prepared for the possibility you may have to do battle to get information. While most assessors and their employees are helpful, you may occasionally encounter resistance. Yes, assessment records are public records. The assessor; however, may take a different view.

Here are a few excuses you may be given as to why records aren't available:

"The property record cards are in the process of being reworked."
"We are short-handed and a year-end report is due."
"The cards are out of the file. Our field staff must have them in the field."
"We are re-doing our file system. Come back in two weeks."

You get the idea.

How do you overcome these objections to access? Be sure to stress you are only compiling research and not looking for mistakes to attack. Be patient, but persistent, if you are asked to come back at a later time; ask for a specific day and time to return. Be sure you express appreciation and be complimentary of their thoroughness, if possible.

You tried all that and it didn't work? You must become forceful -- but not abusive. You can say legal counsel has advised you the information is public record. Or you hope it won't be necessary, but you're prepared to ask a higher authority to make the records available.

If all else fails, contact an attorney or make a formal complaint to the Review Board or appropriate level above the assessor.

RESEARCHING YOUR TAX SYSTEM AND RECORDS

All assessment records are organized according to a properties identification number so you will need to bring your tax bill along when you visit the assessor's office. The staff can help you if you're not sure you're looking for the correct number.

The property record card will be either a card containing your property information or -- if your jurisdiction is computerized -- it may be a computer readout.

The property record card will show how calculations were made when assessing your property. It should include many bits of information including, but not limited to, land and building description, dimensions, amenities and ownership.

After reading this information, you should look at the property record cards for comparable properties, but you'll probably not have their property identification numbers. You may have to ask someone at the assessor's office to cross-reference the property's address for the identification number. If they don't have the means to do that, then look at their map-books for identification numbers. Check (in the state-by-state summary) to see if your state requires your assessor to have map-books. Either way, they should be able to help you find the numbers.

When you have the identification numbers of your comparable's, ask for the property record cards. Copy the information you need from each card or ask the assessor to make copies. Later in this book, I'll detail what information you will be looking for.

An easy method for finding comparable's is to ask if the assessor has cross files for styles of houses (for example, a file of two-story houses or ranch houses for different areas). If not, ask if they file their cards by block, with all properties in a block grouped together. Get the file for your block, along with that for one block higher and one block lower (If your block number is 101, ask for blocks 100,

101, and 102). With these records in hand, you can look through each file for houses that are similar to yours and record pertinent information. You should be able to find many good comparable's this way.

While you are at the assessor's office, ask how they file sales transaction information. If it's available, look to see what properties of similar size and style have been sold recently near your home. When you have those comparable's, request their property record cards and again record the information you need.

QUESTIONS CONCERNING YOUR REAL ESTATE TAX SYSTEM AND ASSESSMENT CYCLES

Each assessor and assessing district has unwritten local customs. Before you approach the assessor with your complaint, gather as much specific information as you can. Use the fourteen questions below to help make your case:

1. What are the filing times for tax appeals in this county? How long is the appeal period held open?

2. What level of appeals are there, such as town or township assessor, county assessor, review board (county), state level?

3. How are assessments determined? Does the assessor base his determination on state-issued Cost Manual, Marshall-Swift Manual, comparable sales of similar properties? Is there some prior base year from which assessments are being calculated?

4. If you were to present evidence and receive a reduction of your assessed valuation, will the official who originated the assessment carry it forward in future years?

5. Is there some type of equalization process (multipliers) between towns (townships) and counties in the state that are applied each year? If so, does this re-open the appeal process for taxpayers?

6. Is an appeal based on inequity of assessments between similar nearby properties considered acceptable evidence?

7. What information is required to get copies of specific property record cards -- property identification number, address, taxpayer's name, etc?

8. How are Real Estate Transfer declarations (recording of sales) filed and where? Are they filed in order by tax numbers, streets, etc? How do I gain access to copies?

9. Are there special valuations in this county for farmland, recreational land, and open space? What special values are assigned?

10. When evidence is submitted at a designated time (assessor, review board or state level hearing), is the taxpayer required to be present?

11. When does vacant land become improved land?

12. If a factual error is found in the assessment, how many years back can recovery be made?

    [FOR COMMERCIAL PROPERTY ONLY]

13. Are there any special requirements for submitting evidence based on an income approach to value? For instance, what is considered an acceptable capitalization rate for commercial and industrial properties?

14. How are personal property items (such as fixtures in restaurants and removable equipment in light-industrial properties) treated? What about appliances transferred with apartment properties?

FINDING ERRORS IN BUILDING DESCRIPTION

When I'm appealing an assessment on a client's behalf, this is where I find most errors on assessment property records. This is also where most of the value is assigned on improved properties. It pays to spend your time carefully in this phase, familiarizing yourself completely with the details pertaining to your property and locating all discrepancies on the assessment building(s) description records. Measure your home to determine total square feet. Remember, always measure the house's exterior to determine square footage. A sample of the house's dimensions is given (figure 3-1).

Most assessors base the initial valuation of properties on the cost approach system. This system involves describing, measuring, classifying and grading building improvements. They multiply the square or cubic feet of the building by a dollar rate amount (taken from a cost manual) to arrive at a replacement cost for the building. This replacement figure is defined as how much it would theoretically cost to reconstruct the building with similar materials. The replacement cost is depreciated for physical age, normal wear and tear, functional items like layout and old facilities and for economic or adverse influences in the area.

This careful mathematical procedure can be sent tumbling on assessment appeal if you can show the building description to be even partly wrong in specification. Such discrepancies can also work to your advantage when comparing the assessments on similar properties, if these errors have caused overvaluation on your property. The following Errors in Building Description and Errors in Land description checklist is a handy tool for your assessment appeal research.

CHECKLIST OF ERRORS IN BUILDING DESCRIPTION:

☐ *Building components wrong.* The assessment card doesn't describe the buildings correctly. For example:

· *Exterior walls*: assessor's card says "brick veneer"; side and rear walls are actually asbestos shingles.

· *Foundation*: property card shows "poured concrete, full basement"; building is actually concrete block, 50 percent basement.

· *Roof*: "slate shingles" on card; asphalt shingles on roof.

· *Floors*: card says "hardwood"; floor is carpet over plywood.

· *Interior finish*: baths shown as "ceramic"; tile in bath is only plastic.

· *Fireplace*: "fireplace" listed; none in house.

· *Electricity*: card says "adequate"; actually inadequate 60 amp.

· *Other*: card shows "enclosed porch"; porch is open.

HOW TO MEASURE YOUR HOME TO DETERMINE SQUARE FOOTAGE

1. Measure your home from the exterior.
2. Draw a diagram like the example below.
3. Divide the building in parts for easier calculating.
4. Multiply sections (such as A) by the number of stories.
5. Do not include garages or unheated areas in total living area.

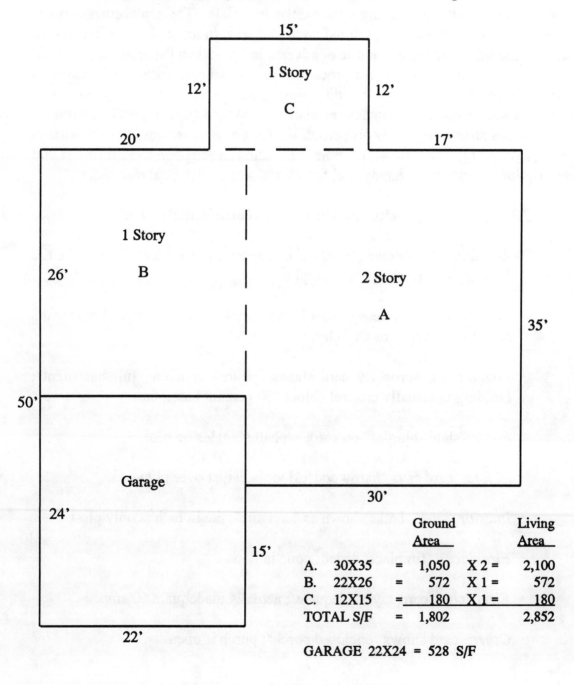

			Ground Area		Living Area
A.	30X35	=	1,050	X 2 =	2,100
B.	22X26	=	572	X 1 =	572
C.	12X15	=	180	X 1 =	180
TOTAL S/F		=	1,802		2,852

GARAGE 22X24 = 528 S/F

Figure 3-1

❏ *Year built is incorrect.* Age of building is wrong.

❏ *Construction grade wrong.* For example, marked "good" when actually less than average because of water in basement and leaking roof.

❏ *Square footage of building wrong.* Marked as a two-story house when it's a one-story with partly-finished below-grade basement (This affects amount of livable square feet).

❏ *Overall description incorrect.* Card identifies building as a three-family type when actually it's a two-family dwelling.

ADDITIONAL BUILDING ERRORS:

❏ Depreciating on-site influences (e.g. flooding basement, inadequate well or septic).

❏ Grade and quality of improvements are wrong.

❏ Important information omitted from record card.

❏ Record out-of-date.

❏ Finished areas wrongly stated.

❏ Personal property, such as appliances, assessed in real estate.

❏ Average maintenance of property used to increase assessments.

❏ Standard Cost Manual improperly used.

❏ Depreciation allowances in error.

❏ Higher than actual construction cost (for new construction).

❏ Radon (see next page).

❏ Asbestos (see next page).

❏ Acid rain damage (see explanation below).

RADON

This is a serious problem that's surfacing in many properties. Radon is radioactive gas produced by uranium decay in soil and rocks. If inhaled, it can cause lung cancer. You should test your property for radon and correct the problem to the recommended level, if possible. Any properties that have been linked to this problem are worth less if left uncorrected and would certainly put someone in line for a sizable reduction in their property taxes.

ASBESTOS

In 1987, John M.L. Gruenstein, a principal economist with Berkeley Planning Association of Berkeley, California, conducted in-depth interviews with real estate professionals, lenders and brokers across the country. He found the effect of asbestos on value is essentially the cost of removal. Less drastic forms of asbestos abatement , such as encapsulation or enclosure combined with an operating and maintenance program, were perceived to be no more than stopgap measures; therefore, unacceptable to many buyers and lenders.

ACID RAIN AND OTHER AIR POLLUTANTS

Acid rain causes more than $2 billion of erosion damage each year to America's buildings.

Air pollutants can be contained in rain, snow, hail, sleet, dew, and frost. This category also includes dry pollutants such as acid soil, sulfur, and nitrogen oxide gases, which contribute to the acid attack on building materials.

- Masonry and stone building exteriors are damaged by chemical reactions, which cause surface erosion, black crust formation, and soiling.

- Brick surfaces are damaged by penetration of the brick itself and by deterioration of the mortar between the bricks.

- Metal surfaces corrode and tarnish. Steel and iron rust; copper and aluminum pit.

• Glass and ceramics are susceptible to surface erosion and surface crust formation.

These flaws lower the building value. Because expensive restoration is involved, they help to reduce the property assessment as well.

ERRORS IN LAND DESCRIPTION

Use the following checklist of errors in land description when you check for overvaluation or improper assessment of your land or property.

ASSESSMENT LAND ERRORS CHECKLIST:

☐ *Wrong property.* Property on the card isn't the correct land.

☐ *Wrong dimensions.* There's more or less road frontage, or more or less total square feet or acreage, than listed.

☐ *Incorrect description.* Property isn't a corner as described, or not level.

☐ *Not in taxing district.* The property is partly or entirely over the boundary line of this taxing district and in another community.

☐ *Wrong classification.* Land is classified as commercial when it's actually zoned residential.

☐ *Outdated description.* Listed and valued as residential even though part or all the building improvements burned down or were demolished long ago.

☐ *Errors in influence.* For example, coded and valued for "view" when the property is level and physically separated from any view by unaesthetic buildings.

☐ *Incomplete data.* The assessor didn't, for example, note the land had deed restrictions when he valued it, even though he received a copy of the deed.

❏ *Calculations wrong.* Front-foot price, depth factors, frontage or any land arithmetic on property card that's in error.

ADDITIONAL LAND ERRORS

❏ Depreciating off-site influences (e.g. trains, industry odors, noise, etc.).

❏ Highest and best use incorrect.

❏ Restrictive covenants not considered.

❏ Easement restrictions not considered.

❏ Zoning restricting property use.

❏ Environmental restrictions.

❏ Poor drainage or wetlands located on property.

❏ Prone to flooding.

❏ Subject to slides or erosion.

❏ Inaccessibility.

❏ Lack of utilities.

❏ See example (figure 3-2 and 3-3).

Check the descriptive comments carefully. They are supposed to be the basis for selecting value figures.

Were building areas figured accurately? In this case, dwelling area should be 1,176 square feet instead of 1,476 square feet, a difference of over 25% because of sloppy math. In the course of your checking, you will also want to measure the dwelling itself.

Also, check these figures. The 20% depreciation allowance was supposedly taken from an official manual for a 1961 dwelling in average condition. It's usually easy to check.

Here again, the math is wrong. $29,270 reflects only 10% depreciation, not 20%.

By now, you can see that this figure is probably about twice as high as it should be.

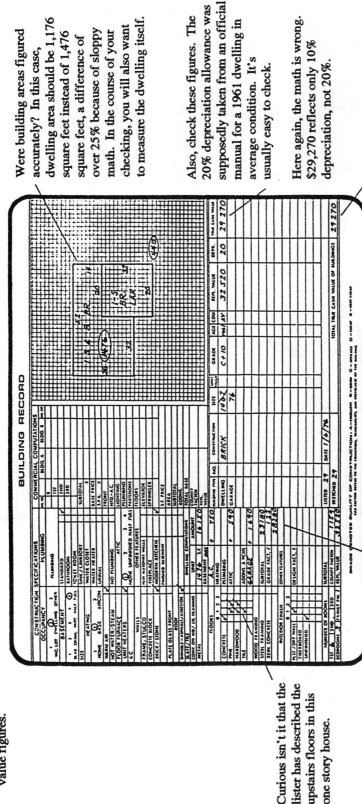

Curious isn't it that the lister has described the upstairs floors in this one story house.

Check these figures very carefully. $590 was added for an attic, but there is no attic. Further, there is a $4,000 error in addition, which is increased by the multiplication. Later, you can check the appropriateness of the cost figures and grade factor and county factors.

Figure 3-2

CHECK THE LAND SIZE. (IS THIS
SITE REALLY 100'X165'?)

The unit value (Here $60 per
front foot for a lot of standard
depth) was supposedly based on
sales of comparable sites.
Later, you may want to check
its fairness.

The depth factor (here 115
percent, presumably because
the site is deeper than ususal)
was supposedly taken from an
official manual. It's usually
easy to check this factor in the
manual.

Was the simple multiplication
done accurately? (In this case,
it was 115% of $60 = $69
and 100 front feet @ $69 =
$6900.)

Was the "true cash value"
converted to assessed value
accurately? (In this jurisdiction,
true cash value is to be divided
by 3, then rounded to nearest
$10. No error here.)

ARE THESE DESCRIPTIVE
ITEMS ACCURATE?

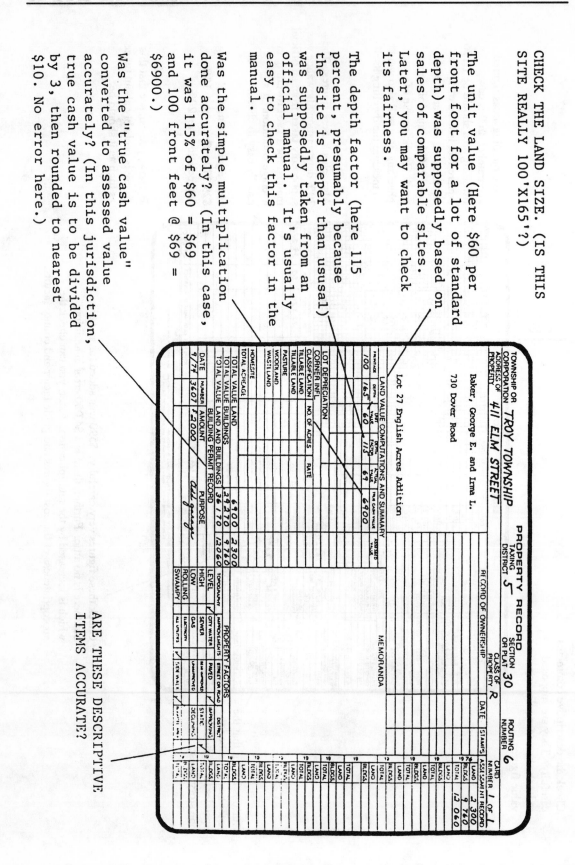

Figure 3-3

CHAPTER 4
METHODS TO REDUCE YOUR ASSESSMENT

MARKET APPROACH

The market data or sales approach is one of three traditional approaches I use to lower assessments. The others, which will be discussed later, are the income approach and the cost approach. The market approach is the most common and useful for single-family residences.

The market data approach is based on market value which I discussed in chapter one. As you may remember, the definition of market value is:

"The highest price in terms of money a property will bring in a competitive and open market under all conditions for a fair sale, the buyer and seller, each acting prudently and knowledgeably, and assuming the price isn't affected by undue stress."

This definition requires both (a) the closing of a sale at a specified date, and (b) the transfer of title from seller to buyer under conditions where:

1. Buyer and seller are typically motivated.

2. Both parties are well-informed or well-advised, and each is acting on what he considers his own best interest.

3. A reasonable time is allowed for exposure in the open market.

4. Payment is made in cash or its equivalent.

5. Financing, if any, is on terms generally available in the community at the specified date and typical for the property type in its locale.

6. The price represents a normal consideration for the property sold, unaffected by special financing amounts and/or terms, services, fees, costs or credits incurred in the transaction.

DETERMINING MARKET VALUE

Determine your house's market value by one of the following:

1. Obtain an appraisal from a certified appraiser. Costs will vary so tell the appraiser why you need the appraisal and ask for the lowest value.

2. Ask for several market analyses from local real estate brokers. While not as detailed and as definitive as an appraisal, they should be adequate for your needs...and are usually free.

3. Go to a real estate office and ask for a printout of recent sales.

4. Some assessor's offices keep a detailed sales record. If yours does, request a copy if possible or review and make notes.

5. There may be data sources in your area, such as title companies and banks, that will give sales comparable's for free or a small charge. REAL ESTATE DATA, INC. is a good source, but does charge for the service.

Keep in mind, however, that none of these approaches are precise. Market valuation isn't an exact science, but rather an opinion of value based on facts.

The best way to show your house's value is if it was recently purchased (within the last two years) in an arm's-length transaction. If your assessment is higher than your purchase price, this alone should be adequate evidence the assessment should be lowered.

Take the case of the taxpayer who owned a one-story residence that included 2,118 square feet of living area, excluding the basement. The taxpayer bought the property for $105,500 the year before it was assessed. The county assessor originally set the property's true value at $124,400 for taxation purposes. Upon request for review by the taxpayer, the board of equalization lowered the amount to $105,500 -- the property's purchase price. The assessor appealed the reduction, citing an earlier appraisal, and he presented eight comparable sales to support submitted written testimony.

The board of tax appeals noted the assessor's original value would only be justified if clear, convincing evidence, justifying such action were offered. The board concluded the purchase price best typified conditions in the community, sustaining a true value of $105,500.

Even Donald Trump challenges his taxes. His estate in Palm Beach may have 58 bedrooms, 38 bathrooms, 3 bomb shelters, a golf course, a theater and a ballroom, but he says there's no way it's worth the $11.5 million at which the county had appraised it. The real estate developer from New York appealed, saying the Mar-a-Largo was worth only the $7 million he paid. He claimed the county was taxing him $208,340 which he felt was $81,524 too much. So you see the procedure is available to *every* taxpayer, no matter what they paid for their property.

STEPS TO DETERMINING MARKET VALUE

If you haven't bought your property within two years or if you haven't had a recent appraisal, you will have to determine your home's market value yourself (Refer to steps 1-5 in the previous section). After you get your sales information, organize it as follows:

1. Get Property record card information for your home.

2. Measure your home from the exterior. Take pictures.

3. Note significant errors.

4. Locate six comparable sales (same style and locale).

LOOKING FOR COMPARABLE SALES

Location (most important)
Style (ranch, split-level, two-story, etc.)
Basement (vs. crawl or slab)
Finished basements
Size (square feet of living area)
Number of bedrooms
Number of baths
Central air conditioning
Fireplaces
Garage capacity (1-, 2- or 3-car) or square footage

Some points to keep in mind...

Location, style and basement should be very similar to your own. A
    dollar adjustment would be difficult to prove.

Overall square footage should be as close to yours as possible.

Number of bedrooms are considered in your final conclusion of value.

Number of baths, finished basements, central air conditioning, fireplaces,
    and garage capacity are important amenities and each has a value in the
    marketplace.

Adjust all comparable's (downward or upward) to yours. Area realtors, local
appraisers or the assessor will have some standard value ranges for adjustments
they use for bank loans or other types of appraisals.

Sometimes a sale may seem high or low compared to similar sales. This can
be checked by looking at the transfer declaration. (Your state may call it something
else.) Here's an example, using an Illinois transfer declaration (figure 4-1).

The SALE INFORMATION box will show if a sale is not arm's length, if
any questions from one through four are answered "no." The FINANCE QUES-
TIONS will influence the true market value. This, in turn, will tell you if it would
be a good sale for comparison purposes. If the real estate purchase included
personal property such as appliances, the value of that personal property is

Illinois Department of Revenue

Property Tax Administration Bureau
REAL ESTATE TRANSFER DECLARATION

THE FOLLOWING INFORMATION IS REQUIRED BY THE **REAL ESTATE TRANSFER TAX ACT** (CHAP. 120, PAR. 1003, IL REV. STAT). PAGES 1 THROUGH 3 ARE TO BE FILLED OUT BY THE SELLERS* AND BUYERS* OR THEIR AGENTS. ANY WILLFUL FALSIFICATION OR WILLFUL OMISSION OF INFORMATION IS A CLASS B MISDEMEANOR (CHAP. 120, PAR. 1005, IL REV. STAT.).

EXCEPT AS TO EXEMPT TRANSACTIONS, THE COUNTY RECORDER IS PROHIBITED BY LAW FROM ACCEPTING ANY DEED OR TRANSFER OF BENEFICIAL INTEREST OF A LAND TRUST (TRUST DOCUMENT) FOR RECORDATION UNLESS IT IS ACCOMPANIED BY THIS DECLARATION CONTAINING ALL OF THE INFORMATION REQUESTED HEREIN (CHAP. 120, PAR. 1003, IL REV. STAT.).

For Use By County Recorder's Office

County

Date

Doc. No.

Vol.

Page

Rec'd. By:

PROPERTY IDENTIFICATION

Address of Property _____
Street / City or Village / Township

Permanent Real Estate Index No. _____ Date of Deed _____ (or Trust Document) (Month/Year)

Enter Legal Description on Page 2 of this form. Type of Deed _____ (or Trust Document)

PROPERTY CHARACTERISTICS

Lot Size _____

Acreage _____
Check type of improvement on property

☐ Vacant land/lot
☐ Residence (Single family or duplex)
☐ Mobile home
☐ Apartment bldg. (6 units or less)
☐ Commercial apartment (Over 6 units)
☐ Store, office, commercial bldg.
☐ Industrial bldg.
☐ Farm, land only
☐ Farm, with bldgs.
☐ Other (Specify) _____

SALE INFORMATION (The following questions must be answered)

NOTE: If the answer to any of the following questions is "Yes", you do not have to complete the Finance Schedule at the top of pages 2 and 3 of this declaration or the Finance Questions at the bottom of this page.

Yes No

1. Is this a transfer between relatives or related corporations? ☐ ☐
2. Is this a compulsory transaction in lieu of foreclosure, divorce, court order, condemnation, probate, etc.? ☐ ☐
3. Was this a transfer in settlement of an installment contract for deed **initiated prior to the CURRENT year**? ☐ ☐
   If "Yes", enter contract year _____
4. Was the deed any of the following types: ☐ ☐

• Sheriff's Deed • Judge's Deed • Quit Claim Deed • Conveyance of Less than full Interest
• Trust Document which Refers to COLLATERAL ASSIGNMENT of Beneficial Interest of Trust

TERMS OF SALE

Full Actual Consideration (Sale Price) .... $ _____
Less amount of personal property included in purchase (Do not deduct value of beneficial interest of a land trust) $ _____
Net consideration for real property .... $ _____
Less value of other real property transferred to seller as part of full consideration .... $ _____
Less outstanding amount of mortgage to which the transferred real property remains subject .. $ _____
Net taxable consideration subject to transfer tax .... $ _____

CALCULATION OF TRANSFER TAX

Amount of State of Illinois tax stamps ($.25 per $500 or part thereof of taxable consideration) . $ _____
Amount of county tax stamps ($_____ per $500 or part thereof of taxable consideration) ..... $ _____
Total Transfer Tax Collected $ _____

Use this space to describe any special circumstances involving this transaction:

FINANCE QUESTIONS: The buyer* and seller* (or their representatives) must answer ALL the following questions *unless one or more of the Sale Information questions above was checked "Yes". If the Sale Information questions are all marked "No" and any of the following questions are answered "Yes", the buyer* or buyer's* representative MUST complete the FINANCE SCHEDULE on pages 2 and 3. If the answer to *all* of the questions below is "No", omit completion of the FINANCE SCHEDULE and go directly to the LEGAL DESCRIPTION on page 2 and signature spaces on page 3.

SPECIAL NOTE: If contract year and recording year are the same, the following questions MUST be answered.

If FINANCE QUESTIONS 1 through 5 are answered "No", DO NOT complete Finance Schedule on Pages 2 and 3.

Yes No

1. Does property REMAIN SUBJECT to a mortgage such as an assumed mortgage? ☐ ☐
2. Did the seller* provide a mortgage in partial or full consideration? ☐ ☐
3. Did the seller* pay points to secure the buyer's* mortgage, including VA and FHA insured loans? ☐ ☐
4. Did the seller's* mortgagee make interest concessions to the buyer*, i.e., offer a "blended" interest rate below market but greater than the seller's existing mortgage rate? ☐ ☐
5. Was the financing in any other manner unique or specifically associated with the property being transferred, e.g., builder "buy down" of interest, etc.? ☐ ☐

PTAB-203 (R-1/88)
IL-492-0027

* If this transaction is a transfer of a beneficial interest of a land trust substitute the word **Assignor for Seller** and **Assignee for Buyer.**

Page 1

Figure 4-1

subtracted from the purchase price. Line two of TERMS OF SALE in the transfer declaration indicates that amount.

NOW DO YOUR RESIDENTIAL MARKET APPROACH ANALYSIS

Of the six comparable's you choose, select three that are most similar and support your case that your home's value should be lowered. Then adjust these sales to determine a fair market value for your property (see figure 4-2). You can use this form unless there's another that's more locally acceptable especially to your assessor or appeal board.

DETERMINING THE MARKET VALUE OF YOUR HOME'S LAND

Separate the land assessment to determine what the assessor thinks the market value is for the land by itself. By getting vacant land comparable's, you may find the assessment is too high.

If you have a large property, and if the assessor has it broken into smaller parcels for assessment purposes, this may be costly. Smaller parcels tend to have a higher market value per square foot -- and conversely, larger parcels will have a lesser market value per square foot.

INCOME APPROACH

The income approach will be useless to homeowners even those living in four-unit-or-less buildings. However, if you own an income-producing property, this is the most useful approach in determining value. You can reduce your assessment if the income approach value of your property is less than what the assessor says it's worth.

From an appraisal standpoint, this generally is the approach that yields the lowest estimate of value. You probably won't see many assessors using this approach to value (it's counter-productive). For certain income-producing properties, it's the only logical approach to value (large apartment complex, for instance). Some taxing jurisdictions are very receptive to evidence based on this approach to value for income-producing properties. It's important for the real estate owner to be well-versed in this area (especially on what's generally acceptable as evidence). Remember the 14 questions of the assessor and tax system (see pages 35-36).

RESIDENTIAL MARKET ANALYSIS

ITEM	SUBJECT PROPERTY	COMPARABLE #1	+(-)$ Adjustment	COMPARABLE #2	+(-)$ Adjustment	COMPARABLE #3	+(-)$ Adjustment
ADDRESS	619 Oak	568 Pine		433 Maple		521 Hickory	
PROXIMITY		within 2 blocks		within 4 blocks		within 3 block	
SALES PRICE	$185,425*	$170,500		$174,500		$169,500	
PRICE PER SQ. FT.	$77.26	$71.04		$69.80		$72.12	
DATE OF SALE	1/1/89	4/12/89		12/20/88		10/13/88	
LOT SIZE	85 X 180	80 X 187		79 X 192		87 X 175	
DESIGN	2 Story	2 Story		2 Story		2 Story	
CONSTRUCTION	Brick	Brick		Brick		Brick	
AGE	27yrs.	25yrs.		28yrs.		24yrs.	
CONDITION	Average	Average		Average		Average	
TOTAL ROOMS, BEDROOMS & BATHS	Total 8 B-Rms 4 Baths 2.5	Total 9 B-Rms 4 Baths 2.5		Total 7 B-Rms 4 Baths 2	+1000	Total 8 B-Rms 4 Baths 1	+1500
GROSS SQ. FT.	2,400	2,400		2,500	-1000	2,350	+500
BASEMENT IF FINISHED	Full Unfinished	Full Unfinished		Full Unfinished		Full Finished	+2000
AIR CONDITIONING	Central	Central		Central		Central	
GARAGE	2 Car Att.	2 Car Att.		3 Car Att.	-2000	1 Car Att.	+2000
OTHER (PATIO, DECK, POOL, FIREPLACE, ETC.)	Deck Fireplace	Patio None	+1200	Deck Fireplace		None Fireplace	+500
NET TOTAL ADJUSTMENTS			+1000		-2000		+1000
NET TOTAL VALUE		$171,700		$172,500		$170,900	
NET VALUE PER SQ. FT		$71.54		$69.00		$72.72	

COMMENTS: All sales are similar in location and style and indicate a narrow adjusted range. Sale #1 is nearest the subject in location and size. Sale #2 is slightly larger indicating a lower sq. ft. value. Sale #3 is slightly smaller indicating a higher sq. ft. value. All 3 sales were given equal consideration to arrive at a final value estimate. The net value per sq. ft. average is $71.08.

INDICATED VALUE BY MARKET APPROACH
2400 sq. ft @ $71.08 per sq. ft. = $170,592

* The **MARKET VALUE** for the subject property are the values set by the assessor not by the sale of the subject property.

Figure 4-2

Income-producing property is typically purchased for investment purposes, and, from the investor's point of view, earning power is the critical element that affects the property's value. The higher the earnings, the higher the value. Supply and demand play a large roie; the rents charged by the owner of a motel, a shopping center, an office building, an apartment building, or any income-producing property usually should not vary greatly from those charged by owners of competing properties that offer the same quality of service. If the demand is great, owners may charge high rents that yield high rates of returns.

The basic steps of the income approach are:

EXAMPLE:

1. Take actual or estimated grossincome	$100,000.00
2. Deduct for vacancy and collection loss at 5%	5,000.00
3. Add miscellaneous income	+1,000.00
Effective Gross Income	96,000.00
4. Determine and deduct operating expenses	-40,000.00
Net Income	56,000.00

5. Determine Capitalization Rate or Gross Income Multiplier from what's locally acceptable.

6. Divide Capitalization Rate into your net income or multiply Gross Income Multiplier times gross income to determine value.

What you're doing is determining the relationship of income to selling prices of property in your area. In some areas, the capitalization rate is more commonly used than gross income multiplier and vice versa. The gross income multiplier is the simplest method in which you determine what buildings are selling for -- say five times the gross income. Taking that multiplier of five, simply multiply it by your building's gross income.

There's a lot of variance in this method, thus it isn't as precise as the capitalization rate method. The capitalization rate method is concerned mostly with net income and its relationship to selling prices. In industry terms, Rate (R) equals Income (I) divided by Value (V).

$$R = \frac{I}{V}$$

Say the income is $56,000 from our earlier example and the building's value or selling price is $560,000. The following rate would result:

$$\frac{\$\ 56,000}{\$560,000} = 10\%$$

So if a similar building in a similar location has a net income of $80,000, you can estimate the building's value using a capitalization rate of 10 percent as follows:

$$\frac{\$80,000\ (I)}{10\%(R)\ or\ .10} = \$800,000$$

To determine the capitalization rate or gross income multiplier in your area, ask the assessor what rates he uses. Compare that with what commercial real estate brokers or appraisers think is acceptable for properties in the area similar to yours.

After you have determined the acceptable rates, use these formulas to estimate your property value. Compare your estimate with the assessor's estimate. If yours is lower, consider appealing your assessment.

You will need to document all your figures -- by showing your most current IRS return on that property or with an income-and-expense statement certified by your accountant.

The *most* important consideration in presenting income information for assessment purposes is that your actual rents reflect the area's market rent. If your rents are lower than market rents, you will have to justify why.

The assessor or board might not accept building expenses higher than a certain percentage for a given area. You may have to show that percentage even though your expenses are higher. A sample is given on the next page (figure 4-3).

APARTMENT COMPLEX
INCOME/EXPENSE ANALYSIS

INCOME

Rental Income	$ 75,422
Other Income	$ 1,096

GROSS INCOME $76,518

EXPENSES

Repair & Maintenance	$ 1,349
Supplies	$ 707
Real Estate Taxes	$ 12,987 **
Scavenger	$ 1,132
Security	$ 98
Sewer	$ 953
Legal & Professional	$ 567
Advertising	$ 243
Management Fees	$ 3,825
Insurance	$ 2,197
Landscaping	$ 125
Utilities	$ 8,934
Exterminating	$ 332
Office Expenses	$ 487
Miscellaneous	$ 176

TOTAL EXPENSES (44.6%) $34,112 *

* Local Acceptable Limit For Expense/Income Ratio (40%)   <u>$30,607</u>
** Real Estate Taxes may be high from overassessment

NET INCOME BEFORE DEPRECIATION & DEBT SERVICE $45,910

<u>**CAPITALIZATION RATE**</u> 9.5%

NET INCOME/CAP. RATE OR $45,910/.095 = $483,263

SAY $483,000

INDICATED VALUE VIA INCOME APPROACH

Figure 4-3

COST APPROACH

Cost approach is the most prevalent approach to value by assessors. The assessor has some type of replacement cost manual, typically divided by property types, from which he extracts a unit value (usually square foot) to be applied to the size of the building being assessed.

The manual generally includes an all-encompassing depreciation table, based on the building's age, so a depreciation factor can be applied to the estimated cost.

The assessor goes through these steps to determine cost:

1. Estimate how much it would cost to reproduce the property and improvements.

2. Deduct an estimate of accrued depreciation for age (the difference in value from that of a proper new structure), adverse physical factors, adverse design factors, adverse location and market factors.

3. Estimate land value (usually site value is estimated from a study of recent sales and current offerings of similar sites).

EXAMPLE:

Estimated Cost New:	$250,000
Less: (four percent from table showing four percent depreciation for 2-year old building)	$ 10,000
Building Value For Tax Purposes	$240,000

Assessors value land either by (1) the square foot or acre; (2) unit price which is a price-per-front (frontage of property)-foot times a depth (depth of property) factor such as 90 percent or 100 percent or 105 percent.

The assessor will add his opinion of the land value on which the building is situated. It may be based on sales of vacant land in the area or some other value he thinks is representative. Let's say, in this case, he adds $50,000, for a one-acre parcel. This brings the total property value to $290,000.

This property value is reduced to an *assessed* value -- depending on the statutory level of assessments. Say, in this instance, it's 33 1/3 percent of value -- the *assessed* value is $96,657 ($290,000 x .3333).

As a building gets older, the cost approach becomes less reliable, and yet it produces the greatest value compared to the market and income approaches. This is one reason assessors like to use this approach -- along with the ease of determining value from a cost manual.

If this method is used most by the assessor in your area, you should be successful finding errors and showing lesser values using the other approaches. There are two ways you can use the cost approach to your advantage. First, by finding that the assessor miscalculated the physical characteristics of your building when making the assessment (refer to the section on Errors in Building Description at the end of chapter three). You can do this by checking your property record card for the correct dimensions and features. Then, whichever cost manual the assessor uses, check to see if he used the correct rates and if the math was accurate.

Another way to use this approach applies to new construction. If the improvement or building assessment is greater than what it cost to build the property, all you need is to document those costs from your contractor as evidence to the assessor or board.

When you check your property record card and compare it with the manual the assessor uses, look for these discrepancies:

1. The cost factors may differ from those in the cost manual.

2. The cost factors may be higher than current construction and material costs.

3. Find a similarly constructed property and compare its cost figures with yours; are they in line with each other?

4. While you are comparing property cards, are you being assessed on the same things or are you being assessed in more categories than your comparable property?

5. Make sure the depreciation is for the exact number of years and for the correct amounts according to the manual.

6. For new construction: is the completion date correct and were you given a prorated credit for uncompleted work as of the assessment date?

Examples of pages from the Illinois State Appraisal Manual for building costs of single family homes follow. (figures 4-4 through 4-10)

EXPLANATION OF DEPRECIATION SCHEDULE (figure 4-4)

This type of depreciation schedule is the basic tool by which the assessment official computes the loss in value for structures within his jurisdiction. This chart measures only the normal physical depreciation referred to as the C.D.U. rating system.

Condition represents a variable measure of the effects of maintenance and remodeling on a building.

Desirability is a measure of the degree of appeal a particular building may have to prospective purchasers.

Usefulness is a measure of the utility value of the structure for the purpose for which it may be used.

C.D.U. RATINGS

Excellent Superior condition; exceptionally desirable; optimum utility.

Good Definitely better than average condition; notably desirable; highly useful.

Average Normal wear and tear for neighborhood; moderate desirability; customary usefulness.

Poor Definitely below average condition; undesirable; inadequate utility.

Unsound Excessively deteriorated condition; absence of desirability; severely deficient in usefulness.

DEFINITIONS OF OTHER TERMS USED WITH DEPRECIATION SYSTEM

Actual Age The number of years elapsed from the year of construction to the present date.

Effective Age An index of relativity for properties of various C.D.U.'s in conjunction with the property age.

REL (Remaining Economic Life)
The period over which a prudent investor would reasonably expect to recapture his investment. In this chart used as an expression of percentage of the 100% value remaining.

USE OF DEPRECIATION TABLE

To use the C.D.U. rating requires the age of the property and its observed physical condition be known. With these to facts in hand the REMAINING ECONOMIC LIFE of residences can be found in the schedule and then be applied to the other schedules as needed.

STEP I Locate the age of subject building in the AGE column of Schedule A.

STEP II Determine the property C.D.U. and locate it along the upper portion of Schedule A.

STEP III Trace the age to its point of intersection with the C.D.U. and find the EFFECTIVE AGE.

STEP IV The effective age determined in Schedule A is then located in the column headed EFF. AGE on Schedule B. The percentage factor indicated in the right column of schedule B. is the net condition based on remaining economic life.

RESIDENTIAL
REL DEPRECIATION TABLES

SCHEDULE A

AGE	E	G	A	P	U
1	1	1	1	25	40
2	1	1	2	25	40
3	1	2	3	26	41
4	1	3	4	26	41
5	1	4	5	26	41
6	1	5	6	27	42
7	1	6	7	27	42
8	1	7	8	27	42
9	1	8	9	28	43
10	1	9	10	29	44
11	2	10	11	29	44
12	2	10	12	30	45
13	2	11	13	30	45
14	3	11	14	31	46
15	3	12	15	32	47
16	4	13	16	33	48
17	4	14	17	33	48
18	5	14	18	34	49
19	6	15	19	35	50
20	7	16	20	36	51
21	8	17	21	37	53
22	9	18	22	38	54
23	10	18	23	38	54
24	10	19	24	39	55
25	11	19	25	40	56
26	11	20	26	41	58
27	12	21	27	42	60
28	13	22	28	43	61
29	13	23	29	44	63
30	14	24	30	45	66
31	14	24	31	46	69
32	15	25	32	47	72
33	16	26	33	48	73
34	17	27	34	49	74
35	17	27	35	50	76
36	18	28	36	51	77
37	18	29	37	53	78
38	19	30	38	54	80
39	19	30	39	55	81
40	20	31	40	56	83
41	21	32	41	58	84
42	22	33	42	60	85
43	23	33	43	61	87
44	23	34	44	63	88
45	24	35	45	66	90
46	24	36	46	69	91
47	25	37	47	72	92
48	26	37	48	73	94
49	26	38	49	74	95
50	27	39	50	76	96
51	28	40	51	77	98
52	28	41	52	78	99
53	29	41	53	78	100
54	29	42	54	80	101
55	30	43	55	81	102
56	31	44	56	83	103
57	31	45	57	83	104
58	32	45	58	84	105
59	33	46	59	84	106
60	33	47	60	85	106
61	34	48	61	87	107
62	34	48	62	87	108
63	35	49	63	88	109
64	36	50	64	89	109
65	36	51	65	90	110
66	37	52	66	90	110
67	38	53	67	90	111
68	38	54	68	90	111
69	39	55	69	91	112
70	40	55	70	91	112
71	40	55	71	92	113
72	40	56	72	93	113
73	41	57	73	94	114
74	41	58	74	95	115
75	42	60	75	95	116
76	42	60	76	96	117
77	42	61	77	98	118
78	43	63	78	99	119
79	43	64	79	100	120
80	44	66	80	101	121
81	44	67	81	102	122
82	45	69	82	102	123
83	45	72	83	103	124
84	45	72	84	105	124
85	46	73	85	106	124
86	46	74	86	106	124
87	47	75	87	107	124
88	47	76	88	109	124
89	48	76	89	110	124
90	48	77	90	111	124
91	48	78	91	112	124
92	49	79	92	113	124
93	49	80	93	113	124
94	50	81	94	114	124
95	50	82	95	116	124
96	50	83	96	117	124
97	51	83	97	117	124
98	52	84	98	118	124
99	53	85	99	120	124
100	53	86	100	121	124
101	54	87	101	122	124
102	54	88	102	123	124
103	54	89	103	124	124
104	55	90	104	124	124
105	55	90	105	124	124
106	56	91	106	124	124
107	57	91	107	124	124
108	58	92	108	124	124
109	59	94	109	124	124
110	59	95	110	124	124
111	60	95	111	124	124
112	60	96	112	124	124
113	61	97	113	124	124
114	62	98	114	124	124
115	63	99	115	124	124
116	64	100	116	124	124
117	65	101	117	124	124
118	66	102	118	124	124
119	67	102	119	124	124
120	69	103	120	124	124
121	70	104	121	124	124
122	71	105	122	124	124
123	72	106	123	124	124
124	72	106	124	124	124

Columns E, G, A, P, U are under the heading EFFECTIVE AGE.

SCHEDULE B

EFF. AGE	REL	EFF. AGE	REL
1	100	63	51
2	100	64	51
3	99	65	51
4	99	66	50
5	99	67	50
6	98	68	50
7	98	69	49
8	98	70	49
9	97	71	49
10	97	72	48
11	96	73	47
12	95	74	46
13	95	75	46
14	94	76	45
15	93	77	44
16	93	78	43
17	92	79	43
18	91	80	42
19	90	81	41
20	89	82	41
21	88	83	40
22	88	84	39
23	87	85	38
24	86	86	38
25	85	87	37
26	84	88	36
27	83	89	36
28	82	90	35
29	81	91	34
30	80	92	33
31	79	93	33
32	78	94	32
33	77	95	31
34	76	96	30
35	75	97	30
36	74	98	29
37	73	99	28
38	72	100	28
39	71	101	27
40	70	102	26
41	69	103	25
42	68	104	25
43	67	105	24
44	66	106	23
45	65	107	22
46	64	108	22
47	63	109	21
48	62	110	20
49	61	111	20
50	60	112	19
51	59	113	18
52	59	114	17
53	58	115	17
54	57	116	16
55	56	117	15
56	55	118	14
57	55	119	14
58	54	120	13
59	54	121	12
60	53	122	12
61	52	123	11
62	52	124	10

Figure 4-4

BASE COST SCHEDULE - MASONRY CONSTRUCTION

Base price schedules include normal construction features, such as foundation, basement and basement walls, all exterior walls, floors, roof, interior finish, central heating, lighting, plumbing (5 fixtures), and average landscaping.

AREA	1 Story & Bsmt.	1½ Story & Bsmt.	Split Level	2 Story & Bsmt.	3 Story & Bsmt.	AREA	1 Story & Bsmt.	1½ Story & Bsmt.	Split Level	2 Story & Bsmt.	3 Story & Bsmt.
100	$ 10,300	$ 13,200	$ 11,200	$ 14,800	$ 18,100	75	$ 60,800	$ 86,350	$ 73,250	$ 96,850	$133,700
25	12,100	15,550	13,150	17,400	21,450	1,600	61,500	87,400	74,150	98,000	135,400
50	13,750	17,700	15,050	19,850	24,600	25	62,200	88,500	75,050	99,200	137,100
75	15,300	19,750	16,750	22,150	27,550	50	62,900	89,550	75,950	100,400	138,850
200	16,700	21,700	18,400	24,350	30,400	75	63,650	90,600	76,850	101,600	140,550
25	18,100	23,550	20,000	26,400	33,150	1,700	64,350	91,700	77,750	102,800	142,300
50	19,350	25,300	21,500	28,400	35,750	25	65,050	92,750	78,700	104,000	144,000
75	20,600	27,000	22,900	30,300	38,300	50	65,800	93,850	79,600	105,200	145,750
300	21,800	28,650	24,300	32,100	40,750	75	66,550	94,900	80,500	106,450	147,500
25	22,900	30,250	25,650	33,900	43,150	1,800	67,300	96,000	81,450	107,650	149,250
50	24,000	31,750	26,950	35,600	45,450	25	68,000	97,100	82,400	108,900	151,000
75	25,050	33,250	28,200	37,250	47,750	50	68,750	98,200	83,300	110,100	152,800
400	26,100	34,650	29,400	38,900	49,950	75	69,500	99,350	84,250	111,350	154,550
25	27,050	36,100	30,600	40,450	52,150	1,900	70,300	100,450	85,200	112,600	156,350
50	28,050	37,450	31,750	42,000	54,250	25	71,050	101,550	86,150	113,900	158,150
75	28,950	38,800	32,900	43,500	56,350	50	71,850	102,700	87,100	115,150	159,950
500	29,850	40,100	34,000	44,950	58,400	75	72,600	103,850	88,100	116,400	161,750
25	30,750	41,350	35,100	46,400	60,400	2,000	73,400	105,000	89,050	117,700	163,550
50	31,600	42,600	36,150	47,800	62,400	25	74,200	106,150	90,050	119,000	165,350
75	32,450	43,850	37,200	49,150	64,350	50	75,000	107,300	91,000	120,300	167,200
600	33,300	45,050	38,250	50,550	66,300	75	75,800	108,450	92,000	121,600	169,050
25	34,100	46,250	39,250	51,850	68,200	2,100	76,600	109,650	93,000	122,900	170,850
50	34,900	47,450	40,250	53,200	70,050	25	77,400	110,800	94,000	124,250	172,750
75	35,700	48,600	41,200	54,500	71,950	50	78,250	112,000	95,000	125,550	174,600
700	36,500	49,750	42,200	55,750	73,800	75	79,050	113,200	96,000	126,900	176,450
25	37,250	50,900	43,150	57,050	75,600	2,200	79,900	114,400	97,050	128,250	178,350
50	38,000	52,000	44,100	58,300	77,400	25	80,750	115,600	98,050	129,600	180,250
75	38,750	53,100	45,050	59,550	79,200	50	81,600	116,850	99,100	131,000	182,150
800	39,450	54,200	46,000	60,750	81,000	75	82,450	118,050	100,150	132,350	184,050
25	40,200	55,300	46,900	62,000	82,750	2,300	83,300	119,300	101,200	133,750	185,950
50	40,900	56,350	47,800	63,200	84,550	25	84,200	120,550	102,250	135,150	187,900
75	41,650	57,450	48,700	64,400	86,250	50	85,050	121,800	103,300	136,550	189,850
900	42,350	58,500	49,600	65,600	88,000	75	85,950	123,050	104,400	137,950	191,800
25	43,050	59,550	50,500	66,750	89,750	2,400	86,850	124,300	105,450	139,400	193,750
50	43,750	60,600	51,400	67,950	91,450	25	87,750	125,600	106,550	140,850	195,700
75	44,400	61,650	52,300	69,100	93,200	50	88,650	126,900	107,650	142,250	197,700
1,000	45,100	62,700	53,200	70,300	94,900	75	89,600	128,200	108,750	143,750	199,700
25	45,800	63,750	54,050	71,450	96,600	2,500	90,500	129,500	109,850	145,200	201,700
50	46,500	64,750	54,950	72,600	98,300	25	91,450	130,800	110,950	146,650	203,700
75	47,150	65,800	55,800	73,750	100,000	50	92,400	132,150	112,100	148,150	205,750
1,100	47,850	66,800	56,700	74,900	101,650	75	93,350	133,500	113,200	149,650	207,750
25	48,500	67,850	57,550	76,050	103,350	2,600	94,300	134,800	114,350	151,150	209,800
50	49,200	68,850	58,400	77,200	105,050	25	95,250	136,200	115,500	152,700	211,850
75	49,850	69,900	59,300	78,350	106,700	50	96,250	137,550	116,650	154,200	213,950
1,200	50,550	70,900	60,150	79,500	108,400	75	97,200	138,900	117,850	155,750	216,000
25	51,200	71,950	61,000	80,650	110,050	2,700	98,200	140,300	119,000	157,300	218,100
50	51,900	72,950	61,900	81,800	111,750	25	99,200	141,700	120,200	158,850	220,200
75	52,550	73,950	62,750	82,950	113,450	50	100,200	143,100	121,400	160,450	222,350
1,300	53,250	75,000	63,600	84,100	115,100	75	101,250	144,500	122,600	162,050	224,450
25	53,900	76,000	64,500	85,250	116,800	2,800	102,250	145,950	123,800	163,600	226,600
50	54,600	77,050	65,350	86,400	118,450	25	103,300	147,350	125,000	165,250	228,750
75	55,250	78,050	66,200	87,550	120,150	50	104,350	148,800	126,250	166,850	230,900
1,400	55,950	79,100	67,100	88,700	121,850	75	105,400	150,250	127,450	168,500	233,100
25	56,650	80,100	67,950	89,850	123,500	2,900	106,450	151,750	128,700	170,100	235,300
50	57,300	81,150	68,850	91,000	125,200	25	107,550	153,200	129,950	171,800	237,500
75	58,000	82,200	69,700	92,150	126,900	50	108,600	154,700	131,200	173,450	239,700
1,500	58,700	83,250	70,600	93,300	128,600	75	109,700	156,200	132,500	175,100	241,900
25	59,400	84,250	71,500	94,500	130,300	3,000	110,800	157,700	133,750	176,800	244,150
50	60,100	85,300	72,350	95,650	132,000	Over	$36.95/SF	$52.55/SF	$44.60/SF	$58.95/SF	$81.40/SF

Figure 4-5

BASE COST SCHEDULE - WOOD FRAME CONSTRUCTION

Base price schedules include normal construction features, such as foundation, basement and basement walls, all exterior walls, floors, roof, interior finish, central heating, lighting, plumbing (5 fixtures), and average landscaping.

AREA	1 Story & Bsmt.	1½ Story & Bsmt.	Split Level	2 Story & Bsmt.	3 Story & Bsmt.	AREA	1 Story & Bsmt.	1½ Story & Bsmt.	Split Level	2 Story & Bsmt.	3 Story & Bsmt.
100	$ 9,300	$ 11,800	$ 9,700	$ 12,550	$ 15,800	75	$54,800	$ 77,400	$ 66,500	$ 85,550	$116,650
25	10,900	13,900	11,450	14,800	18,700	1,600	55,450	78,350	67,300	86,600	118,150
50	12,400	15,850	13,050	16,900	21,450	25	56,100	79,300	68,150	87,650	119,650
75	13,800	17,700	14,600	18,900	24,050	50	56,750	80,250	69,000	88,700	121,150
200	15,050	19,450	16,050	20,800	26,550	75	57,400	81,200	69,800	89,800	122,650
25	16,300	21,100	17,450	22,600	28,900	1,700	58,050	82,150	70,650	90,850	124,150
50	17,450	22,700	18,800	24,300	31,200	25	58,700	83,150	71,500	91,950	125,650
75	18,600	24,200	20,100	26,000	33,400	50	59,350	84,100	72,350	93,050	127,200
300	19,650	25,700	21,300	27,600	35,550	75	60,000	85,050	73,200	94,150	128,700
25	20,650	27,100	22,550	29,150	37,650	1,800	60,650	86,050	74,050	95,200	130,250
50	21,650	28,450	23,700	30,650	39,700	25	61,350	87,050	74,950	96,300	131,800
75	22,600	29,800	24,800	32,100	41,650	50	62,000	88,000	75,800	97,450	133,300
400	23,500	31,100	25,950	33,500	43,600	75	62,700	89,000	76,650	98,550	134,850
25	24,400	32,350	27,000	34,900	45,500	1,900	63,400	90,000	77,550	99,650	136,400
50	25,300	33,550	28,050	36,250	47,350	25	64,100	91,050	78,400	100,800	138,000
75	26,100	34,750	29,100	37,600	49,150	50	64,750	92,050	79,300	101,900	139,550
500	26,950	35,950	30,100	38,900	50,950	75	65,500	93,050	80,200	103,050	141,150
25	27,750	37,050	31,100	40,150	52,700	2,000	66,200	94,100	81,100	104,200	142,700
50	28,500	38,200	32,050	41,400	54,450	25	66,900	95,100	82,000	105,350	144,300
75	29,300	39,300	33,000	42,650	56,150	50	67,600	96,150	82,900	106,500	145,900
600	30,050	40,400	33,950	43,850	57,850	75	68,350	97,200	83,800	107,650	147,500
25	30,750	41,450	34,900	45,050	59,500	2,100	69,050	98,250	84,700	108,800	149,100
50	31,500	42,500	35,800	46,250	61,150	25	69,800	99,300	85,650	110,000	150,700
75	32,200	43,550	36,700	47,400	62,750	50	70,550	100,350	86,550	111,150	152,350
700	32,900	44,600	37,600	48,550	64,400	75	71,300	101,450	87,500	112,350	154,000
25	33,600	45,600	38,500	49,700	65,950	2,200	72,050	102,500	88,400	113,550	155,600
50	34,250	46,600	39,400	50,800	67,550	25	72,800	103,600	89,350	114,750	157,250
75	34,950	47,600	40,250	51,950	69,100	50	73,600	104,700	90,300	115,950	158,950
800	35,600	48,550	41,100	53,050	70,700	75	74,350	105,800	91,250	117,200	160,600
25	36,250	49,550	41,950	54,150	72,200	2,300	75,150	106,900	92,200	118,400	162,250
50	36,900	50,500	42,800	55,200	73,750	25	75,900	108,050	93,200	119,650	163,950
75	37,550	51,450	43,650	56,300	75,300	50	76,700	109,150	94,150	120,900	165,650
900	38,150	52,450	44,500	57,400	76,800	75	77,500	110,300	95,150	122,150	167,350
25	38,800	53,350	45,300	58,450	78,300	2,400	78,300	111,400	96,100	123,400	169,050
50	39,450	54,300	46,150	59,500	79,800	25	79,150	112,550	97,100	124,650	170,800
75	40,050	55,250	46,950	60,550	81,300	50	79,950	113,700	98,100	125,900	172,500
1,000	40,700	56,200	47,800	61,600	82,800	75	80,800	114,900	99,100	127,200	174,250
25	41,300	57,100	48,600	62,650	84,300	2,500	81,600	116,050	100,100	128,500	176,000
50	41,900	58,050	49,450	63,700	85,750	25	82,450	117,250	101,100	129,800	177,750
75	42,550	58,950	50,250	64,750	87,250	50	83,300	118,450	102,150	131,100	179,500
1,100	43,150	59,900	51,050	65,800	88,700	75	84,150	119,600	103,150	132,400	181,300
25	43,750	60,800	51,850	66,800	90,200	2,600	85,050	120,850	104,200	133,750	183,100
50	44,350	61,700	52,650	67,850	91,650	25	85,900	122,050	105,250	135,050	184,900
75	44,950	62,650	53,500	68,900	93,100	50	86,800	123,250	106,300	136,400	186,700
1,200	45,550	63,550	54,300	69,900	94,600	75	87,650	124,500	107,350	137,750	188,500
25	46,200	64,450	55,100	70,950	96,050	2,700	88,550	125,750	108,400	139,100	190,300
50	46,800	65,400	55,900	72,000	97,500	25	89,450	127,000	109,500	140,500	192,150
75	47,400	66,300	56,700	73,000	99,000	50	90,400	128,250	110,550	141,850	194,000
1,300	48,000	67,200	57,500	74,050	100,450	75	91,300	129,500	111,650	143,250	195,850
25	48,600	68,150	58,300	75,100	101,900	2,800	92,250	130,800	112,750	144,650	197,750
50	49,250	69,050	59,150	76,100	103,350	25	93,150	132,050	113,850	146,050	199,600
75	49,850	69,950	59,950	77,150	104,850	50	94,100	133,350	114,950	147,450	201,500
1,400	50,450	70,900	60,750	78,200	106,300	75	95,050	134,650	116,050	148,850	203,400
25	51,050	71,800	61,550	79,250	107,800	2,900	96,000	136,000	117,150	150,300	205,300
50	51,700	72,750	62,400	80,300	109,250	25	97,000	137,300	118,300	151,750	207,250
75	52,300	73,650	63,200	81,300	110,700	50	97,950	138,650	119,450	153,200	209,150
1,500	52,950	74,600	64,000	82,350	112,200	75	98,950	140,000	120,600	154,650	211,100
25	53,550	75,550	64,850	83,400	113,700	3,000	99,950	141,350	121,750	156,150	213,050
50	54,200	76,450	65,650	84,450	115,150	Over	$33.30/SF	$47.10/SF	$40.60/SF	$52.05/SF	$71.00/SF

Figure 4-6

SCHEDULE COMBINING - FRAME (−)

SFGA	NO. OF STORIES				
	1 Story	1½ Story	Split	2 Story	3 Story
100	$ 6,350	$ 6,400	$ 6,400	$ 6,500	$ 6,600
200	6,850	6,900	6,900	7,050	7,250
300	7,200	7,350	7,350	7,450	7,750
400	7,500	7,650	7,650	7,850	8,200
500	7,750	8,000	8,000	8,150	8,600
600	8,000	8,250	8,250	8,500	8,950
700	8,200	8,550	8,550	8,750	9,300
800	8,400	8,800	8,800	9,050	9,650
900	8,600	9,000	9,000	9,300	9,950
1,000	8,800	9,250	9,250	9,550	10,300
1,100	9,000	9,450	9,450	9,800	10,600
1,200	9,150	9,700	9,700	10,000	10,900
1,300	9,350	9,900	9,900	10,250	11,200
1,400	9,500	10,100	10,100	10,500	11,450
1,500	9,700	10,300	10,300	10,700	11,750
1,600	9,850	10,550	10,550	10,950	12,050
1,700	10,000	10,750	10,750	11,150	12,350
1,800	10,200	10,950	10,950	11,400	12,600
1,900	10,350	11,150	11,150	11,600	12,900
2,000	10,500	11,350	11,350	11,850	13,200
2,100	10,700	11,550	11,550	12,100	13,500
2,200	10,850	11,800	11,800	12,300	13,800
2,300	11,050	12,000	12,000	12,550	14,100
2,400	11,200	12,200	12,200	12,800	14,400
2,500	11,400	12,450	12,450	13,000	14,700
2,600	11,550	12,650	12,650	13,250	15,000
2,700	11,750	12,900	12,900	13,500	15,300
2,800	11,950	13,100	13,100	13,750	15,650
2,900	12,150	13,350	13,350	14,050	15,950
3,000	12,300	13,550	13,550	14,300	16,300

Note: When using Schedule Combining with houses that have central air conditioning, subtract (−) an additional $1,000 (see page R7).

SCHEDULE COMBINING - MASONRY (−)

SFGA	NO. OF STORIES				
	1 Story	1½ Story	Split	2 Story	3 Story
100	$ 6,550	$ 6,600	$ 6,600	$ 6,700	$ 6,800
200	7,100	7,200	7,200	7,350	7,550
300	7,500	7,700	7,700	7,850	8,150
400	7,850	8,100	8,100	8,300	8,700
500	8,150	8,450	8,450	8,700	9,150
600	8,450	8,750	8,750	9,050	9,600
700	8,700	9,050	9,050	9,400	10,000
800	8,950	9,350	9,350	9,700	10,400
900	9,200	9,650	9,650	10,000	10,800
1,000	9,400	9,900	9,900	10,300	11,150
1,100	9,600	10,150	10,150	10,550	11,500
1,200	9,800	10,400	10,400	10,850	11,850
1,300	10,000	10,650	10,650	11,100	12,200
1,400	10,200	10,900	10,900	11,350	12,550
1,500	10,400	11,100	11,100	11,650	12,850
1,600	10,600	11,350	11,350	11,900	13,200
1,700	10,800	11,600	11,600	12,150	13,550
1,800	11,000	11,800	11,800	12,400	13,850
1,900	11,200	12,050	12,050	12,650	14,200
2,000	11,400	12,300	12,300	12,950	14,550
2,100	11,600	12,550	12,550	13,200	14,900
2,200	11,800	12,750	12,750	13,450	15,200
2,300	12,000	13,000	13,000	13,750	15,550
2,400	12,200	13,250	13,250	14,000	15,900
2,500	12,400	13,500	13,500	14,300	16,300
2,600	12,600	13,750	13,750	14,600	16,650
2,700	12,800	14,000	14,000	14,850	17,000
2,800	13,000	14,250	14,250	15,150	17,350
2,900	13,250	14,550	14,550	15,450	17,750
3,000	13,450	14,850	14,800	15,750	18,150

NO HEAT (−)

SFGA	NO. OF STORIES				
	1 Story	1½ Story	Split	2 Story	3 Story
200	$1,200	$1,300	$1,450	$1,450	$ 1,650
400	1,450	1,750	2,000	2,000	2,600
600	1,750	2,150	2,650	2,650	3,550
800	2,000	2,750	3,400	3,400	4,350
1,000	2,300	3,150	3,950	3,950	5,100
1,200	2,750	3,750	4,500	4,500	5,850
1,400	3,000	4,200	5,050	5,050	6,650
1,600	3,500	4,600	5,550	5,550	7,400
1,800	3,750	5,050	6,100	6,100	8,200
2,000	4,050	5,450	6,650	6,650	8,950
2,200	4,350	5,850	7,200	7,200	9,700
2,400	4,600	6,300	7,750	7,750	10,500
2,600	4,900	6,700	8,250	8,250	11,250
2,800	5,150	7,150	8,800	8,800	12,050
3,000	5,450	7,550	9,350	9,350	12,800

CENTRAL AIR CONDITIONING (+)

SFGA	NO. OF STORIES				
	1 Story	1½ Story	Split	2 Story	3 Story
200	$1,200	$1,200	$1,200	$1,200	$1,200
400	1,200	1,200	1,200	1,200	1,300
600	1,200	1,300	1,300	1,300	1,550
800	1,200	1,400	1,400	1,550	1,900
1,000	1,300	1,550	1,550	1,650	2,500
1,200	1,300	1,650	1,650	1,900	3,100
1,400	1,400	1,750	1,750	2,500	3,300
1,600	1,550	2,500	2,500	2,500	3,550
1,800	1,550	2,500	2,500	3,100	4,250
2,000	1,650	3,100	3,100	3,200	4,950
2,200	1,900	3,300	3,300	3,400	5,100
2,400	1,900	3,300	3,300	3,550	5,300
2,600	1,900	3,400	3,400	3,800	6,500
2,800	2,500	3,550	3,550	4,250	6,750
3,000	2,500	3,550	3,550	4,950	7,450

FIREPLACE(+)

QUALITY	A	B	C	D
Fireplace & Stack	$4,200	$3,200	$1,800	$1,000
2nd Fireplace on Same Stack	3,500	2,500	1,300	800

NOTE: 100% Masonry Fireplaces are 'B' Quality or Better.

FINISHED BASEMENT (+)
Per SF of Finished Floor Area

QUALITY	A	B	C	D
Recreation Room	$ 8.45	$ 6.90	$5.65	$4.60
Living Quarters	12.70	10.35	8.00	6.95

PARTIAL MASONRY TRIM (+)
Per SF of Surface Area

QUALITY	AB	CD
Brick	$6.90	$5.50
Stone	9.50	7.15
Artificial Stone	—	6.00

Figure 4-7

FOUNDATION (−)

AREA	Crawl	Slab
100	$ 450	$ 850
200	900	1,750
300	1,350	2,600
400	1,800	3,450
500	2,250	4,350
600	2,650	5,200
700	3,100	6,050
800	3,550	6,900
900	4,000	7,800
1,000	4,450	8,650
1,100	4,900	9,500
1,200	5,350	10,400
1,300	5,800	11,250
1,400	6,250	12,100
1,500	6,700	13,000
Over	$4.45/SF	$8.65/SF

GARAGES (+)

AREA	Frame	Masonry
140	$1,350	$1,700
160	1,550	1,900
180	1,750	2,150
200	1,950	2,400
220	2,150	2,650
240	2,350	2,900
260	2,550	3,100
280	2,750	3,350
300	2,950	3,600
320	3,100	3,850
340	3,300	4,100
360	3,500	4,300
380	3,700	4,550
400	3,900	4,800
420	4,100	5,050
440	4,300	5,300
460	4,500	5,500
480	4,700	5,750
500	4,900	6,000
520	5,050	6,250
540	5,250	6,500
560	5,450	6,700
580	5,650	6,950
Over	$9.75/SF	$12.00/SF

QUALITY

Grade	Factor
AA	225
A	150
B	122
C	100
D	82
E	50

RESIDENTIAL POOLS IN GROUND (+)

Price includes excavation, filtering system, pump, chlorinator, and ladder.

Running SF	Concrete	Vinyl Liner
300	$ 7,650	$3,950
400	8,400	4,850
500	9,750	5,350
600	10,500	6,000
800	11,750	6,950
1,000	12,650	7,800

Price permanent type above ground pools at 50% of Vinyl Liner price.

PAVING (+)

Crushed Stone	$ .30/SF
Concrete	1.75/SF
Asphalt	1.10/SF

STOOP, DECKS, PATIOS (+)

Stoop - Masonry	$5.00/SF
Deck - Wood	6.25/SF
Patio - Concrete	1.75/SF
Patio - Brick	5.00/SF

PLUMBING (±)

Per Fixture less than standard	Deduct $800
Per Fixture greater than standard	Add $800

POOL ADDITIONS (+)

Heater	$850
Diving Board	250

PORCHES (+)

AREA	OFP	EFP	OMP	EMP
12	$ 550	$ 800	$ 550	$ 950
16	550	850	600	1,050
20	600	900	650	1,100
30	700	1,100	800	1,300
40	800	1,250	950	1,450
60	950	1,600	1,200	1,800
80	1,150	1,900	1,450	2,200
100	1,350	2,250	1,700	2,550
125	1,550	2,650	2,050	3,000
150	1,800	3,050	2,350	3,450
175	2,000	3,500	2,700	3,900
200	2,250	3,900	3,000	4,350
250	2,900	4,700	3,750	5,350
300	3,400	5,550	4,400	6,250
350	3,850	6,350	5,050	7,150
400	4,300	7,200	5,700	8,050
450	4,750	8,000	6,350	8,950
Over	$10.55/SF	$17.75/SF	$14.10/SF	$19.90/SF

ATTIC (+)

SFGA	Unfinished	½ Finished	Finished
600	$3,200	$ 5,350	$ 7,500
800	3,450	5,900	8,350
1,000	3,650	6,450	9,250
1,200	3,850	7,000	10,150
1,400	4,050	7,550	11,050
1,600	4,300	8,100	11,900
1,800	4,500	8,650	12,800
2,000	4,700	9,200	13,700
2,200	4,900	9,750	14,600
2,400	5,150	10,300	15,450
2,600	5,350	10,850	16,350
2,800	5,550	11,400	17,250
3,000	5,800	12,000	18,150

BASE COST SCHEDULE - MOBILE HOMES

Base cost includes average construction features, permanent inexpensive crawl space foundation, steps, plumbing (5 fixtures), lighting, and central heating. Furniture is not included.

WIDTH	40'	45'	50'	55'	60'	65'	70'
10'	$11,030	$12,160	$13,260	$14,390	$15,400	$16,450	$17,490
12'	12,130	13,340	14,520	15,680	16,810	17,940	19,030
14'	13,150	14,430	15,680	16,910	18,110	19,290	20,450
20'	23,230	25,540	27,110	28,960	30,730	32,490	34,190
24'	25,160	27,150	29,060	30,880	32,640	34,380	36,060

AGE	REL	AGE	REL	AGE	REL
1	87	8	55	15	41
2	80	9	52	16	40
3	74	10	50	17	39
4	69	11	48	18	38
5	65	12	46	19	37
6	61	13	44	20	36
7	58	14	43	Over 20	35

Figure 4-8

DEMONSTRATION APPRAISAL

(Building Record on following page.)

CONSTRUCTION SPECIFICATIONS

Subject property is a two story brick dwelling with full basement, attached garage, and three open frame porches. There are six rooms on the first and second floors including three bedrooms, kitchen, living and dining rooms. The dwelling has one full bath, two half baths, 405 sq. ft. of recreation room in basement, and one wood burning fireplace. The interior is finished with lath and plaster walls, hardwood trim and flooring, with some carpet and tile on the first floor. The dwelling is heated with a central warm air systyem and is equipped with a central air conditioning system. The building was erected twenty-four years ago, has a grade factor of C and a CDU of Good.

PROCEDURE

1. Record construction specifications in the appropriate sections of property record card number 2.

2. Sketch diagram of dwelling and:

    a. Identify all sections as to story height, construction type, and foundation.

    b. Label main structure and all appendages with proper dimensions and square feet of ground area.

3. Establish the quality grade in accordance with the explanations and procedures described in the Property Record Card System Section.

4. Establish the CDU rating in accordance with the explanations and procedures described in the Property Record Card System Section.

5. Price the dwelling in the pricing ladder under "Dwelling Computations" on the Property Record Card by completing the following items:

    a. The story height and the construction (masonry or frame) of the dwelling.

    b. The square foot area of the dwelling and the corresponding base price from the Dwelling Pricing Schedule.

    c. Make the necessary additions and/or deductions from the Dwelling Adjustment Schedules.

    • Basement: Base price includes basement; no adjustment is necessary.

    • Heating: Base price includes central warm air system; no adjustment is necessary.

    • Plumbing: Base price includes a standard complement of plumbing consisting of 1 full bathroom, a kitchen sink and automatic water heater; add for 2 extra toilet rooms.

    • Attic: Base price does not include an attic; no adjustment is necessary.

    • Porches: Base price does not include any porches. List and price porches separately in computation ladder.

    • Attached Garage: Enter price of garage in computation ladder. Detached garages are listed separately in summary of other buildings.

    d. Compute total price after adjustments thus far.

    e. Apply grade factor that was determined during inspection.

    f. Compute prices for other features:

    • Part Masonry Walls: Not applicable for this property.

    • Fireplace: Enter price of one (Grade C) fireplace and stack.

    • Finished Basement: Enter price of (Grade C) recreation room.

    g. Add "other features" to total computed above to obtain new total. Apply cost, design, neighborhood or appraiser factor to arrive at replacement value.

6. Establish the depreciation allowance from the REL depreciation system, insert the REL factor in the pricing ladder and compute the full value.

Figure 4-9

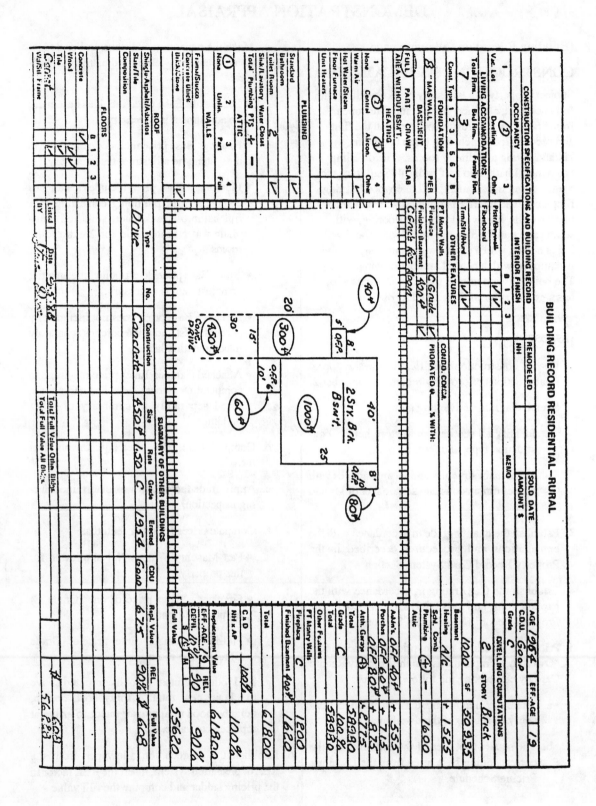

Figure 4-10

EQUITY APPROACH

Depending on your area's acceptable grounds for appeal, most homeowners will find this method to be very useful in lowering property assessment.

It's the intent of most state laws that each taxpayer pay taxes in direct proportion to the value of his property. The conscientious assessor tries to maintain standards, methods and procedures which will result in fair assessments. Perfectly accurate assessments are impossible because appraising is based on observation and is therefore inexact. The size and complexity of the assessor's duties, the statutory and budgetary limitations facing him, also restrict his capabilities.

You may find your assessor is intentionally keeping residential assessments down. If he is elected, he may be trying to give the homeowners in his district a break. Then, if the assessments are equalized upward by the county or state, the assessor can remain the good guy. Or, by keeping assessments down, the assessor will keep the homeowner from appealing. If this is the case, it doesn't mean assessments are equitable for everyone. If anything, it probably means there's more inequity. Let's examine the procedure to prove inequity of assessments. The procedure is similar to market value approach, again finding six similar-style homes located near yours. These homes don't have to have been sold. However, entry to assessment information and property record cards are needed for all comparable's including your own. You are looking for assessment per square foot for the building, and for land, to determine inequity in assessment.

STEPS TO DETERMINING EQUITY

1. Get Property record card information for your home.

2. Measure your home from the exterior. Take pictures.

3. Note significant errors.

4. Locate six comparable properties (same style and locale). These do not have to be actual sales.

5. Get Property record card information for the comparable properties from the assessor's office.

6. Determine the following information for each property:

EQUITY APPROACH CRITERIA

Location (most important)
Style (ranch, split-level, two-story, etc.)
Basement (vs. crawl or slab)
Finished basements
Size (square feet of living area)
Number of bedrooms
Number of baths
Central air conditioning
Fireplaces
Garage capacity (1-, 2- or 3-car) or square footage

Some points to keep in mind:

Location, style and basement should be very similar to your own. A
   dollar adjustment would be difficult to prove.

Overall square footage should be as close to yours as possible.

Number of bedrooms are considered in your final conclusion of value.

Number of baths, finished basement, central air conditioning, fireplaces,
   and garage capacity are important amenities, and each has a value in the
   marketplace.

NOW DO YOUR RESIDENTIAL EQUITY ANALYSIS

Of the six comparable's you choose, use the three that are most similar and
support your case that your home's assessment should be lowered. Adjust these
comparable's to arrive at a fair assessment for your home. Two forms are shown
as examples; one where you have to find dollar amounts for adjustments (figure
4-11). . .the other where you estimate upward and downward adjustments in the
analysis (figure 4-12). Use whichever form is easier or acceptable to the assessor
or appeal board.

RESIDENTIAL EQUITY ANALYSIS

ITEM	SUBJECT PROPERTY	COMPARABLE #1		COMPARABLE #2		COMPARABLE #3	
ADDRESS	419 Grant	218 Jefferson		233 Jefferson		522 Lincoln	
PROXIMITY		within 3 blocks		within 3 blocks		within 1 block	
ASSESSED VALUE	$34,419	$30,041		$30,165		$30,655	
A/V PER SQ. FT.	$26.47	$23.11		$23.69		$22.72	
			+ (-) $ Adjustment		+ (-) $ Adjustment		+ (-) $ Adjustment
DATE OF SALE	n/a	n/a		n/a		n/a	
LOT SIZE	65 X 130	65 X 132		62 X 132		67 X 130	
DESIGN	Ranch	Ranch		Ranch		Ranch	
CONSTRUCTION	Frame	Frame		Frame		Frame	
AGE	17yrs.	15yrs.		15yrs.		17yrs.	
CONDITION	Average	Average		Average		Average	
TOTAL ROOMS, BEDROOMS & BATHS	Total 6, B-rms 3, Bath 2	Total 6, B-rms 3, Bath 1.5	+300	Total 6, B-rms 3, Bath 2		Total 6, B-rms 3, Bath 2	
GROSS SQ. FT.	1,300	1,300		1,273		1,346	
BASEMENT IF FINISHED	Slab n/a	Slab n/a		Slab n/a		Slab n/a	
AIR CONDITIONING	Central	Central		Central		Central	
GARAGE	2 Car Det.	2 Car Det.		1 Car Det.	+500	2 Car Det.	
OTHER (PATIO, DECK, POOL, FIREPLACE, ETC.)	Patio Fireplace	Patio Fireplace		Patio Fireplace		Patio None	+400
NET TOTAL ADJUSTMENTS			+300		+500		+400
NET TOTAL VALUE		$30,341		$30,665		$31,055	
NET VALUE PER SQ. FT.		$23.34		$24.09		$23.07	

COMMENTS: All three comparables are similar track type homes in the same subdivision. Minimal adjustments were required. The adjusted assessed value per square foot average is $23.50 per square foot.

INDICATED ASSESSED VALUATION BY EQUITY ANALYSIS
1,300 sq./ft. @ $23.50 per sq./ft. = $30,550

Note: This property is assessed at 1/3 of market value, therefore all adjustments are at 1/3 of full value.

If this reduction is successful, the assessment will be lowered by $3869. If the tax rate is $8.00 per hundred dollars of assessment, the tax savings will approximately be $300.00.

Figure 4-11

EQUITY ANALYSIS
COMPARABLE RANCH STYLE HOMES

COMP. NO.	P.I.N.	ADDRESS	AGE	S/F G/A	ASSESSMENT	A/V PERS/F
1.	01-11-211-017	218 Jefferson	15yrs.	1,300	$30,041	$23.11
2.	01-11-210-009	233 Jefferson	15yrs.	1,273	$30,165	$23.69
3.	01-11-212-009	522 Lincoln	17yrs.	1,346	$30,655	$22.72
4.	01-11-212-014	514 Lincoln	18yrs.	1,638	$33,986	$20.75
5.	01-11-207-024	505 Grant	16yrs.	1,640	$35,169	$21.44
6.	01-11-407-030	201 Grant	16yrs.	1,609	$34,038	$21.15
7.	01-11-407-024	221 Grant	18yrs.	1,769	$35,330	$19.97
8.	01-11-407-026	211 Grant	18yrs.	1,300	$34,557	$26.47
SUBJECT						
	01-11-207-055	419 Grant	17yrs.	1,300	$34,419	$26.47

ANALYSIS

All comparables are similar in style, location and indicate an assessed square foot value of $19.97 to a high of $23.69. Comparables #1- #3 are most similar in size and are at the upper end of the value range. Comparables #4- #8 (the lower end of the value range) are larger in square footage. Based on this analysis, a fair and equitable square foot assessed value for the subject would be $23.00.

1,300 square feet @ $23.00 per square foot = $29,900

Figure 4-12

SALE RATIO STUDIES

This is another method to uncover inequity of assessments. I lowered the assessment of a house in Cook County, Illinois, by using the latest sales ratio figures provided by the Illinois Department of Revenue. Since the house was recently purchased, value was easily determined. Instead of the assessment being at the legal level of 16 percent of value, it was lowered to the median sales ratio of 10.26 percent for residential property in Cook County in the most recent year that the sales ratio study was completed...a 36 percent reduction in taxes!

The purpose of the sales ratio study is to determine at what level property is assessed, compared to the actual sales price. Even if your state assesses at full value, the assessment is usually less than 100 percent. Your state may do detailed sales ratio studies for your township or county (see state-by-state summary). Check with the highest appeal board to see which sales ratio information has the best reliability; they might not accept the state study if it's too broad or outdated. You may have to do your own study locally -- especially if your local assessor won't provide you with such information.

To do your own study, obtain data about sales of comparable homes during the one-year period before the assessment date, using any methods mentioned earlier. If, for example, the assessment date is January 1, 1989, then get sales from January 1, 1988 to January 1, 1989. You don't have to be as specific when it comes to finding homes similar to yours, but the sales should come from the same geographic region as your property. The more sales you can show, the better -- quantity is important for determining a ratio. You don't omit sales because they don't help your case. The assessor may notice those sales missing and dismiss your evidence.

Divide the property's sale price by its current assessment as of the assessment date, giving you its sales-to-assessment ratio. Note examples of ratio studies (figure 4-13). Total all the percentages and divide by the number of properties to give you the average sales ratio.

Determine the average sales ratio for the six property sales you used to get your market value. You can use either or both of those studies to show whether your property has been assessed at a higher-than-average rate.

This method is most effective if you recently bought your home. It could also be used with the market data approach to first determine your property's value, then to determine if your assessment-to-value percentage is higher than the sales ratio average. You base your appeal on that evidence.

SALES RATIO STUDY

P.I.N.	LOCATION	DATE OF SALE	SALES PRICE	DOCUMENT NO.	1988 EQUAL ASSD. VALUATION	PERCENTAGE A/V TO SP
01-18-106-020	220 JEFFERSON	12/21/88	$42,000	R88-51198	13,352	.318
01-18-106-035	211 JEFFERSON	05/10/88	$36,500	R88-16744	10,539	.289
01-18-106-041	201 JEFFERSON	07/20/88	$40,500	R88-16744	11,924	.294
01-18-107-031	219 WASHINGTON	04/23/88	$41,900	R88-13671	12,378	.295
01-18-110-027	205 WASHINGTON	03/26/88	$44,100	R88-09899	14,791	.335
01-18-110-032	225 WASHINGTON	10/18/88	$53,000	R88-38736	16,750	.316
01-18-112-020	115 LINCOLN	01/12/88	$35,500	R88-09147	10,528	.297
01-18-113-025	117 LINCOLN	10/04/88	$39,000	R88-37096	12,227	.314
01-18-116-026	110 LINCOLN	05/24/88	$39,500	R88-17678	12,324	.312
01-18-116-036	217 GRANT	08/16/88	$41,900	R88-30154	12,064	.288
01-18-116-042	100 GRANT	11/05/88	$41,900	R88-41199	12,973	.310
01-18-118-035	208 GRANT	07/12/88	$31,000	R88-24943	10,344	.333
01-18-118-040	220 GRANT	06/27/88	$37,900	R88-22517	11,902	.314
MEAN AVERAGE ASSESSMENT LEVEL FOR 13 SALES						.309
SUBJECT						
01-18-116-038	211 GRANT	05/25/88	$39,900	R88-17609	13,398	.336

We request a reduction based on an average assessment of .309 for our area. The revised assessment should be $39,900 X .309 = $12,329, a reduction of $1,069 assessed valuation.

Figure 4-13

HOW THE ASSESSOR OR STATE MAY
CONDUCT THEIR SALES RATIO STUDY

The degree of equality achieved by an assessment program can best be measured by a sales ratio study. The first thing the assessor (or state) does is to collect samples of properties sold in the community which can be verified. To verify that a sale is bona fide, it must be an arm's-length transaction (refer to definition of market value).

Verification of the sales to be used in the sales ratio study is necessary to drop any transactions which were influenced by non-market oriented factors. The assessor does this by examining transfer declarations (figure 4-1).

Sales ratio study may be conducted according to location within the community, property type or sales value. The assessor's office may divide some cities into geographic regions, such as subdivisions, and conduct a sales ratio study for each area. Or they might consider divisions by property type: residential; commercial; industrial; and agricultural (additional property types may be included according to your community's needs and financial limitations).

Another type of stratification program -- generally used with either of the other two programs -- focuses on the value of the properties sold. Under this program, for example, it would be possible to conduct a sales ratio study of all residential property with a value range of 0 to $100,000 and perhaps another for a value range of $100,000 and up. If needed, this same structure can be applied to different geographic regions within the community.

Whatever method of stratification they select, the primary reason for using the sales ratio study is to test the assessment's quality. In a large centralized city, a highly sophisticated system may be required to isolate problems in the assessment. A sparsely populated agricultural county, otherwise, may require only the most rudimentary program to examine its assessments. The selection of a sales ratio program must be tailored to the community's needs and will therefore vary widely from place to place.

Once the system has been developed and the sales being used have been verified, they can analyze how much each deviates from its assessed value. This is accomplished by resorting to any three deviations:

1. Mean deviation (most prevalent use)
2. Median deviation
3. Standard deviation

A sample page from the Illinois Department of Revenue (Findings of 1987 Assessment/Sales ratio study) is shown (figure 4-14).

A SPECIAL NOTE ON CONDOS

In a populous area with a lot of condominium developments, a condominium owner may be able to reduce his assessment. There are several reasons why this special type of residential property can be so difficult for the assessor to value fairly and according to true market value.

1. If a cost approach alone is used for valuing each unit with its common areas, varying locations within the condominium complex make it a natural for factual errors and inequities.

2. Assessors generally base assessments on their analysis of current sales of the condo units and identify current market value "right on the button." If an analysis of other nearby condo properties show they are assessed 20 percent below the statutory level of assessments, isn't that a case for a reduction using the sales ratio study method? Generally, the sales ratio approach is the most viable approach for condominium appeals.

3. Did the sales used to develop the assessments contain a measure of personal property (refrigerator, stoves, etc)? Many tax jurisdictions allow this personal property value to be deducted from the sales price to reflect a lower real property value.

4. In areas with a glut of condominiums, there may be decreasing sales prices of units. In this case, you can show lesser value using the market approach...especially in brand-new developments where, due to slow sales, developers had to lower prices.

TABLE I
ASSESSMENT RATIOS 1987

GEOGRAPHIC AREA	CATEGORY	ADJUSTED MEDIAN	MEDIAN	COEF. OF DISP.	QUARTILES 1ST	QUARTILES 3RD	RANGE	NO. OF TRANS.
DEWITT								
Total County	Urban	-*	33.77	41.66	29.51	40.52	344	198
TOWNSHIPS								
Clintonia	Urban	-	33.37	39.09	29.38	40.52	168	118
Santa Anna	Urban	-	35.81	15.71	31.17	38.93	40	31
All Others	Urban	-	33.33	64.88	28.70	47.31	344	49

* *

GEOGRAPHIC AREA	CATEGORY	ADJUSTED MEDIAN	MEDIAN	COEF. OF DISP.	QUARTILES 1ST	QUARTILES 3RD	RANGE	NO. OF TRANS.
DOUGLAS								
Total County	Urban	-*	31.96	45.42	25.20	41.24	190	204
TOWNSHIPS								
Arcola	Urban	-	27.19	51.59	21.54	39.20	187	38
Camargo	Urban	-	31.01	49.39	26.57	42.45	136	33
Tuscola	Urban	-	31.37	29.23	25.61	37.01	137	87
All Others	Urban	-	37.75	61.83	27.56	54.59	139	46

* *

GEOGRAPHIC AREA	CATEGORY	ADJUSTED MEDIAN	MEDIAN	COEF. OF DISP.	QUARTILES 1ST	QUARTILES 3RD	RANGE	NO. OF TRANS.
DUPAGE								
Total County	Urban	-	26.49	14.31	24.00	29.31	396	16,221
TOWNSHIPS								
Addison	Urban	28.42	27.14	16.96	24.31	30.65	216	1,335
	Unimp.	-	25.59	49.78	18.50	33.32	216	111
	Imp.	-	27.22	14.13	24.49	30.58	78	1,224
Bloomingdale	Urban	28.45	26.54	13.81	24.38	29.30	282	2,196
	Unimp.	-	16.16	57.64	12.40	18.86	280	84
	Imp.	-	26.67	12.01	24.61	29.46	236	2,112
Downers Grove	Urban	27.98	26.43	17.20	23.07	30.25	89	2,794
	Unimp.	-	17.95	39.82	12.72	23.97	88	97
	Imp.	-	26.58	16.29	23.27	30.33	74	2,697
Lisle	Urban	28.26	26.46	10.44	24.70	28.61	97	2,579
	Unimp.	-	23.27	31.87	14.09	26.80	43	57
	Imp.	-	26.51	9.95	24.76	28.64	93	2,522
Milton	Urban	27.94	25.81	13.67	23.29	28.52	80	2,345
	Unimp.	-	22.92	48.60	13.36	32.74	80	102
	Imp.	-	25.84	12.28	23.44	28.48	57	2,243
Naperville	Urban	29.27	27.56	10.14	25.76	29.95	72	1,094
	Unimp.	-	16.22	24.39	14.17	20.26	22	25
	Imp.	-	27.62	9.46	25.88	30.02	63	1,069
Wayne	Urban	28.30	26.01	11.87	24.11	28.56	108	896
	Unimp.	-	23.84	33.74	15.68	29.43	63	41
	Imp.	-	26.08	10.87	24.25	28.54	103	855
Winfield	Urban	28.31	26.76	14.46	24.20	29.29	126	742
	Unimp.	-	21.03	58.98	15.33	32.91	126	58
	Imp.	-	26.87	11.41	24.72	29.23	92	684
York	Urban	28.52	26.31	17.19	22.91	29.18	394	2,240
	Unimp.	-	15.43	71.70	8.01	19.82	335	79
	Imp.	-	26.46	15.45	23.23	29.28	390	2,161

*No adjustments necessary because there were no significant assessment changes in 1987.

Figure 4-14

CHAPTER 5
HOW TO APPEAL AND WIN

Finally! You have done the research. You are certain you have evidence of overassessment. Now you will have to decide whether the tax savings will justify the further trouble and expense of an appeal. Consider this: you have already done most of the work by this point, so if you anticipate enough savings to justify a few more hours of your time, then why not go for it? Remember, your savings will be realized every year you're living in the property.

BEGIN WITH AN INFORMAL APPEAL

Informal hearings take place between the assessor and you. This is the time to present your evidence in a convincing and professional manner.

- Take a proper attitude going in.

- Assume they will try to be fair.

- Remember this is their job and they have nothing personal against you.

- Keep in mind they are concerned with assessment, not tax rates.

• Do not get emotional or abusive.

• Remember you have the formal hearing if you aren't successful here.

When you are prepared, arrange for an informal conference with the assessor or his representative.

At your meeting, here are five questions the assessor may ask you, along with some ways you should be prepared to respond:

Question #1: Would you be willing to sell your house for the market value indicated by the assessment?

That question is not relevant if I'm not assessed fairly compared with my neighbors.

Question #2: What did you pay for the property and when did you buy it?

You can answer, but it shouldn't be relevant if the sale is older than two years.

Question #3: What is the home insured for?

Assessors sometimes think insurance has some relationship to the house's cost. Remind them it has no relation to market or equity value or you can say it's the amount your mortgage lender required.

Question #4: Have any recent improvements been made to the house? When? How much did they cost? Who was the contractor or did you do it yourself?

Answer honestly but don't volunteer more information than necessary. Remember, the cost of improvement is seldom matched by an equal increase in the property's value. Real estate brokers or an appraiser could back that up.

Question #5: Are you familiar with such-and-such house in the neighborhood? Are you aware that it just sold for $$$? Do you think it's reasonably comparable to your home?

This would be a good time to present your evidence if you haven't already done so.

Remember, you are presenting fact and logic, not begging or demanding an assessment reduction.

PRESENTATION OF EVIDENCE

You may have to develop a thick skin. Sometimes property owners -- and even real estate appraisers -- are discouraged from getting involved in the appeal process because of the antagonistic attitude of some assessment officials. Keep in mind, it's the assessor's job to defend the assessment. If the assessment is relatively indefensible, the only course left to them (they think) is to refute your evidence.

State your case concisely, alluding only to those facts concerned with value. For example, that a building has a steep roof has little to do with value.

Presentation to the local assessor should recognize the following:

· The assessor is convinced his methods are proper.

· He or she doesn't like the idea of reducing his aggregate assessments.

· You have to convince the assessor of your determination for equitywithout criticizing his work (if possible). Be tactful.

· Your best opportunity for a reduction at this level is a case of factual error or a flagrant case of inequity. Remember, at the next appeal level, the assessor is not going to like having his mistakes "highlighted."

Some assessors will not cooperate, no matter how glaring the evidence -- especially if they believe the board will take their side no matter what the evidence shows. If this is the case, don't use any more of your time, and just request the proper forms to file with the board. Make notes of any threats to increase your assessment if you file; you may want to double check your evidence to make sure there's no basis for an increase. This is usually done to discourage you from appealing.

Perhaps, in your research, you found that your entire subdivision, neighborhood or condo complex is assessed differently from others. In this case, you might consider appealing as part of a group. You will be more successful as one of a large number, provided you have the evidence to back your case. This is especially so if the only objection the assessor has to granting you a reduction is that others in your subdivision may find out and want a reduction, too. Let everyone know, and you may all get the same reduction.

If the assessor agrees with your evidence -- whether it's is an error or based on any method described earlier -- ask when the reduction will be reflected. Also ask for documentation for your records. At this point, your work has paid off with tax savings. Congratulations!

WHEN TO APPEAL

If, you aren't satisfied with the outcome after your meeting with the assessor -- perhaps you only received a partial reduction or no reduction at all -- then the procedure to follow is:

1. Find out the deadline for filing an appeal with the local appeal board to request a formal hearing.

2. Get the proper forms needed to file.

3. Complete the appeal forms exactly as specified.

4. Complete your evidence in written form and make as many copies as are needed for the appeal board.

5. Submit the forms and evidence by the deadline specified in your juridiction.

6. Attend the formal hearing. (If attendance is optional, you can rely on your written evidence, but you will yield your chance to question the

assessor and discredit his evidence. You may also give the impression that your case isn't strong enough for you to attend.)

7. Repeat this process with the next higher appeal board if you are denied or given only a partial, unacceptable reduction.

Check your state's appeal process in the state-by-state summary and double-check it against your local deadline for filing an appeal by asking your assessor. The appeal period usually begins the date the assessment notice was mailed. You must take the responsibility of finding out the appeal deadlines. Claiming that you didn't receive a notice makes no difference because the assessor doesn't have to prove he sent you a notice. (You would have to prove he didn't, and that's difficult.)

Read preparation instructions carefully. In many jurisdictions, it's not necessary to complete the entire form. You may simply write, "evidence to follow." Find out if this is the case in your jurisdiction. In some states you don't have to present your evidence in advance with your appeal form, but may submit it before your hearing date or bring it with you to the appeal board hearing.

In most states, a written grievance or complaint is filed in accordance with state law and local regulations. This usually consists of a specific form -- mandated by state or developed locally. There are specific forms for each level of the appeal process. It's your responsibility to find what form to use. Many grievance forms will require your signature to be witnessed by a notary public.

The government office making the assessment can tell how and when to file a grievance. The period between the opening of the tentative assessment roll and the deadline is usually between ten and thirty days. If you miss the deadline, you must wait another year to file.

When you submit formal appeal forms, get a receipt from the clerk. When mailing, use certified or return receipt mail.

PRESENTATION OF EVIDENCE TO THE LOCAL APPEAL BOARD

These hearings vary in style from state to state or even between counties or townships within a state. Some are very informal, others are court-like to the point of including oaths and tape recordings.

A review board consists of one to three members (it varies from one jurisdiction to another). You are allowed to state your case, be questioned and interrogate the local assessor.

There are two ways to present your case to the assessment review board on grievance day:

1. Present the grievance statement and supporting documents. No appearance is necessary.

2. Either the property owner and/or a designated knowledgeable person may support the written statement.

HOW TO PRESENT YOUR CASE TO AN APPEAL BOARD AND BE SUCCESSFUL

Be prepared! Please follow all the steps presented in this book. If you cut any corners, you may discover you do not have all the ammunition you need for the assessor and the appeal board to change your assessment.

Generally, appeal board hearings are public hearings and notice of hearings are published. Before you attend your hearing, try to sit in on another one as an observer -- to get the feel of the order of proceedings, type of questions and the type of evidence submitted.

Evidence submitted at these hearings is considered public record; you may review evidence submitted by other successful appellants. Check the type of evidence submitted by expert witnesses (usually appraisers), by looking up specific property where a reduction was granted. Even if you must buy a copy of the public record (from the Office of the Appeal Board, usually at a minimal fee), you will have a great source for comparative data and that adds to your confidence.

Write down everything you are going to say and make copies for everyone present. Please include a summary at the end for later reference.

Be brief and to the point. Short, concise statements and summaries have more impact than long-winded stories. Stick to the subject of assessment. Complaining that taxes are too high, for example, gets into the subject of tax rates and that is not their responsibility. Tell the truth, but only present information that supports your case. Know when to quit when you're ahead, and do not present information that isn't needed.

But do make full use of your evidence. Use all the information that highlights the overassessment between your property and the comparable's, particularly when most favorable to the point you're trying to make.

Be agreeable when possible. You want to demonstrate that you're reasonable and not critical of their entire process, but rather a few areas involving your case. If the assessor is hostile or incompetent, this may not be possible.

Be confident. Show no doubt that you are right. If you show doubt, the board will have doubts. Do not become emotional, abusive or lecturing. This will surely turn off your audience and distract them from your evidence.

After you present your evidence, state what you think the assessment should be. Do not leave that open for them to decide because it may not be what you intended. Even if they don't agree with you, they may concede some reduction in your favor.

Here are some ways to challenge the assessor's comparable's:

Ask to see a written copy of the comparable's at the hearing. Ask where they're located in relation to your property.

Point out when they are not similarly located or if the buildings don't have similar physical characteristics.

Question or establish improper method of valuation, incomplete appraisal of data, or other information they may have left out in their statement.

A ROLE PLAY

Let's run through a role play of a presentation to a county review board.

Review Board Chairman:	This is a proceeding before the Jackson County Appeal Board. For all those who are about to testify. Raise your right hand and repeat after me, I promise to tell the whole truth and nothing but the truth, so help me God.
	(Pause)
	Mr. or Mrs. Property owner, would you like to tell us the basis of your appeal?

Property Owner:	Yes, Mr. Chairman. I'm here regarding 45 West State Street with property identification number 01-12-104-103. I would like to present evidence requesting the assessment for my property be reduced to reflect a more equitable level compared to similar properties in my subdivision.
Chairman:	Go right ahead.
Property Owner:	I have found three comparable brick ranch houses in my subdivision that were built within a three-year range and have similar amenities, as you can see from my analysis. The building assessment per square foot of living space for each comparable building is within less than 10 percent range of each other -- from $21.00 per square foot to $22.60 per square foot. As you can see, my home is at $31.70 per square foot. I have examined the property record cards of each comparable and found they weren't constructed differently and my property doesn't include any features or materials that would increase the cost so significantly.
	I request a reduction to a level of $22.00 per square foot of living space, which is 2,187 square feet. This is the total square footage that I calculated by measuring the exterior of my house. This is 120 square feet less than the assessor has shown in the property record card. [Note: show blueprints, if you have them.] The total building assessment would be $48,114. Adding the land assessment of $22,600 would result in a total assessment of $70,714 instead of $91,860.
Chairman:	Has ownership of your comparable properties been transferred in the last two years?
Property Owner:	No, they weren't.
Chairman:	Mr. Assessor, would you like to present your evidence?

Assessor:	Yes, I would. I have three comparable sales that indicate to me that the total assessment of $91,680 is close to the market value of the subject property.
Chairman:	Mr. Property Owner, would you like to ask the assessor any questions?
Property Owner:	Mr. Assessor, you show the sale prices of the three comparable properties, but not the assessments. Do you recall what they are?
Assessor:	No, I don't.
Property Owner:	Would you say your property assessments tend to be more or less than their selling prices?
Assessor:	I would say less.
Property Owner:	How much less as a percentage?
Assessor:	I don't have any idea.
Property Owner:	Then you didn't test to see if the assessments were equitable?
Assessor:	No, I didn't.
Property Owner:	I don't have any further questions. Thank you.
Chairman:	There being no other evidence in the record, this hearing is closed. A decision will be rendered within a 60-day time period and notice will be sent in the mail. If you aren't satisfied with the decision, you may appeal with the State Appeal Board within 30 days of the date on the notice.

[Note: Remember, all the evidence you referred to in your testimony should have been submitted in writing to the Appeal Board.]

From my experience, assessors don't spend much time preparing their evidence. When the property is truly overassessed, their evidence may even support your case.

The appeals board may not make its decision immediately. Having heard the evidence and read the documents submitted, they may proceed to the next case and meet later to resolve all cases. Once their decision is reached, the board will direct the assessor to make whatever changes are determined. Most likely, you will be notified of the board's action by mail or by checking with the assessor's office.

After all complaints are heard by the local appeal board, the final assessment roll is completed and the tax rates are determined. It may be open for public inspection, but in most states taxpayers no longer can file grievances (check with your state).

If you are successful at the local appeal board level you will realize a tax reduction, based on the lowered assessment on your next tax bill.

If you aren't satisfied with the results of the local appeal board, you may carry the case to the next higher level -- state appeal board or judicial review (court).

PRESENTATION TO A STATE APPEAL BOARD

Most states have statutes allowing the taxpayer to appeal their assessment before a state board, if they aren't satisfied at the local level. If the local board was not agreeable to your case, there may either be a state board or judicial review (court) that you can further appeal to. Each higher board or appeal level tends to be more objective and less biased in the assessor's favor.

The rules for these hearings are very specific, including when to file. The appeal process in your state is listed in the state-by-state summary.

Presentation to a state appeal board will be similar to the previous role play, but now you are trying to reverse the board's decision. The appeal board acts as a referee between you and the combined forces of the assessor and board of review.

Here are some points to keep in mind:

- Proceedings are somewhat more formal and can be intimidating to the newcomer. Again, try to attend one hearing as an observer. It can be very distracting to your presentation to be interrupted because you have proceeded in the improper order of events. If they are available, read the pamphlets detailing the appeal board rules.

- The hearing officer is usually unfamiliar with local market conditions and is mainly concerned with facts about value.

- The hearing officer will enforce statutory requirements that may be ignored by local review boards. Equity is served, personal property is separated from real property, etc.

- In some states there may be such a volume of appeals that it sometimes takes months before a decision is finally rendered.

In Illinois, for example, the highest appeal board is the property tax appeal board. Check the state-by-state summary under "Appeals & Protests" to see which is your state's equivalent.

Call or write that office, asking them to provide you with a list of all written material available to the public, including the cost. You will find this information useful to help you understand their rules, to decide what grounds for appeal will be most successful and see what evidence is acceptable.

In Illinois, the property tax appeal board publishes a synopsis of its decisions each calendar year. This synopsis summarizes successful and non-successful cases and describes how decisions were made in each case. If a similar book is available in your state, it would be a valuable piece of information to prepare for your state appeal board hearing. And since your local appeal board tries to mirror the state board decision-making process, it could also help when preparing for the local board hearing.

JUDICIAL REVIEW

Judicial review is an appeal of an assessment to a jurisdiction higher than the local administrative review. In some states this review is conducted by a court;

others use an agency, such as the state appeal board. Either has the power to sustain or overturn an assessment made locally.

Judicial review in most states is available only to those who seek and get local appeal board hearings, but aren't satisfied with the decision. If you didn't file a grievance with the local appeal board before the deadline, you may not be able to appeal to a higher jurisdiction.

You can appeal again -- for the second year -- to the local appeal board during the next appeal year, even if last year's appeal hasn't yet been resolved. If the first year's decision eventually isn't in your favor, you can still appeal again. If the decision is in your favor, you can roll over the decision and get the same reduction for the second year -- and every year in the assessment period.

If you are successful at the state or judicial level, you will probably have already paid the tax under appeal. If so, you will get a refund, usually with interest. You may also "carry over" or freeze your new assessment for one or more years in the future (check your state law).

As with the original grievance procedure, there is a limited time to file an appeal. Be sure to check this for your state. The information is accessible through your state's real property tax laws, and it is usually provided by the state agency which is listed in your state summary.

CONCLUSION

This book is intended to be a complete guide to lowering your real estate taxes. Now you won't be intimidated by what you don't know. It will help you understand the entire process even though you may not have to go through the entire appeal process, or use all the methods of reduction to get satisfaction.

As a homeowner, you should question your assessment. The people determining your property's value are not perfect. They make mistakes. Just consider the number of properties in your neighborhood. Since each property is unique, probably each assessment is different. But realistically, what are the chances that each assessment is correct? Examine your assessment and how it compares to your neighbors'.

Remember, when you reduce your assessment, the tax savings are realized for not just one year, but *every year* during the valuation period -- if not for the entire time you're in your home. But that's not all, when mistakes are found, you can often get refunds for past years.

If, after reading this book, you aren't sure you're ready or able to investigate and reduce your assessment, I may be able to help. You may write me at any point in your research and appeal process, in care of R.E.I. Press at 36 S. Washington, Hinsdale, IL. 60521, with your questions. If you would like to speak with me personally, call 708-985-4550. I'm also interested in your success stories. Let me know how this edition worked for you. If I use your story in future editions, I'll send you a check for $50.00.

Approximately 70 percent of the states responded to my request for verification of the information included. Of those 70 percent, only one state made major changes. The others provided few or no changes. With your help, I will continue to try to verify the remainder of the information.

Help us update future editions. Mail us a postcard correcting any mistake or wrong name, address, phone number, typographical error you come across. In appreciation, we will include your name under Contributing Research Editors on our next printing.

If you'd like to be included on a mailing list to be notified of updated information on this book or the availability of other related information or services, send me a request on the Reader's Feedback sheet at the end of this book.

If time is a problem, you may have to find a professional -- a consultant, appraiser, or attorney -- who can help you. For a set fee, an appraiser will help determine your property's value and will defend his or her appraisal, if necessary, with the assessor or board. Look for a certified appraiser familiar with your area, preferably with experience in tax appeal work. Make sure the appraiser you hire understands the need for finding comparable's and facts that will help your case, rather than hurt it. An M.A.I. designation is the highest appraiser certification in the industry this can be costly.

A consultant or attorney specializing in real estate tax reduction may charge you by the hour, set fee, or contingency. Your best option is to hire a professional who is willing to take the case contingent on his or her own success. That way, if they aren't successful, you have lost nothing. If you can't find someone willing to work on a contingency basis, you may want to do your own research and have them represent you before the assessor or appeal boards. When choosing a consultant or attorney, make sure they have successful experience in assessment reduction. Ask for names of clients you could call for references.

When deciding to use a professional to research and appeal your assessment, ask the following questions. The answers will enable you to choose the right consultant and avoid misunderstandings.

❑ Do you work on a contingency or flat fee basis?

❑ How much is your fee and what is it based on?

❑ Is it based on one tax year or the entire assessment period?

❑ When is your fee due, ie. when a reduction is granted by notice, by reduced tax bill or tax refund?

❑ Do you give a reduced rate for appealing future tax years?

❑ What costs will I be responsible for, ie. appraisal, court reporter, land survey, etc.?

❑ What methods do you use to determine if I'm overassessed?

❑ What kinds of information do you use as evidence?

❑ Do you do all the research yourselves or do you need an appraisal?

❑ Will you do all the research before filling any appeal?

❑ Do you act as my agent at every level of hearing?

❑ Will I need to be present at any level of hearing?

❑ Are you responsible for filing all paperwork?

❑ Do you have any professional designations, ie. appraisal, real estate or attorney?

❑ If you aren't an attorney, do I need one at any level?

Get most of these questions answered before entering into any agreement. Ask to look over their contracts to determine exactly how they will act as your agent and how you will be billed.

The time you take to investigate and appeal your assessment can be rewarding. Many people before you have reaped high financial benefits compared to the time they invested. Remember, if you have clear-cut evidence of your overassessment, you'll prevail. When you are successful with your tax-reduction efforts, you'll have enjoyed doing it, you may want to offer your services to other homeowners as a new part-time occupation that will be needed and appreciated -- especially if real estate taxes continue to rise. How likely is that to happen?

PART II

STATE
BY
STATE
SUMMARY

EXPLANATION OF YOUR STATE BY STATE SUMMARY

NAME OF TAX:
Name by which your state and local assessor refers to the tax on your real property.

VALUATION STANDARD:
How your state defines your real property value for assessment purposes.

REVALUATION CYCLE:
The minimum time between reassessments as prescribed by law in your state.

ASSESSMENT LEVEL:
The percentage basis of the value of your real property. Either 100% for full value or downward for a fraction of full value as specified by state law.

HOMEOWNERS EXEMPTIONS:
Exemptions and their restrictions available to homeowners in your state.

ASSESSMENT DATE:
The day of the tax year at which the property value is determined and used as the basis for assessment.

LEVEL OF GOVERNMENT RESPONSIBLE FOR ASSESSMENT:
Such as village, town, city, township, county, parish or state. This is the level at which you begin your research and appeal.

EQUALIZATION:
State and/or local level adjustments of assessments to achieve equality before tax roll is issued.

ASSESSORS:
Tells if the assessor is appointed or elected, for how long and whether certification or education is required or recommended.

STATE ISSUED MANUALS:
What the manuals used by assessors are called.

PROPERTY OWNERSHIP MAPS REQUIRED:

Does your state require your local assessor to provide the public with maps showing where your property is located, lot size and corresponding property index number, etc.

PERMIT REAL PROPERTY TO BE VALUED IN A CURRENT USE RATHER THAN IN A FINANCIALLY BETTER USE:

Yes, means your residences and lots are assessed at the current value in its present use. No, means you can be assessed at your properties "best use" value. For example, if your land can be better used for commercial property, then the land will be assessed accordingly.

MEDIAN AREA ASSESSMENT TO SALES PRICE RATIOS:

The ratio between what the property was sold for and the assessment. Source is from the U.S. Bureau of the Census, Taxable Property Values and Assessment - Sales Price Ratios (Washington, D.C., GPO, 1984), page 50.

FREQUENCY OF STATE RATIO STUDIES:

How often Sales Ratio Studies are performed by your state.

STATE RATIO STUDY AVAILABLE TO PUBLIC:

Answers the question of whether the State Ratio Study is available to the general public upon request.

ADMINISTRATION OF ASSESSMENTS AND TAX LAWS:

How and by whom the property tax laws are carried out.

APPEALS AND PROTESTS:

Details the steps a taxpayer must follow to appeal his property taxes and what level of appeal is available to him.

REFER TO STATE LAW IMPOSED BY:

Where to look up the laws and statues pertaining to property tax assessments in your states law book.

CHANGES:

Changes in the law pertaining to real property taxation.

ADDRESS (STATE):

Address of the person and department responsible for real property taxation in your state.

TELEPHONE:
The telephone number of the above person or department.

VERIFIED BY THIS OFFICE:
A request was sent to each State office to the above office to review a copy of their respective State's summary to verify the contents for accuracy and return the summary with corrections. A "yes" response means the State has responded and a "no" means the State hasn't responded as of this edition.

COMMENTS:
Additional information specific to your state that may assist you in reducing your real estate assessment.

ALABAMA

NAME OF TAX:
Ad Valorem Tax.

VALUATION STANDARD:
Fair and Reasonable Market Value, defined as being "estimated price property would bring at fair and voluntary sale."

REVALUATION CYCLE:
Not specified by statute, but Department of Revenue periodically inspects and supervises statewide reappraisals on a county-by-county basis according to a definite schedule.

ASSESSMENT LEVEL:

Class I: Public Utility Operating property - 30%.
Class II: Property not in Class I or III - 20%.
Class III: Single family residences, agricultural property,
                    historic buildings - 10%.

HOMEOWNERS EXEMPTIONS:

1. Property of deaf and insane to extent of $3,000 actual value; incompetent veterans to extent of $3,000 actual value; and blind veterans to extent of $12,000 actual value.

2. Homesteads for homeowners less than 65 years old are exempt up to $4,000 assessed value for state ad valorem and up to $2,000 for county ad valorem.

3. Homesteads for homeowners over 65 years old or retired due to total and permanent disability or blindness regardless of age are exempt up to $5,000 assessed if annual adjusted gross income is less than $12,000.

4. Homesteads of persons disabled or 65 years and older with a net annual of $7,500 or less is exempt.

5. Homes of vets acquired through federal government assistance while owned and occupied by such veteran or his unmarried widow are exempt.

ASSESSMENT DATES:
October 1.

LEVEL OF GOVERNMENT RESPONSIBLE FOR ASSESSMENT:
County.

EQUALIZATION:
None.

ASSESSORS:
Elected to six year terms.

STATE ISSUES MANUALS:
Appraisal Manuals.

PROPERTY OWNERSHIP MAPS REQUIRED:
Yes. Failure of assessor to maintain plat book (tax maps) according to department standards, i.e., updated annually, can result in a $500.00 fine.

PERMIT REAL PROPERTY TO BE VALUES IN CURRENT USE RATHER THAN IN A FINANCIALLY BETTER USE:
Yes.

MEDIAN AREA ASSESSMENT TO SALES PRICE RATIOS:
94.18 for 1988.

FREQUENCY OF STATE RATIO STUDIES:
Annual.

STATE RATIO STUDY AVAILABLE TO PUBLIC:
No.

ADMINISTRATION OF ASSESSMENTS AND TAX LAWS:
The valuation of property is administered by the various counties as is the collecting of taxes. However, the Department of Revenue generally supervises the valuation of property to maintain an equitable assessment among the counties that's representative of fair market value.

APPEALS AND PROTESTS:
An appeal must be filed within 10 days of the date of final publication of notice of assessed value. The appeal must be in writing and be submitted to the Secretary of the County Board of Equalization. The deadline for filing an appeal is generally given on any assessment notice. Depending on the county's size involved, the appeals will be filed on counties with low populations before the last Monday in April and on counties with higher populations before May 15. Board hearings commence on the first Monday in June each year and continue as long as required, but not beyond the second Monday of July.

Dissatisfaction with the county board's decision may be filed in the Circuit Court of the county where the property is located within 30 days from the date of the board's notice of its decision. The notice must be filed with the Secretary of the Board of Equalization and the Clerk of the Circuit Court. The taxpayer must either pay the protested tax by its delinquency date or post a bond for twice the amount of the tax due.

The decision of the Circuit Court may be appealed within 30 days of the decision to the Court of Civil Appeals or directly to the State Supreme Court.

REFER TO STATE LAW IMPOSED BY:
Title 40 of the Code of Alabama, 1975, as amended, covers all revenue and taxation including the taxing of property.

CHANGES:
1.   10/1/78 - Established current classified assessment system.

ADDRESS (STATE):
State of Alabama
Department of Revenue
Ad Valorem Tax Division
Montgomery, Alabama 36132-7210

TELEPHONE:
(205) 242-1525

VERIFIED BY THIS OFFICE:
Yes.

ALASKA

NAME OF TAX:
Property Taxes.

VALUATION STANDARD:
Full and True Value, defined as the "estimated price which property would bring in an open market under the prevailing market conditions in a sale between a willing seller and a willing buyer, both conversant with the property and with the prevailing general price levels."

REVALUATION CYCLE:
Not specified by statute, but borough assembly has authority to pass a resolution ordering borough-wide property revaluation by local assessor.

ASSESSMENT LEVEL:
100% of full and true value.

HOMEOWNERS EXEMPTIONS:
1. Property owned and occupied as the primary residence by a resident aged 65 or older, by a disabled veteran or be a resident at least 60 years old who is the widow or widower of a person who qualified for the exemption is exempt from tax on the first $150,000 of assessed value (municipalities may provide for exemption beyond $150,000 in hardship cases).

2. Municipalities may exempt, or partially exempt, from taxation (1) residential property subject to voter approval, but an exemption may not exceed $10,000 for any one residence, and (2) privately owned land, wetland and water areas for which a scenic, conservation or public recreation use easement is granted to a governmental body.

ASSESSMENT DATE:
January 1.

LEVEL OF GOVERNMENT RESPONSIBLE FOR ASSESSMENT:
Municipal.

EQUALIZATION:
None.

ASSESSORS:
Appointed to indefinite terms with no certification required.

STATE ISSUED MANUALS:
Appraisal Manuals.

PROPERTY OWNERSHIP MAPS REQUIRED:
No.

PERMIT REAL PROPERTY TO BE VALUED IN CURRENT USE RATHER THAN IN A FINANCIALLY BETTER USE:
No.

MEDIAN AREA ASSESSMENT TO SALES PRICE RATIOS:
74.30.

FREQUENCY OF STATE RATIO STUDIES:
Annual.

STATE RATIO STUDY AVAILABLE TO PUBLIC:
No.

ADMINISTRATION OF ASSESSMENTS:
All assessments other than those on oil and gas related property are fully administered at the local level.

APPEALS AND PROTESTS:
A taxpayer dissatisfied with an assessment received from a local assessor may file an appeal with the local board of equalization in writing, within thirty (30) days of issuing the assessment notice. If the taxpayer isn't satisfied with the local board of equalization's decision, there is no recourse available with the state through a board of equalization. The board's decision must be appealed directly to the state superior court.

REFER TO STATE LAW IMPOSED BY:
Title 29 of the Alaska Statutes grants authority to impose property taxes to local governments (first and second class cities and first, second and third class boroughs).

CHANGES:
None.

ADDRESS (STATE):
State of Alaska
Department of Revenue
Petroleum Revenue Division
550 West 7th Avenue - Suite 300
Anchorage, Alaska 99501

TELEPHONE:
(907) 276-2678

VERIFIED BY THIS OFFICE:
No.

ARIZONA

NAME OF TAX:
Property Taxes.

VALUATION STANDARD:
1. Primary tax purposes, i.e., state, county, municipal and school district taxes: Limited Property Value, which cannot exceed the greater of (a) 110% of prior year limited property value (generally used when property ownership or character remains unchanged); or (b) prior year limited property value plus 25% of the difference between prior year limited property value and current year full cash value (generally used when property ownership or character changes). In no case can the limited property value exceed the full cash value.

2. Secondary tax purposes, i.e., special district levies and assessments: Full Cash Value, defined as being "synonymous with market value, which means that estimate of value that's derived annually by use of standard appraisal methods and techniques or as provided by law."

REVALUATION CYCLE:
Not specified by statute.

ASSESSMENT LEVEL:
Class I: Flight property and producing mines - 38%.
Class II: Public utility property - 38%*.
Class III: Commercial and industrial property not in other classes - 25%.
Class IV: Agricultural and vacant property - 16%.
Class V: Residential property - 10%.
Class VI: Rental residential - 18%**.
Class VII: Railroad and private car companies - average of Classes I, II, III.
Class VIII: Historic property - 5%.
Class IX: Scenic or historic railroad property - 50% of Class VII.

 * 1983 level, to decrease by 2% per year to 25% by 1990
** 1984 level, to decrease by 1% per year to 14% by 1988

HOMEOWNERS EXEMPTION:
1. Exemptions are allowed for the property of honorably discharged veterans, disabled persons, widows and widowers in the amount of:
   $2,340 if the total assessment doesn't exceed $5,460.
   $1,560 if the total assessment doesn't exceed $6,240.
   $780 if the total assessment doesn't exceed $7,020.
   $390 if the total assessment doesn't exceed $7,800.

   Veterans with a service-connected disability of more than 60%, and veterans with a non-service connected disability that's total and permanent are entitled to a double exemption. Veterans with a service-connected disability of 60% or less are entitled to the full exemption plus a percentage of a second exemption equal to the percentage of disability.

For a widow, widower or disabled person to qualify, the total income of the widow, widower or disabled person and spouse and all children living in the residence may not exceed $8,400 if no children under age 18 dwell in the residence or $12,000 if children under age 18 or totally and permanently disabled reside in the home.

ASSESSMENT DATES:
November 30 and value determined as of January of next year.

LEVEL OF GOVERNMENT RESPONSIBLE FOR ASSESSMENT:
County.

EQUALIZATION:
State Board of Tax Appeals equalizes assessed values between or within counties by adjusting property classes, geographic areas or individual parcels.

ASSESSORS:
Elected to four-year term, certification required.

STATE ISSUED MANUALS:
Assessment practice manual.

PROPERTY OWNERSHIP MAPS REQUIRED:
Yes.

PERMIT REAL PROPERTY TO BE VALUED IN CURRENT USE RATHER THAN IN A FINANCIALLY BETTER USE:
Yes.

MEDIAN AREA ASSESSMENT TO SALES PRICE RATIOS:
6.30.

FREQUENCY OF STATE RATIO STUDIES:
Annual.

STATE RATIO STUDY AVAILABLE TO PUBLIC:
Yes.

ADMINISTRATION OF ASSESSMENTS AND TAX LAWS:
Real property and unsecured personal property are assessed by the county assessor using the "Assessment Practice Manual" issued by the Arizona Department of Revenue as a guideline for determining value.

APPEALS AND PROTESTS:
A taxpayer dissatisfied with the assessment received from the county assessor on real property and secured personal property may, within 15 days of the mailing of the Notice of Value, file a written appeal with the assessor. If the taxpayer isn't satisfied with the county assessor's decision on the real property and secured personal property, he must file an appeal with the County Board of Equalization within 15 days of the mailing of the county assessor's decision.

Any action by the County Board of Equalization may be appealed to the State Board of Tax Appeals. Decisions on real property and secured personal property may appeal within 15 days of the mailing of the decision of the County Board of Equalization. Any taxpayer not satisfied with the decision of the State Board of Tax Appeals on real property and secured personal property may file an appeal with the State Superior Court. A taxpayer dissatisfied with the assessment determined by the county assessor may appeal, whether he files an appeal with the assessor, county board or state to the State Superior Court.

Assessments determined by the Department of Revenue will be appealed to the State Board of Tax Appeals and the State Superior Court. Effective 9/30/88, the Arizona Tax Court was created under the administrative supervision of the presiding judge of the superior court of Maricopa County. The tax department of the superior court in Maricopa County, when exercising the original jurisdiction of the superior court over cases of law and equity involving the legality of any tax assessment, shall be known as the Arizona Tax Court. The principal office of the Arizona Tax Court is at the superior court in Maricopa County; however, the tax court may hold hearings in any county seat in the state to provide reasonable opportunity for taxpayers to appear before the court.

Except when sitting on a small claims tax case, the tax court is final unless a notice of appeal is filed with the clerk of the tax court within 30 days after entry of the tax court judgement. The appeal will be heard by the Court of Appeals. A judgment in a small claims case in the tax court is conclusive on all parties and cannot be appealed. The small claims tax court only hears cases involving real or personal property with a full cash value not exceeding $100,000 or an assessment (including interest and penalties) not exceeding $5,000.

REFER TO STATE LAW IMPOSED BY:
Title 42, Chapters 1-4 of the Arizona Revised Statutes, as amended.

CHANGES:
1.   1979 - Required assessor examination.

2.   6/1/80 - Allowed Department of Revenue to contest valuation - See State Control #1.C.

3.   1983 - Legislated valuation standard for primary tax purposes - See Valuation Standard #1.

ADDRESS (STATE):
Arizona Department of Revenue
Division of Property Valuation
Jane McVey Assistant Director
1600 W Monroe St. - 8th Floor
Phoenix, Arizona 85038

TELEPHONE:
(602) 542-5221

VERIFIED BY THIS OFFICE:
Yes.

ARKANSAS

NAME OF TAX:
Property Tax

VALUATION STANDARD:
True Market Value in Money, determined by "valuing each separate piece of real estate at its true value in money, excluding the value of crops growing thereon, but the price at which such real estate would sell at auction or at a forced sale shall not be taken as the criteria of such value."

REVALUATION CYCLE:
Not specified by statute.

ASSESSMENT VALUE:
A percentage of true market value in money, as determined by the Public Service Commission through the Department of Assessment Coordination (maximum: 20%).

HOMEOWNERS EXEMPTIONS:
Disabled veterans and widow or widowers of those who were killed or missing in action in the service are totally exempt.

ASSESSMENT DATES:
January 1.

LEVEL OF GOVERNMENT RESPONSIBLE FOR ASSESSMENT:
County.

EQUALIZATION:
State Equalization Board equalizes assessed values within and among counties by percentage adjustments to counties.

ASSESSORS:
Elected to two year term, certification required.

STATE ISSUED MANUALS:
Appraisal.

PROPERTY OWNERSHIP MAPS REQUIRED:
No.

PERMIT REAL PROPERTY TO BE VALUED IN CURRENT USE RATHER THAN IN A FINANCIALLY BETTER USE:
Yes.

MEDIAN AREA ASSESSMENT TO SALES PRICE RATIOS:
7.70.

FREQUENCY OF STATE RATIO STUDIES:
Annual.

STATE RATIO STUDY AVAILABLE TO PUBLIC:
Yes.

ADMINISTRATION OF ASSESSMENTS AND TAX LAWS:
Although the tax returns are filed with the county assessors and each county collects its own tax, the administration of the property tax law, to ensure equitable assessments throughout the state, is the responsibility of the Arkansas Public Service Commission.

APPEALS AND PROTESTS:
The taxpayer must file a petition with the County Board of Equalization on or before the third Monday of August. Where the Board raises an assessment, the taxpayer has until the Saturday following the third Monday of September to apply for a hearing. If the taxpayer isn't satisfied with the Board's decision, he may appeal to the county court on or before the second Monday of October. The court generally finishes hearing cases by the first Monday of November. The ruling of the County Court may be further appealed to the Circuit Court. All administrative remedies must be pursued. If no decision is rendered on the appeal prior to the delinquency date of a tax payment, the taxpayer must pay the tax due within 30 days of the finalization date of the appeal.

REFER TO STATE LAW IMPOSED BY:
Arkansas Code of 1987, Title 26, Chapters 1-52.

CHANGES:
1.   1/1/80 - Court-ordered revaluation was to begin. Completion was scheduled for 12/31/85 by revaluing 15 counties per year.

2.   12/80 - Modified revaluation start date to 1/1/81. Completion by 12/31/83 (25 counties per year).

ADDRESS (STATE):
Assessment Coordination Division
Public Service Commission
John Zimpel
1614 West Third
Little Rock, Arkansas 72201

TELEPHONE:
(501) 371-1261

VERIFIED BY THIS OFFICE:
No.

COMMENTS:
A test of residential assessments in the metropolitan areas indicate a significant "under assessment." Therefore, the only viable and acceptable protest would be inequity of assessments between similar properties.

CALIFORNIA

NAME OF TAX:
Property Tax

VALUATION STANDARD:
Full Cash Value or Fair Market Value, defined as "the amount of cash or its equivalent which the property would bring if exposed for sale in the open market under conditions in which neither buyer nor seller could take advantage of the exigencies of the other and both with all the knowledge of the uses and purposes to which the property is adapted and for which it's capable of being used and of the enforceable restrictions upon those uses and purposes."

 Note: Except for state-assessed public utilities and railroads, and changes due to new construction or ownership, valuation changes are limited to the consumer price index (CPI), but cannot exceed 2% per year from the base year of 1975.

REVALUATION CYCLE:
Property is revalued only when ownership changes or improvements are newly constructed.

ASSESSMENT LEVEL:
100% of full cash value or fair market value.

HOMEOWNERS EXEMPTION:

1. Homes of veterans or their unmarried surviving spouse are exempt on that part of the assessed value not over $40,000 if the veteran is blind, totally disabled or has lost the use of two or more limbs (value of not over $60,000 if the disabled veteran has a household income of not more than $24,000 or $34,000 if the taxpayer filed and qualified for either of the $40,000 or $60,000 exemption in 1983). Totally disabled veterans are entitled to an exemption of up to $100,000 of assessed value for property which constitutes the home of a veteran or the home of the unmarried surviving spouse of the veterans, who, because of injury or disease incurred during military service, is totally disabled. This exemption equals $150,000 of assessed value if household income for the previous year didn't exceed $24,000.

2. Tax assistance is available to California homeowners and renters who are 62 or older, blind, or disabled and whose gross household income does not exceed $24,000. The percentage of assistance ranges from 96% of the tax on the first $34,000 of assessed value if household income is not over $3,300 to 4% of the tax on the first $34,000 if household income is not over $13,200.

3. Residents whose household income is under $20,000, who own their dwelling and who are either age 62 or older or blind or disabled may postpone residential property taxes, assessments and user charges. Tenant-stockholders aged 62 or older, blind or disabled whose household income doesn't exceed $20,000 and who occupy as a principal residence a residential unit in a cooperative housing corporation may postpone taxes on their proportionate share of real estate. Persons 62 or older, blind or disabled who own and occupy a qualified mobile home may postpone property taxes if household income is $24,000 or less. The postponement won't be allowed if household income exceeds $20,000.

4.   Homeowners are provided property tax relief as follows: an exemption of $7,000 of full cash value is allowed for each dwelling occupied by an owner as his principal place of residence. The exemption does not apply to property rented, vacant or under construction on the lien date or to a vacation or second home. The homeowners' exemption doesn't apply to property on which the owner received the veterans' exemption.

5.   Owners of disaster damaged property in eligible counties who file a claim for reassessment may defer payment of taxes on the property.

ASSESSMENT DATES:
March 1.

LEVEL OF GOVERNMENT RESPONSIBLE FOR ASSESSMENT:
County.

EQUALIZATION:
Performed within the county.

ASSESSORS:
Elected to four year term.

STATE ISSUED MANUALS:
Assessment manual.

PROPERTY OWNERSHIP MAPS REQUIRED:
Yes.

PERMIT REAL PROPERTY TO BE VALUED IN CURRENT USE RATHER THAN IN A FINANCIALLY BETTER USE:
Yes.

MEDIAN AREA ASSESSMENT TO SALES PRICE RATIOS:
65.

FREQUENCY OF STATE RATIO STUDIES:
None; uses conformity studies.

STATE RATIO STUDY AVAILABLE TO PUBLIC:
No.

ADMINISTRATION OF ASSESSMENTS AND TAX LAWS:
The responsibility for the administration over assessing and collecting of property taxes has been delegated to the county assessor and county tax collector, respectively. The State Board of Equalization maintains an "Assessors' Handbook" as a guide to all assessors, appraisers and local boards of equalization to ensure a uniform understanding of the basic concepts of value so a standard means of determining values throughout the state might be realized.

APPEALS AND PROTESTS:
A taxpayer who's dissatisfied with the assessment determined by the county assessor may appeal the assessment to the county assessor. Prior to a hearing with the assessor, the taxpayer and

assessor will have a prehearing conference to try to resolve the matter. If an agreement cannot be reached, a formal hearing will be held. If the taxpayer isn't satisfied with the county assessor's decision, an appeal may be filed in writing with the clerk of the Board of Supervisors between July 2 and September 15 requesting a hearing before the County Board of Equalization (County Board of Supervisors) or an Assessment Appeals Board (delegated by the County Board of Supervisors). An appeal of an assessment made outside the regular period may be filed within 60 days from the date the taxpayer was notified.

If the board's decision doesn't satisfy the taxpayer, the tax must be paid under protest and a claim for a refund filed. After the taxing authorities have denied the refund, the taxpayer has six months in which to file a refund suit with the superior court in the county in which the tax was paid. The courts won't receive any new evidence of value. They can only review the record of the hearing in the local equalization proceedings. The court will only hear the case for the following reasons: lack of due process, actual or constructive fraud, abuse of discretion or an erroneous appraisal method that could prove incapable of producing the correct value. The court won't render a decision on the taxes that should be paid if it finds an assessment to be arbitrary or invalid, but it will resubmit the case to the board of equalization for a redetermination of value and a settling of the tax due. The court may retain jurisdiction in the case until resolved. The court will render decisions in any question of law.

REFER TO STATE LAW IMPOSED BY:
Division 1 of the California Revenue and Taxation Code, as amended.

CHANGES:
1.   6/6/78 - Limitation on valuation increases, i.e., proposition 13 - see Valuation Standard Note.

ADDRESS (STATE):
California State Board of Equalization
Department of Property Taxes
Assessment Standards Division
Verne Walton, Chief
1719 24th Street (P.O. Box 942879)
Sacramento, California 94279-0001

TELEPHONE:
(916) 445-4982

VERIFIED BY THIS OFFICE:
Yes.

COMMENTS:
Proposition 13 precludes any attempt to appeal based on sales ratio studies or comparable assessments but one possible appeal would be if proof can be presented of personal property being included in the sales price. This would double taxation since the sale would create a new assessment for real property. The only other viable possibility would be via Proposition 8 which allows for reduction by assessors if physical or economic regression of value can be proven (quake damage, condominium market glut, etc.).

PROPOSITION 13 UPDATE

Twelve years ago it was thought that California voters initiated a national tax revolt by passing Proposition 13. "Prop 13" rolled back property tax assessments to those prevailing in 1975 and limited property tax hikes to one percent a year, regardless of increases in a home's market value, as long as the property didn't change ownership. Prop 13 cut local property taxes (California property taxes are collected locally) by more than 50 percent and dropped California from fourth to twenty-fifth in a ranking of the highest-taxed state residents. Unfortunately, cash strapped local governments have had to engage in damage control programs.

Many new impact fees and other charges have been placed on developers, whereby severely increasing the cost of finished real estate (residential and commercial) to occupants and users. The lack of necessary tax revenue has restricted the construction of much infrastructure (roads, utilities, etc) and many public educational systems and has directly resulted in a major increase in slow-growth and no-growth voter initiatives. The "home feeding frenzy" in California can be traced to the undersupply of houses priced in the range of most buyers and is a primary result of Prop 13. In addition, certain California localities will be faced with declining local economies if new businesses decide to locate elsewhere due to the high occupancy and operational costs traceable to Prop 13.

The major adverse impact, however, continues to be felt by home buyers. In a survey conducted in the fall of 1987 by the National Association of Home Builders, California builders reported impact fees and infrastructure charges on residential construction more than doubled since 1983 and added an average of nearly $12,000 to the cost of a new single-family home. And we can bet that cost has increased over the last few years.

The problem continues. Most local governments demand builders contribute land and absorb major costs of building schools, parks, fire stations, roads, and utilities as well as provide various other public services to receive building permits. Such costs were previously (prior to the passing of Prop 13) covered primarily by taxes on residential real estate.

Prop 13 has actually had the reverse impact of that expected by California voters in 1978. Rather than limit costs to the users of residential and commercial property, Prop 13 has increased such costs. The dried-up coffers of local governments necessitate that property users bear costs in many unexpected forms that unaltered property tax law would have covered.

COLORADO

NAME OF TAX:
General Property Tax

VALUATION STANDARD:
Actual Value, defined as "other than agricultural lands exclusive of building improvements thereon and other than residential real property and other than producing mines and lands or leaseholds producing oil or gas, that value determined by the appropriate consideration of the cost approach, the market approach and the income approach to value."

REVALUATION CYCLE:
Every two years, 1985 base year values will be used for the 1987-1988 assessment cycle. For assessment years 1989-1990 and 1991-1992, the level of value employed will be from an 18-month period ending June 30 prior to the assessment date. Commencing in 1993, Colorado law will require annual valuation utilizing an advanced level of value annually.

ASSESSMENT LEVEL:
Residential property - 15% of actual value.

Nonresidential property, other than oil and gas production and producing mines - 29% of actual value.

Note: Starting in 1987 and every two years thereafter, the general assembly may adjust the assessment rate of residential property to ensure the aggregate residential assessed value remains the same as it was in the preceding revaluation year.

HOMEOWNERS EXEMPTIONS:
1. Property occupied by individuals age 62 or over or disabled, whose incomes are within 150% of the limits prescribed for similar individuals and families who occupy nearby low rent public housing operated by a local housing authority.

2. Persons who are 65 or older may defer their previous year's realty taxes by filing a claim after January 1 and on or before April 1, of each year in which they claim a deferral. To qualify, the property must be the homestead (including a mobile home) of the taxpayer, the taxpayer must own or be purchasing the fee simple estate, the property must not be income-producing, all realty taxes for years prior to the year for which election is made must be paid and the property must not be subject to any lien of a mortgage or deed of trust which has been of record for less than five years prior to the date on which the claim for deferral is submitted. Interest accrues on the deferred rate of 8% per year. The spouse of the taxpayer may elect to continue the tax deferral if the spouse is 60 years old or older.

3. Individuals having resided within Colorado for the entire taxable year who are age 65 or older or who are disabled are eligible for a grant based upon payment of their real estate taxes. A surviving spouse age 58 or older will be treated as qualifying for the grant if the surviving spouse meets all the other limitations. Homeowners income from all sources for the tax year must be less than $7,500 if single or less than $11,200 in the case of a husband

and wife. The grant equals the amount of the general property taxes actually paid on the residence up to $500 depending on household income. The grant can't exceed the amount of general property taxes actually paid.

ASSESSMENT DATES:
January 1.

LEVEL OF GOVERNMENT RESPONSIBLE FOR ASSESSMENT:
County.

EQUALIZATION:
Yes.

ASSESSORS:
Elected to four-year term, certification not required.

STATE ISSUES MANUALS:
Appraisal assessment manuals.

PROPERTY OWNERSHIP MAPS REQUIRED:
Yes.

PERMIT REAL PROPERTY TO BE VALUED IN CURRENT USE RATHER THAN IN A FINANCIALLY BETTER USE:
No.

MEDIAN AREA ASSESSMENT TO SALES PRICE RATIOS:
15.99.

FREQUENCY OF STATE RATIO STUDIES:
Yearly.

STATE RATIO STUDY AVAILABLE TO PUBLIC:
Yes.

ADMINISTRATION OF ASSESSMENTS AND TAX LAWS:
The direct administration of property assessment and collecting property taxes, other than the assessment of public utilities (which are assessed by the Property Tax Administrator) is at the county level. The assessments determined by the county assessor are subject to review by the County Board of Equalization, which may adjust the assessment if it finds it not to be just and equitable.

The State Board of Equalization shall appoint a State Property Tax Administrator, who will have the duty of administering the property tax laws and such other duties as may be prescribed by law, and shall be subject to the supervision and control of the State Board of Equalization. The Administrator shall issue and update property tax manuals to be furnished to all county assessors with recommended guidelines for determining equitable valuations for assessment purposes.

APPEALS AND PROTESTS:

The initial protest must be made to the county assessor between May 15 and June 15 of each year for real property and between June 15 and July 5 for personal property. An appeal may be made to the board of county commissioners, sitting as the county board of equalization. An appeal to the CBOE must be made on or before July 10 for real property and July 15 for personal property. An appeal of the county board's decision can be filed within 30 days with either the State Board of Assessment Appeals (BAA) or district court; or the taxpayer may request binding arbitration. The BAA's decision and the district court's decision may be appealed to the Court of Appeals, and the Court of Appeals' decisions appealed, finally, to the Colorado Supreme Court.

REFER TO STATE LAW IMPOSED BY:

Title 39 of the Colorado Revised Statutes, as amended, and Article X of the Colorado Constitution.

CHANGES:

1. 1/1/83 - Required annual audit of local assessment practices.

2. 4/22/83 - Established current valuation standard.

ADDRESS (STATE):

Colorado Division of Property Taxation
1313 Sherman Street - Room 419
Denver, Colorado 80203

TELEPHONE:

(303) 866-2371

VERIFIED BY THIS OFFICE:

Yes.

COMMENTS:

Re-evaluation every 2 years would tend to create considerable overassessments. Remember, current year assessments are based on a prior year value, so if proving value, it must be based on market data circa the valuation period NOT the assessment.

CONNECTICUT

NAME OF TAX:
Property Tax

VALUATION STANDARD:
Present, True, and Actual Value, defined as "the fair market value, and not the value at a forced or auction sale."

REVALUATION CYCLE:
Within 10 years of last revaluation.

ASSESSMENT LEVEL
70% of present, true and actual value.

HOMEOWNERS EXEMPTION:

1. Property of blind residents, property of pensioned or disabled war veterans or their surviving spouses while unmarried or minor children of deceased servicemen, to the value of $1,500 to $3,000 depending on age and disability rating. Property of veterans or members of armed forces or of their surviving spouses, minor children or parents of veterans, to the value of $1,000. Local exemptions include: dwelling house and lot belonging to veterans with service-connected disabilities or their surviving spouse, who served in the U.S. Army, Navy, Marine Corps, Coast Guard or Air Force to the extent of $10,000; loss of use of one arm or leg due to a service-connected injury entitles the veteran to a $5,000 exemption; subject to municipal approval, the dwelling and lot of a veteran who uses federal financial assistance for specially adapted housing to acquire the dwelling are fully exempt.

2. $1,000 in property belonging to any resident eligible to receive permanent total disability benefits under a federal, state or local plan.

3. Persons 65 or over may have real property tax frozen if (1) federal adjusted gross income and tax exempt interest for the preceding year isn't over $6,000, (2) the taxpayer has occupied the property as his home, and (3) either he or his spouse has resided in Connecticut for at least one year. The tax is calculated after deducting $1,000 from assessed value for 1966 or the year when first qualified.

4. Residential property owners in certain municipalities which have undergone revaluation within the past six years, or in certain municipalities in which a general revaluation becomes effective in any assessment year beginning October 1, 1987, to October 1, 1991, may qualify for property tax credit. The credits range from $40 to $250 depending on the year in which a revaluation is effective. In order to qualify for the tax credits, the amount of property tax must have been increased by at least $200 due to the revaluation.

5. A reduction in the assessed value of residential realty as follows is allowed for persons totally and permanently disabled and persons age 65 or older (or whose spouse is 65 or older) or who are 50 or older and the surviving spouse of a taxpayer who qualified for the reduction at the time of death, if they occupy the property as a primary residence and have total federal

adjusted gross income plus other qualifying income (excluding medicaid payments) for the prior tax year of not over $20,000 if married or $16,200 if unmarried.

6. Municipalities may allow totally disabled persons an additional $1,000 exemption if federal adjusted gross income plus any other income is not more than $16,000 if married or $14,000 if unmarried. Municipalities may also allow an additional $2,000 exemption to blind persons whose federal adjusted gross income plus any other income isn't more than $16,000 if married or $14,000 if unmarried.

7. Municipalities may allow veterans an additional exemption to the assessed value of property up to $1,000 if federal adjusted gross income plus any other income isn't more than $16,000 if the veteran is married or $14,000 if the veteran is unmarried. Municipalities may also allow an additional $1,000 exemption to a veteran's surviving spouse if the spouse's federal adjusted gross income plus other income isn't more than $14,000.

8. Municipalities may exempt buildings equipped with solar heating or cooling systems or buildings to which a solar energy heating or cooling system is added, to the extent the assessed value of the building so equipped exceeds its value equipped with a conventional heating or cooling system. The exemption applies to the first 15 assessment years following construction and is allowed for construction begun on or after October 1, 1976, but before October 1, 1991.

9. Municipalities may abate property taxes on any residential dwelling occupied by the owner as the primary place of residence to the range the taxes exceed 8% or more of total household income from any source for the prior calendar year. The owner must agree to reimburse the municipality for the taxes abated with interest at 6% per year or a rate approved by the municipality. The amount of abated taxes is due in full upon the sale or transfer of the property or the owner's death.

ASSESSMENT DATES:
October 1.

LEVEL OF GOVERNMENT RESPONSIBLE FOR ASSESSMENT:
Township.

EQUALIZATION:
Performed between counties.

ASSESSORS:
Elected and appointed, terms for elected varies and indefinite for appointments, certification not required.

STATE ISSUED MANUALS:
Assessment manuals.

PROPERTY OWNERSHIP MAPS REQUIRED:
No.

PERMIT REAL PROPERTY TO BE VALUED IN CURRENT USE RATHER THAN IN A FINANCIALLY BETTER USE:
No.

MEDIAN AREA ASSESSMENT TO SALES PRICE RATIOS:
40.50.

FREQUENCY OF STATE RATIO STUDIES:
Annual.

STATE RATIO STUDY AVAILABLE TO PUBLIC:
Yes.

ADMINISTRATION OF ASSESSMENTS AND TAX LAWS:
The valuation of property is controlled by state statute but administering assessments and collecting taxes is at the town level.

APPEALS AND PROTESTS:
The initial step would be to have an informal meeting with the assessor. If differences cannot be resolved, excessive assessments may be appealed before the City Board of Review during the month of February. The decision of the Board of Review may be appealed to the superior court of the judicial district where the property is located. Any person, including a lessee of real property whose lease has been recorded and who's bound under the terms of the lease to pay real property taxes, claiming to be aggrieved by the action of the Board of Tax Review in any town or city with respect to the assessment list for the assessment year beginning October 1, 1988, may appeal from that assessment to the superior court for the judicial district in which the city or town is located.

REFER TO STATE LAW IMPOSED BY:
Title 12, Chapters 201 through 206 of the General Statutes of Connecticut, as amended.

CHANGES:
1.   1/1/78 - Established current revaluation cycle.

2.   7/1/84 - Created voluntary assessor certification.

ADDRESS (STATE):
State of Connecticut
Office of Policy and Management
Intergovernmental Relations Division
Donald Zimbouski
80 Washington Street
Hartford, Connecticut 06106

TELEPHONE:
(203) 566-8070

VERIFIED BY THIS OFFICE:
Yes.

COMMENTS:
Properties are reassessed on a town-wide basis staggered throughout the State (every 10 years). The best time, therefore, to effectively petition an assessment appears to be in the re-evaluation year.

DELAWARE

NAME OF TAX:
Property Tax.

VALUATION STANDARD:
True Value in Money (not defined by statute).

REVALUATION CYCLE:
Not specified by statute.

ASSESSMENT LEVEL:
Not specified by statute, other than to state "all property subject to taxation shall be assessed at its true value in money."

HOMEOWNERS EXEMPTIONS:
1. Up to $5,000 of the assessed value of residential property of persons 65 or over provided the annual income of the taxpayer or his spouse is not over $3,000 and they have owned and occupied the property for three years. The exemption is also allowed on owner-occupied mobile homes.

2. Residents of Delaware municipalities who own realty in the city and who are 65 years old or older are eligible for an exemption on such realty, subject to adopting local law by the municipality.

ASSESSMENT DATES:
January 1.

LEVEL OF GOVERNMENT RESPONSIBLE FOR ASSESSMENT:
County.

EQUALIZATION:
None.

ASSESSORS:
Appointed to four year term, certification not required.

STATE ISSUED MANUALS:
None.

PROPERTY OWNERSHIP MAPS REQUIRED:
No.

PERMIT REAL PROPERTY TO BE VALUED IN CURRENT USE RATHER THAN IN A FINANCIALLY BETTER USE:
No.

MEDIAN AREA ASSESSMENT TO SALES PRICE RATIOS:
26.10.

FREQUENCY OF STATE RATIO STUDIES:
None.

STATE RATIO STUDY AVAILABLE TO PUBLIC:
None.

ADMINISTRATION OF ASSESSMENTS AND TAX LAWS:
Counties assess and collect taxes under general law and municipalities assess and collect under the provisions of the particular municipality's charter. School taxes and many municipal taxes are determined by adopting the county's assessment.

APPEALS AND PROTESTS:
Appeal dates to protest county or municipal assessments vary. Appeals may be made to the county or municipal assessor or the respective Board of Appeals. Dissatisfaction with the decision at the local level may be appealed to the Superior Court within the period established by statute or court rule.

REFER TO STATE LAW IMPOSED BY:
Title 5, 9, 14 and 30 of the Delaware Code, Revised 1974, as amended.

CHANGES:
None.

ADDRESS (STATE):
Director of Revenue
Delaware Division of Revenue
Wilmington, Delaware

TELEPHONE:
(302) 571-3315

VERIFIED BY THIS OFFICE:
Yes.

DISTRICT OF COLUMBIA

NAME OF TAX:
Property Tax.

VALUATION STANDARD:
Estimated Market Value, defined as "100% of the most probable price at which a particular piece of real property, if exposed for sale in the open market with a reasonable time for the seller to find a purchaser, would be expected to transfer under prevailing market conditions between parties who have knowledge of the uses to which the property may be put, both seeking to maximize their gains and neither being in a position to take advantage of exigencies of the other."

REVALUATION CYCLE:
Not specified by statute.

ASSESSMENT LEVEL:
100% of the estimated market value.

Note: For tax purposes, property is classified as follows:

Class 1:   Residential, owner-occupied, less than five units.

Class 2:   Residential, not owner-occupied, less than five units, non-transient accommodations.

Class 3:   Commercial realty providing transient accommodations, e.g., hotel, motels and inns.

Class 4:   All property other than classes 1, 2 and 3.

HOMEOWNERS EXEMPTIONS:
1.   Historic property exemption credit.

2.   Property transferred to a qualifying lower income homeownership household.

3.   A $2200 deduction from the estimated market value of improved residential real property is allowed if the property is occupied by the owner, contains not more than 5 dwelling units or is a single dwelling unit owned as a condominium and is used exclusively for non-transient residential dwelling purposes. A deduction from the estimated market value of residential real property owned by a cooperative housing association is allowed equal to 44% of the estimated market value, but not to exceed $22,000 multiplied by the number of dwelling units that are occupied by the shareholders or members of the association.

4.   All Class I property owners age 65 or older who receive retirement income, social security benefits or both as their primary means of support are eligible for a 50% decrease in property tax liability.

5. Qualified owners of residential realty may apply for deferral each year of residential realty tax owed in excess of 100% of the preceding year's tax.

6. The real property tax liability of qualified property located within an approved economic development zone is reduced by 80% in the first tax year beginning after the date of issuance of a certificate of occupancy for the property and by 64%, 48%, 32% and 16% in the second, third, fourth and fifth tax years respectively after issuance of the occupancy certificate.

ASSESSMENT DATES:
January 1.

LEVEL OF GOVERNMENT RESPONSIBLE FOR ASSESSMENT:
Municipal.

EQUALIZATION:
Board of Equalization and Review equalizes assessed values that are more than 5% above or below the estimated market value standard.

ASSESSORS:
Elected to indefinite term, certification not required.

STATE ISSUED MANUALS:
Assessment manuals.

PROPERTY OWNERSHIP MAPS REQUIRED:
No.

PERMIT REAL PROPERTY TO BE VALUED IN CURRENT USE RATHER THAN IN A FINANCIALLY BETTER USE:
No.

MEDIAN AREA ASSESSMENT TO SALES PRICE RATIOS:
81.30.

FREQUENCY OF STATE RATIO STUDIES:
Annual.

STATE RATIO STUDY AVAILABLE TO PUBLIC:
No.

ADMINISTRATION OF ASSESSMENTS AND TAX LAW:
The assessing and collecting of property taxes is administered by the District of Columbia Department of Finance and Revenue.

APPEALS AND PROTEST:
A taxpayer may appeal the property assessment that he feels is excessive by filing a protest on or before April 15 with the District of Columbia Board of Equalization and Review. If not satisfied with the Board's decision, the taxpayer has within six months of October 1 following the

assessment (April 1) to appeal the decision to the Tax Court Division of the Superior Court. An unfavorable decision by the Tax Court can be appealed to the Supreme Court of the District of Columbia.

REFER TO STATE LAW IMPOSED BY:
Title 47, Chapters 8, 10 and 15 of the District of Columbia Code, 1981.

CHANGES:
1.   1978 - Changed from 2-year assessment cycle to current 1-year cycle.

ADDRESS (DISTRICT):
Real Property:
Robert L. King
Associate Director
Real Property Assessments
300 Indiana Avenue NW - Room 2132
Washington, DC 20001

TELEPHONE:
(202) 727-6460

VERIFIED BY THIS OFFICE:
No.

COMMENTS:
Overevaluation appears to be the only basis of appeal and because of spiraling values in this district, properties are generally underassessed.

FLORIDA

NAME OF TAX:
Ad Valorem Tax

VALUATION STANDARD:
Just Value, which must consider "1. The present cash value of the property, which is the amount a willing purchaser would pay a willing seller, exclusive of reasonable fees and costs of purchase, in cash or the immediate equivalent thereof in a transaction at arm's length; 2. the highest and best use, as well as the present use of the property taking into consideration applicable land use regulations and moratoriums; 3. the property's location; 4. the quantity or size of the property; 5. the cost of the property and the present replacement value of the improvements; 6. the property's condition; 7. the income from the property; and 8. the net proceeds of the sale of the property, exclusive of personal property and reasonable fees and costs of the sale."

REVALUATION CYCLE:
Physical inspection of all property at not greater than three-year intervals is required, but owners may request more frequent inspections.

ASSESSMENT LEVEL:
100% of just value.

HOMEOWNERS EXEMPTIONS:
1. Historic property exemption credit.

2. Homesteads up to the assessed value of $25,000 for a person who is a Florida resident; additional exemptions for persons 65 or older who are permanent residents of Florida, for widows, blind persons and totally and permanently disabled persons, homestead of a quadriplegic. Homesteads of totally and permanently disabled persons confined to a wheelchair or blind with household gross income not more than $12,000.

3. Real estate owned and used as a homestead by a totally disabled veteran or veteran confined to a wheelchair, who's a permanent resident of Florida or his widow but only until she remarries or sells the property.

4. Improved real property upon which a renewable energy source device is installed and operated equal to the lesser of (1) the assessed value of the real property less any other property tax exemptions; (2) the original cost of the device; or (3) 8% of the property's assessed value immediately following installation.

5. Persons entitled to claim the homestead tax exemption may defer payment of a portion of the property taxes levied on their homestead. The amount deferred is that portion of taxes exceeding 5% of the applicant's household income. (Persons entitled to the increased homestead exemption may defer that portion of the taxes which exceeds 3% of the applicant's household income.) Interest is imposed on the taxes deferred.

ASSESSMENT DATES:
January 1.

LEVEL OF GOVERNMENT RESPONSIBLE FOR ASSESSMENT:
County.

EQUALIZATION:
None.

ASSESSORS:
Elected to four-year term, certification required.

STATE ISSUED MANUALS:
Assessment Manuals.

PROPERTY OWNERSHIP MAPS REQUIRED:
Yes.

PERMIT REAL PROPERTY TO BE VALUED IN CURRENT USE RATHER THAN IN A FINANCIALLY BETTER USE:
No.

MEDIAN AREA ASSESSMENT TO SALES PRICE:
69.20.

FREQUENCY OF STATE RATIO STUDIES:
Triennial.

STATE RATIO STUDY AVAILABLE TO PUBLIC:
Yes.

ADMINISTRATION OF ASSESSMENTS AND TAX LAWS:
All real property is assessed and collected at the local level but the assessment rolls must be submitted to the executive director of the Department of Revenue for review to determine if the rolls meet all appropriate requirements of law relating to form and just value.

APPEALS AND PROTESTS:
Any taxpayer objecting to the assessment of his tangible property may request an informal conference with the property appraiser (revised from tax assessor by 1976 amendment to the law). If not successful, the taxpayer may petition in writing, under oath, with the clerk of the Property Appraisal Adjustment Board of the county on or before the 25th day following the mailing of the Notice of Value. The Board will meet not earlier than 30 days and not later than 45 days after the mailing of the Notice of Value. The Board will render its decision, in writing, within 20 calendar days of the last day the Board is in session.

Either the taxpayer or the appraiser may appeal the decision of the Board to the Circuit Court in the county where the property is located. No action shall be taken to contest a tax assessment after

60 days from the date the assessment being contested is certified for collection or 60 days from the date of the Board's decision .

The taxpayer may appeal the decision of the Circuit Court to the State Supreme Court.

REFER TO STATE LAW IMPOSED BY:
Title XIV of the Florida Statutes, as amended, covers all taxation and finance including the taxing of property.

CHANGES

1. 1973 - Provided for withholding of state revenue sharing funds for assessing at other than just value.

2. 1982 - Required Department of Revenue review of county assessment rolls.

ADDRESS (STATE):
Florida Department of Revenue
Division of Ad Valorem Tax
Alton B. Parker
Woodcrest Office Building (P.O. Box 3000)
Tallahassee, Florida 32315

TELEPHONE:
(904) 488-0108

VERIFIED BY THIS OFFICE:
No.

COMMENTS:
Properties are, in effect, re-valued each year. If you have your assessment reduced, it most probably can/will be changed the next year. If you enlist the services of a consultant to present evidence on your behalf in this State, the assessing officials CAN require the consultant/expert witness have a real estate license in this State.

NOTE: It is common practice for the assessor in this State to value properties at a level less than 100% of value ie. 95%, or 93%, etc. The intent being to dissuade appeals. Therefore you must determine from the assessor in your county what's the actual level of assessment currently being utilized.

GEORGIA

NAME OF TAX:
Ad Valorem Taxation of Property.

VALUATION STANDARD:
Fair Market Value, denied as "the amount a knowledgeable buyer would pay for the property and a willing seller would accept for the property at an arm's length, bona fide sale."

REVALUATION CYCLE:
Not specified by statute.

ASSESSMENT LEVEL:
40% of fair market value.

HOMEOWNERS EXEMPTIONS:

1. Homesteads to the amount of $2,000.

2. Homesteads of persons 65 or older to the amount of $4,000 if owned and occupied as their residence and if their net income (excluding federal old-age, survivor or disability benefits), together with that of their spouse, doesn't exceed $10,000 for the prior taxable year; homesteads of resident disabled veterans or their unremarried surviving widows or minor children to the amount of $35,000.

3. Up to $10,000 of assessed value of homesteads of persons 62 or older residing in an independent school district or county school district if their annual gross income is under $10,000.

4. Counties or municipalities may exempt the value of qualified solar heating or cooling systems, including machinery and equipment directly used in the manufacture of such heating or cooling systems.

5. The first $35,000, or the maximum amount allowed to a disabled veteran under Sec.802 of Title 38 of the U.S. Code, of the value of a resident disabled veteran's homestead.

6. Persons age 62 or older with a household gross income or less than $15,000 may defer all or a part of the taxes on the first $50,000 of assessed value of a homestead. In lieu of the statewide tax deferral plan, persons 62 or older living in Fulton County (Atlanta) may defer all or any portion of their homestead property taxes in excess of 4% of gross household income for the preceding year. The assessed value of the home or the applicant's gross household income doesn't limit this deferral.

ASSESSMENT DATES:
January 1.

LEVEL OF GOVERNMENT RESPONSIBLE FOR ASSESSMENT:
County.

EQUALIZATION:
Performed between counties. Department of Revenue equalizes assessed values by fixed percentage adjustments to property classes or to taxpayer classes.

ASSESSORS:
Appointed for six-year term; certification required.

STATE ISSUED MANUALS:
Assessment manuals.

PROPERTY OWNERSHIP MAPS REQUIRED:
Yes.

PERMIT REAL PROPERTY TO BE VALUED IN CURRENT USE RATHER THAN IN A FINANCIALLY BETTER USE:
No.

MEDIAN AREA ASSESSMENT TO SALES PRICE RATIOS:
30.

FREQUENCY OF STATE RATIO STUDIES:
Annual.

STATE RATIO STUDY AVAILABLE TO PUBLIC:
Yes.

ADMINISTRATION OF ASSESSMENTS AND TAX LAWS:
The real property is made by the various counties but the assessments must be submitted to and must be approved by the State Revenue Commissioner.

APPEALS AND PROTESTS:
A taxpayer who's dissatisfied with his tangible property assessment must file an appeal with the County Board of Tax Assessors within 30 days of receipt of the assessment notice. The Board may either act upon the appeal or forward it to the County Board of Equalization without a decision. Within 10 days of such forwarding, the dissatisfied taxpayer will be notified by the County Board of Equalization of a scheduled hearing within 30 days. Notice of the decision of the Board of Equalization will be mailed within 15 days of the hearing.

The taxpayer may appeal the decision of the Board of Equalization to the Superior Court within thirty (30) days of the Board's notice. The tax must be paid in full under protest before the Superior Court will hear the case.

An aggrieved party may review the final judgment of the Superior Court by the Court of Appeals or the State Supreme Court.

REFER TO STATE LAW IMPOSED BY:
Title 48, Chapters 5 and 6 of the Official Code of Georgia Annotated.

CHANGES:
1.   1972 - Established Department of Revenue control measures.

ADDRESS (STATE):
Georgia Department of Revenue
Property Tax Division
Larry Griggers, Director
405 Trinity-Washington Building
Atlanta, Georgia 30334

TELEPHONE:
(404) 656-4240

VERIFIED BY THIS OFFICE:
No.

COMMENTS:
Inequity of assessments, sales/ratio studies and overassessment are all considered viable appeals. The counties that comprise the Atlanta area have historically "underassessed" residential properties.

HAWAII

NAME OF TAX:
Real Property Taxation

VALUATION STANDARD:
Fair Market Value (not defined by state statute - see note below).

Note: Each of the Hawaiian counties specifies its own language for the definition of fair market value, but all counties have the same requirements imposed by the state constitution. The City and County of Honolulu determines the fair market value, "by the market data and cost approaches to value using appropriate systematic methods suitable for mass valuation of properties, so selected and applied to obtain, as far as possible, uniform and equalized assessments throughout the county."

REVALUATION CYCLE:
Not specified by law.

ASSESSMENT LEVEL:
100% of fair market value, as determined by local county ordinances.

HOMEOWNERS EXEMPTIONS:
1. Property owned and occupied as a principal home on the date by the owner is totally exempt if its value is not over $20,000, plus an additional exemption for persons aged 60 or over based solely on age. Persons 60 or over but not over 70 use a multiple of 2.0 in computing the exemption; persons 70 or over use a multiple of 2.5.

2. Property owned and occupied as a home by a totally disabled veteran of the U.S. armed forces.

3. Property belonging to a Hansen's disease sufferer, to the extent of $25,000 (increased from $15,000 to reflect increased tax base of 100% of fair market value).

4. Property of certain persons with impaired sight or hearing, or who are totally disabled, to the extent of $25,000 (increased from $15,000 to reflect increased tax base of 100% of fair market value).

5. Property used for an alternate energy improvement if installed and placed in service after June 30, 1976, but before December 31, 1981.

ASSESSMENT DATE:
January 1.

LEVEL OF GOVERNMENT RESPONSIBLE FOR ASSESSMENT:
County.

EQUALIZATION:
None.

ASSESSORS:
Appointed to indefinite term, certification not required.

STATE ISSUED MANUALS:
None.

PROPERTY OWNERSHIP MAPS REQUIRED:
Yes.

PERMIT REAL PROPERTY TO BE VALUED IN CURRENT USE RATHER THAN IN A FINANCIALLY BETTER USE:
No.

MEDIAN AREA ASSESSMENT TO SALES PRICE RATIOS:
37.30.

FREQUENCY OF STATE RATIO STUDIES.
Annual.

STATE RATIO STUDY AVAILABLE TO PUBLIC:
Yes.

ADMINISTRATION OF ASSESSMENTS AND TAX LAWS:
Only real property is taxable in the state of Hawaii, and the full responsibility for the administration of the taxation of real property was assigned to the counties.

APPEALS AND PROTESTS:
The county (district) assessor must issue the assessment notice to the taxpayer by March 15 preceding the tax year. The taxpayer should try to obtain relief for any excessive assessment through meeting with the assessor. If the taxpayer is dissatisfied with any relief received from the assessor, he may appeal, by April 9 preceding the tax year, to the district Board of Review. The board will publish a notice no later than the first week of September specifying a period of a least 10 days within which complaints will be heard. The appeal is filed through the assessor.

Taxpayers may appeal their assessment directly with the Tax Appeal Court by April 9 preceding the tax year, instead of going to the district board. Or appeal to the Tax Appeal Court within 30 days of the board's decision. The decision of the Tax Appeal Court may be further appealed by filing an appeal with the State Supreme Court within 30 days of the decision of the Tax Appeal Court.

REFER TO STATE LAW IMPOSED BY:
Chapter 246A of the Revised Hawaii Statutes, which assigns all functions, powers and duties relating to the taxation of real property previously reserved to the state,s counties with the exception of the county of Kalawao.

CHANGES

1. 1/7/81 - Prior system of state assumption of all assessment functions abolished and returned to the counties until at least 11/89.

2. 1/1/83 - Assessment level changed from 60% of fair market value to current 100%.

ADDRESS (STATE):

The state has no responsibility for property. Full administrative responsibility for the taxing of property is at the county level.

TELEPHONE:

Not applicable.

VERIFIED BY THIS OFFICE:

Not applicable.

COMMENTS:

Limited testing of assessment to value sample indicate that properties are considerably underassessed the 100% statutory level. No indication has been determined of how receptive assessors are to comparing assessments of similar properties.

IDAHO

NAME OF TAX:
Property Tax.

VALUATION STANDARD:
Market Value, True Cash Value, Cash Value, True Value, and Assessed Value are all considered to be "market value for assessment purposes" which is defined by the rules and regulations of the State Tax Commission.

REVALUATION CYCLE:
Every five years, by the annual appraisal of 20% of each property category. Annual appraisal results are used to index properties not reappraised.

ASSESSMENT LEVEL:
100% of market value.

HOMEOWNERS EXEMPTIONS:
1. Property of persons who, because of unusual circumstances which affect their ability to pay the tax, should be relieved from paying the tax to avoid undue hardship.

2. The first $50,000 of the market value for assessment purposes of residential improvements, or 50% of the market value for assessment purposes of residential improvements, whichever is less.

3. The following persons, if Idaho residents and homestead owners during the preceding year, are eligible for the property tax reduction: (1) fatherless children under age 18; (2) persons 65 or older; (3) widows or widowers; (4) disabled persons receiving social security disability insurance benefits, Civil Service disability benefits or Railroad Retirement Act disability benefits; (5) disabled veterans or veterans receiving a pension for a non-service connected disability; (6) person entitled to benefits as prisoners of war; and (7) blind persons. The final tax reduction on the homestead is based on the taxpayer's current year's assessed value and levy.

ASSESSMENT DATES:
January 1.

LEVEL OF GOVERNMENT RESPONSIBLE FOR ASSESSMENT:
County.

EQUALIZATION:
Performed both within and between counties. State Tax Commission equalizes assessed values between counties by adjustment of property categories or by ordering reassessment of categories.

ASSESSORS:
Elected four-year terms, certification required.

STATE ISSUED MANUALS:
Appraisal manuals.

PROPERTY OWNERSHIP MAPS REQUIRED:
Yes.

PERMIT REAL PROPERTY TO BE VALUED IN CURRENT USE RATHER THAN IN A FINANCIALLY BETTER USE:
No.

MEDIAN AREA ASSESSMENT TO SALES PRICE RATIO:
86.80.

FREQUENCY OF STATE RATIO STUDIES:
No, special requests subject to approval.

STATE RATIO STUDY AVAILABLE TO PUBLIC:
Yes.

ADMINISTRATION OF ASSESSMENTS AND TAX LAWS:
The actual administering of assessing property and collecting taxes is retained at the county level. The State Tax Commission does furnish the county assessors with index factors and depreciation tables. Although the assessors aren't required to follow the recommendations of the commission; most assessors follow them closely.

APPEALS AND PROTESTS:
A taxpayer dissatisfied with an assessment should appeal it with the county assessor. Should the taxpayer not obtain the relief sought, he may file an appeal with the County Board of Equalization prior to the fourth Monday in June. The board will hold its hearings between the fourth Monday in June and the second Monday in July.

A taxpayer dissatisfied with the decision of the County Board of Equalization may elect to file an appeal with the State Board of Tax Appeals or bypass the State Board and take his appeal directly to the District Court of the county where the property is located. If the taxpayer elects to appeal to the State Board of Tax Appeal, he may still appeal any unfavorable decision of the State Board to the District Court. The decision of the District Court may be appealed to the State Supreme Court.

REFER TO STATE LAW IMPOSED BY:
Title 63, Chapters 1 through 22, of the Idaho Code, 1947 (as amended to date).

CHANGES:
1. 1979 - Tax Commission ordered to revalue or to index all property to 12/31/78 price level by 6/1/80. Assessment level changed from 20% of cash value to 100% of 12/31/78 market value.
2. 1982 - a. Established current valuation standard.

     b. Provided Tax Commission with authority to assume county revaluation program.

ADDRESS (STATE):
State of Idaho
Department of Revenue and Taxation
State Tax Commission
Real and Personal Property Bureau
700 West State Street (P.O. Box 36)
Boise, Idaho 83722

TELEPHONE:
(208) 334-7733

VERIFIED BY THIS OFFICE:
Yes.

ILLINOIS

NAME OF TAX:
Property Tax.

VALUATION STANDARD:
Fair cash value (not defined by statute).

REVALUATION CYCLE:
Every four-years, counties are assigned to one of four assessment districts, one of which is revalued each year, except for Lake and St. Clair Counties which are each divided into four districts, one of which is revalued each year. Cook County is now divided into three disticts, one of which is the City of Chicago, and revalued every three years.

ASSESSMENT LEVEL:
33-1/3% of fair cash value except in counties with populations of 200,000 or more, where a classification system is allowed. Cook County is the only one to implement such a system.

Class I:	Unimproved real estate - 22%.
Class II:	Agricultural and residential (6 units or less) - 16%.
Class III:	Residential other than Class II - 33%.
Class IV:	Real estate owned by nonprofit corporation - 30%.
Class V:	All others - 36%.

Note: Assessment level of the highest class cannot exceed 2.5 times the lowest class - classes locally determined in applicable counties.

HOMEOWNERS EXEMPTIONS:
1. Homestead of a person aged 65 or over, limited to a $2,000 maximum reduction from equalized or assessed value (or $2,000 multiplied by the number of apartments or units in a cooperative building occupied by persons 65 or older who are liable for realty taxes and are owners of record).

2. Specially adapted housing purchased with federal funds to the assessed value of $47,500 owned and used by a disabled veteran, the spouse or unmarried surviving spouse as a home.

3. Homesteads, to a reduction in the equalized assessed value of homestead property of $3,500 (or $3,500 multiplied by the number of apartments or units in a cooperative building occupied by persons who are liable for realty taxes and are owners or record).

4. Individuals 65 or older, or who will become 65 during a year in which a claim is filed, and disabled persons whose annual household income is less than $14,000, who lived in Illinois when filing their claims are entitled to claim a grant equal to the amount by which such taxes were paid or payable during the prior tax year, but the grant may not exceed $700 less 4.5% of such income. In addition, any individual who (1) is 65 or older or who will become 65 during a year in which a claim is filed or is disabled, (2) is domiciled in Illinois when filing

his claim, and (3) has a maximum household income of less than $14,000 is entitled to claim an additional grant (regardless of whether he's liable for property taxes) of $80.

5. Persons aged 65 or older or 60 or older who are disabled, whose household incomes are no greater than the maximum household income specified for claimants under the tax relief for senior citizens and disabled persons may have realty taxes (or installments of special assessments) on their homesteads deferred.

6. An exemption of up to $30,000 in actual value is allowed for new improvements to existing residential structures for four years. Maintenance and repairs to residential realty won't increase the assessed value of the realty.

7. A certificate of rehabilitation may be issued upon the renovation, restoration, preservation or rehabilitation of a historic building. For the eight years from the date of issuance of such certificate, the valuation will be in an amount not to exceed the base year value for the entire eight-year valuation period. For the first year after the expiration of the eight-year valuation period, the value for purposes of computing the assessed value is the base year value plus 25% of the adjustment in value; for the second year, the base year value plus 50% of the adjustment in value; for the third year, the base year value plus 75% of the adjustment in value; and for the fourth year, the assessed value is based upon the current fair cash value. A taxing district may elect not to participate in the incentive program.

ASSESSMENT DATES:
January 1.

LEVEL OF GOVERNMENT RESPONSIBLE FOR ASSESSMENT:
Township and some county.

EQUALIZATION:
Performed both within and between counties. Department of Revenue equalizes assessed values by percentage adjustments to county or town aggregate assessment roll.

ASSESSORS:
Elected to four-year term, certification required.

STATE ISSUED MANUALS:
Appraisal manuals.

PROPERTY OWNERSHIP MAPS REQUIRED:
Yes.

PERMIT REAL PROPERTY TO BE VALUED IN CURRENT USE RATHER THAN IN A FINANCIALLY BETTER USE:
No.

MEDIAN AREA ASSESSMENT TO SALES PRICE RATIOS:
31.20.

FREQUENCY OF STATE RATIO STUDIES:
Annual.

STATE RATIO STUDY AVAILABLE TO PUBLIC:
Yes.

ADMINISTRATION OF ASSESSMENTS AND TAX LAWS:
The Department of Revenue reviews the assessments for each county as they relate to fair cash value each year. The ratio of fair cash value to the current assessment' is determined and an equalization rate is assigned to each county. The Department of Revenue generates only a county-wide equalization factor (multiplier) and township multipliers are determined at the local level. The assigned equalization factor is applied uniformly to all assessments previously established by the assessor of the taxing jurisdiction. The equalization factor won't appear separately on the notice of assessment, but will be incorporated in the assessment notice. The preparation of the initial assessment that's reviewed by the State Department of Revenue varies from county to county as follows:

County Assessor - In counties such as Cook County where population exceeds 1,000,000.

Board of Assessors - In counties where the population exceeds 150,000 but is less than 1,000,000.

Township Assessors - In counties divided by township organizations (predominant form in Illinois).

County Treasurer - In counties without township organization the County Treasurer is the ex officio assessor (Alexander, Calhoun, Edwards, Hardin, Johnson, Massac, Menard, Monroe, Morgan, Perry, Pope, Pulaski, Randolph, Scott, Union, Wabash, Williamson).

APPEALS AND PROTESTS:
A taxpayer may contest his assessment by writing to the County Board of Review (except Cook County) prior to September 1 (August 1 in counties with a population of under $150,000 or later if there's a delay in completing the assessment rolls. The Board can meet according to its needs from the third Monday in June until anywhere from October 7 to December 31 depending on the county's size. Larger counties have longer hearing time tables that can be extended by 30 days in quadrennial assessment years.

Taxpayers dissatisfied with the County Board of Review's decision may file, within 20 days of receipt of the written notice of the County Board decision, for a hearing before the State Property Tax Appeal Board. The petition must be in writing and filed with the Clerk of the State Board. The decision of the State Board may be appealed to the Circuit and Superior Courts if the appeal is concerned with fraud or equality. The taxpayer also has the alternative of paying the tax under protest and appealing directly from the county board of review to the circuit court.

Cook County is the only exception to the above procedure. A taxpayer appealing an assessment in Cook County would first seek an informal hearing with the Cook County Assessor. If the taxpayer fails to obtain relief from the assessor, an appeal may be filed in writing with the Cook County Board of Appeals prior to the dates published in the local newspapers (dates may vary for each district).

The Cook County Board of Appeals starts its meeting by the third Monday in June with the hearing dates being published and the taxpayers being notified. Hearing dates usually begin on or about August 1 and continue until at least 60 days after receipt of the last tax roll. If the taxpayer isn't satisfied with the decision, the tax must be paid under protest and appealed to the Circuit Court of Cook County.

REFER TO STATE LAW IMPOSED BY:
The Illinois Revenue Act of 1939, as amended.

CHANGES:
1. 1974 - Cook County adoption of classified assessment system.

2. 4/81 - Required certain assessors to meet minimum training qualifications.

ADDRESS (STATE):
Illinois Property Tax Appeal Board
404 Statton Building
P.O. Box 19278
Springfield, Illinois 62794-9278

TELEPHONE:
(217) 782-6076

INDIANA

NAME OF TAX:
Property Taxes.

VALUATION STANDARD:
True Tax Value, defined as "not meaning market value", but "that value determined under the rules of the State Board of Tax Commissioners."

REVALUATION CYCLE:
After March 1, 1989, a state-wide revaluation must be completed every four years.

Note: Statewide revaluation will begin July 1, 1991.

ASSESSMENT LEVEL:
33-1/3% of true cash value.

HOMEOWNERS EXEMPTIONS:
1.   An honorably discharged veteran having a service-connected disability is allowed a $4,000 deduction from assessed value.

Totally disabled veterans or veterans who are at least 62 years of age and have a disability of at least 10%, or their surviving spouses, are allowed a $2,000 deduction if the value of the property doesn't exceed $9,500.

Surviving spouses of servicemen who served prior to November 12, 1918, are allowed a $3,000 deduction.

World War I veterans are allowed a $3,000 deduction from the assessed value of their principal place of residence if its assessed value is under $14,000.

2.   Mortgage or contract indebtedness on real estate to the amount of $1,000, the balance of the mortgage or contract indebtedness on the assessment date or one-half of the realty's assessed value, whichever is less.

3.   Residents 65 or older whose federal adjusted gross income, when combined with that of (1) their spouse, or (2) the individuals with whom the individual shares ownership or is purchasing the property under a contract as joint tenants or tenants in common, doesn't exceed $15,000 a year (the value of the real property or mobile home may not exceed $19,000. They must have owned the real property or mobile home for a least 1 year, must live on the real property or mobile home and receive no other property tax exemption except the mortgage deduction are allowed a $1,000 exemption for the real property or mobile home. An unremarried surviving spouse who's at least 60 years old and whose spouse was at least 65 at the time of death can claim the exemption if all other requirements are satisfied.

4.   A limited deduction is allowed from the assessed value of qualified rehabilitated residential realty. Assessed value may be reduced, for a five-year period, by either the increase in

assessed v..lue due to the rehabilitation, or $3,000 per dwelling unit rehabilitated, whichever is less. Only improvements to the following property qualify for the deduction (value shown is that prio: to rehabilitation): (1) single-family dwellings with an assessed value of not more than $6,000;' (2) two-family dwellings with an assessed value of not more than $8,000; and (3) dwellings with three or more family unit with an assessed value of not more than $3,000 per unit. As an alternative, owners of rehabilitated realty (except land) erected at least ten years prior to applying for the deduction may have deducted from the increased assessed value of the realty 50% of the increase in value resulting from the rehabilitation. The deduction may be taken annually for a five-year period, but the maximum annual deduction is $5,000 for a single-family dwelling or $25,000 for any other type of property.

5. Owners of property in an economic revitalization area are entitled to a 3-, 6- or 10-year deduction if the property has been rehabilitated or is located on realty that has been redeveloped.

6. A homestead credit is allowed for property taxes paid on a principal residence and the surrounding real estate, not exceeding one acre, at a rate of 6%. The credit may be increased if funds are available. A county in which the county option income tax is in effect may increase the percentage credit allowed, but not to exceed 8%.

7. An annual deduction is allowed to the owner of real property, or a mobile home that's not assessed as real property, that's equipped with a hydroelectric power device or geothermal energy heating or cooling device.

8. Taxpayers owning property in blighted or deteriorating areas are eligible for a tax credit if a local ordinance is adopted. A formula sets the maximum credit available. Also, a credit may be granted from a blighted area housing program allocation fund if its amount exceed prescribed limits.

ASSESSMENT DATE:
March 1.

LEVEL OF GOVERNMENT RESPONSIBLE FOR ASSESSMENT:
Township.

EQUALIZATION:
Performed both within and between counties.

ASSESSORS:
Elected to four-year terms, certification required.

STATE ISSUED MANUALS:
Appraisal manuals.

PROPERTY OWNERSHIP MAPS REQUIRED:
Yes.

PERMIT REAL PROPERTY TO BE VALUED IN CURRENT USE RATHER THAN IN A FINANCIALLY BETTER USE:
No.

MEDIAN AREA ASSESSMENT TO SALES PRICE RATIOS:
17.20.

FREQUENCY OF STATE RATIO STUDIES:
Each reassessment

STATE RATIO STUDY AVAILABLE TO PUBLIC:
Yes.

ADMINISTRATION OF ASSESSMENTS AND TAX LAWS:
The State Board of Tax Commissioners has been authorized to oversee the local assessing practices to insure that uniformity is maintained throughout the state. Real property of all counties must be reassessed every four years beginning July 1, 1991. Previously, the reassessment was to occur every eight years beginning July 1, 1987.

APPEALS AND PROTESTS:
A taxpayer who is not satisfied with an assessment should contact the township assessor to resolve the problem. Failure to arrive at an acceptable conclusion on value with the township would require the taxpayer to seek relief through the County Board of Review by filing a written petition with the county auditor within 30 days of the mailing of the notice by the township assessor. The taxpayer should use Form 130 in filing the petition. The County Board of Review will notify the taxpayer of the hearing date and send a notice him after the hearing to advise him of the board's decision.

A taxpayer dissatisfied with the decision of the County Board of Review may file a petition for review by the State Board of Tax Commissioners (using Form 131) with the county auditor within 30 days after notice of the County Board of Review's action is given to the taxpayer. The county, upon receipt of the petition, has 10 days within which to prepare a statement showing concisely the substance of the petitioner's complaint and the action of the County Board of Review, and to transmit it to the State Board of Tax Commissioners. At least 10 days prior to the hearing, the state board will notify the taxpayer, township assessor, county assessor of the hearing date and advise all parties of its decision, giving the reasons which the determination was based, and advising them of the procedures to obtain a review through the courts. If the taxpayer doesn't agree with the assessment recommended by the hearing office, he may petition, after completing of the hearing and review, the state board will consider additional information, provided the petition is filed before the final assessment. Prior to an additional hearing by the state board, the taxpayer must file a brief with the State Board furnishing the additional information to be considered.

State Board of Tax Commissioners, upon petition of a required number of taxpayers for reassessment in non-election or non-reassessment year, can order a reassessment of inequitably assessed property.

The final determination of the State Board may be appealed by the taxpayer to the Indiana Tax Court. The tax court has exclusive jurisdiction over any case that arises under the state tax laws on and after July 1, 1986. Earlier cases may be transferred to the tax court if all parties agree to the transfer. Any decision of the tax court that isn't to the taxpayer's satisfaction may be appealed to the State Supreme Court.

REFER TO STATE LAW IMPOSED BY:
Title 6, Article 1.1 of the Indiana Code.

CHANGES:
1. 9/1/84 - Established current valuation stand, previously undefined.

ADDRESS:
State of Indiana
State Board of Tax Commissioners
Katrina Hall
State Office Building - Room 201
Indianapolis, Indiana 46204

TELEPHONE:
(317) 232-3761

VERIFIED BY THIS OFFICE:
Yes.

COMMENTS:
This State has limited appeals to only the assessor's use of the State-provided assessor's manual. No income or market data is considered unless a case can be built on economic regression of value. Example - an apartment property that has developed a severe vacancy problem. The assessor's manual is very comprehensive.

IOWA

NAME OF TAX:
Property Taxes.

VALUATION STANDARD:
Actual Value (Fair and Reasonable Market Value), defined as "the fair and reasonable exchange in the year in which the property is listed and valued between a willing buyer and a willing seller, neither being under any compulsion to buy nor sell and each being familiar with all the facts relating to the particular piece of property."

REVALUATION CYCLE:
Every two years, but assessor may revalue as change in value occurs.

ASSESSMENT LEVEL:
100% of actual value.

HOMEOWNERS EXEMPTION:
1. Property owned by veterans on July 1 of the year for which exemption is claimed, their spouses or surviving spouse, their surviving widowed parent and the minor children of deceased veterans is exempt up to various amounts depending upon the military action in which they served.

2. A homestead credit fund is apportioned annually to give a tax credit to the owner of a dwelling, which the owner occupies for six months or more in the year the credit is claimed. The credit is in an amount equal to the first $4,850 of actual value for each homestead, with a minimum credit of $62.50. Disabled veterans are allowed the credit in an amount equal to the tax levied on the homestead if the annual income of the veteran and his spouse does not exceed $10,000. The credit may be continued to the unremarried surviving spouse and any child of a deceased veteran.
Persons aged 65 or older, surviving spouses who were 56 or older before 1989 and totally disabled persons are eligible for a tax credit or reimbursement in addition to the homestead tax credit allowed all taxpayers if they are Iowa residents.

3. Normal and necessary repairs to a building don't increase the taxable value of the building if the repairs do not exceed $2,500 per year.

4. Owners of real estate in revitalization areas are allowed to elect full or partial exemption for improvements which increase the actual value of the property by at least 15% or at least 10% in the case of residential realty.

ASSESSMENT DATES:
January 1.

LEVEL OF GOVERNMENT RESPONSIBLE FOR ASSESSMENT:
County, some city.

EQUALIZATION:
Performed both within and between counties.

ASSESSORS:
Appointed for six-year terms, certification and continuing education required.

STATE ISSUED MANUALS:
Appraisal manuals.

PROPERTY OWNERSHIP MAPS REQUIRED:
Yes.

PERMIT REAL PROPERTY TO BE VALUED IN CURRENT USE RATHER THAN IN A FINANCIALLY BETTER USE:
Valued according to Current Primary use.

MEDIAN AREA ASSESSMENT TO SALES PRICE RATIOS:
64.10.

FREQUENCY OF STATE RATIO STUDIES:
Annual.

STATE RATIO STUDY AVAILABLE TO PUBLIC:
Yes.

ADMINISTRATION OF ASSESSMENTS AND TAX LAWS:
The Director of Revenue and Finance has the power and duty to exercise general supervision over administration of the assessment and tax laws of the state, over the activities of all assessors, boards of review, boards of supervisors and all other officers or boards of assessment and levy in the performance of their duties, in all matters relating to assessments and taxation, to the end that all assessments of property and taxes levied thereon are made relatively just and uniform in substantial compliance with the property tax law in Iowa.

Department of Revenue and Finance:

A.   Can order reassessment of any and all property in any tax district in any year.

B.   Can order uniform increases or decreases of any and all property classes in any tax district.

C.   Can order county or city board of review to reconvene and adjust improperly assessed properties.

D.   Equalizes assessed values in revaluation year by percentage adjustments to property classes that show a minimum of 5% deviation from actual value.

E.   Cannot change individual parcel values unless obvious errors or injustice is present or except upon recommendation of local board of review.

APPEALS AND PROTESTS:

The assessor must have the tax rolls completed by April 15 and any taxpayer not satisfied with the assessment received may file an appeal with the Board of Review at any time between April 16 and May 5. It's the duty of the Board of Review to examine evidence and decisions issued by the Director of Revenue and Finance for the identification of taxable property, classification of property as real or personal and for collecting taxes. The Board of Review will commence hearings on May 1 and will remain open until May 31. However, if the Board completes its work prior to May 31, it may adjourn. If the Board of Review hasn't disposed of all the protests by May 31, the Director of Revenue may extend that time but not beyond July 15. The local Board of Review will reconvene in special session from October 15 to November 15 to hear the protests of affected taxpayers within its jurisdiction whose valuation of property is increased pursuant to the equalization order issued by the Director of Revenue and will result in a value greater than the actual value.

If a taxpayer isn't satisfied with the decision of the Board of Review, he may file an appeal with the district court of the county in which the Board holds its sessions within 20 days after the Board adjourns or May 31, whichever is later. The appeal must be in writing with a copy to the chairman of the Board of Review. No new grounds may be added to the protest, but additional evidence regarding the initial grounds will be accepted. The decision of the County District Court may be appealed to the State Supreme Court. The Iowa Supreme Court has ruled that a taxpayer may appeal directly to the District Court without first requesting a review by the Director of Revenue and Finance where the taxpayer receives an adverse property tax assessment issued pursuant to an equalization order.

REFER TO STATE LAW IMPOSED BY:

Title XVI, chapters 425 through 448, of the Code of Iowa, as amended.

CHANGES:

1.   1980 - Established assessor certification and continuing education requirements.

ADDRESS (STATE):

Iowa Department of Revenue and Finance
Local Government Services Division
Hoover State Office Building
Des Moines, Iowa 50319

TELEPHONE:

(515) 281-4040

VERIFIED BY THIS OFFICE:

Yes.

COMMENTS:

This is one of the States where the State-Issued Cost Manual is almost the sole source of an assessment valuation and a means of appealing assessments. The manual is very comprehensive and is given significant weight by Appeal Boards in lieu of market data.

KANSAS

NAME OF TAX:
Property Taxes.

VALUATION STANDARD:
Fair Market Value in Money, defined at "The amount in terms of money that a well informed buyer is justified in paying and a well-informed seller is justified in accepting for property in an open and competitive market, assuming the parties are acting without undue compulsion."

REVALUATION CYCLE:
Every 4 years, after statewide reappraisal valuations are established.

ASSESSMENT LEVEL:
Classification system:

Class I:	Real property.
Subclass A:	Residential property, including apartments - 12%.
Subclass B:	Agricultural property - 30% of use value.
Subclass C:	Vacant land - 12%.
Subclass D:	All other real property - 30%.

HOMEOWNERS EXEMPTIONS:
1. Circuit Breakers programs qualified for age and disability, etc.

2. The following Kansas residents are eligible for a homestead property tax refund with respect to taxes: (1) persons who are disabled; (2) persons who are at least 55; or (3) persons, other than persons included in (1) or (2) above, having one or more dependent children under 18 residing in the homestead during the calendar year immediately preceding the year in which a claim is filed.

ASSESSMENT DATES:
January 1.

LEVEL OF GOVERNMENT RESPONSIBLE FOR ASSESSMENT:
County.

EQUALIZATION:
Performed both within and between counties. State Board of Tax Appeals equalizes assessed values by adjustments to any and all property in any county, city, town or district. County Boards of Equalization cannot adjust entire property classes without State Board approval.

ASSESSORS:
Known as appraisers, appointed for four-year term, certification required.

STATE ISSUED MANUALS:
Appraisals manual, CAMA user's manual, appraisal guides and course manuals.

PROPERTY OWNERSHIP MAPS REQUIRED:
Yes.

PERMIT REAL PROPERTY TO BE VALUED IN CURRENT USE RATHER THAN IN A FINANCIALLY BETTER USE:
Agricultural use only.

MEDIAN AREA ASSESSMENT TO SALES PRICE RATIOS:
9.50, close to 12 after reappraisal.

FREQUENCY OF STATE RATIO STUDIES:
Annual.

STATE RATIO STUDY AVAILABLE TO PUBLIC:
Yes.

ADMINISTRATION OF ASSESSMENTS AND TAX LAWS:
Cities and townships administer the assessments within their jurisdiction, but the assessments must be certified by the county clerk and the tax is collected by the county treasurer. The Director of Property Valuation prescribes uniform assessment forms, records and renders all the assistance possible toward uniform assessments within the counties and throughout the state. Commencing in 1990, every parcel of real property must be actually viewed and inspected by the county or district appraiser once every four years. The Director of Property Valuation must require the compliance with this program of statewide reappraisal immediately after the 7/1/88 effective date thereof.

APPEALS AND PROTESTS:
The appeal procedure has been substantially revised in Kansas effective 7/1/88 to state that a taxpayer aggrieved of the classification or appraised value of property may appeal to the county appraiser by giving notice of such dissatisfaction to the assessor within 21 days of the mailing of the assessment notice. The county appraiser must then arrange an informal meeting with the taxpayer. Informal hearings involving real property must not be scheduled after April 1 (May 1 for 1989 only) and a final determination by the county appraiser must not be given after April 15 (May 15 for 1989 only) in the year in which valuation of real property established pursuant to the program of statewide reappraisal is first applied as a basis for the levy of taxes.

Any taxpayer dissatisfied with the determination of the county appraiser may appeal to the hearing officer or panel appointed by the board of county commissioners or, where no hearing officer or panel has been appointed, to the county board of equalization. Appeals must be heard by the hearing officer or panel on or before May 15, and by the county board of equalization on or before May 30. The board may reconvene of June 6 to hear appeals for a period not exceeding 10 days. Notice of the decision of the hearing office, panel or county board of equalization shall be mailed within five days after the date of the making of the decision or the date of approval of the director of property valuation, whichever is later. The taxpayer may also appeal the determination of the hearing officer or panel to the board of equalization.

Authorizing for disclosure of the certificates of value that are retained in the office of the register of deeds has been extended to any property owner who has appealed the valuation of property, to the county appraiser, the hearing officers, and county boards of equalization, but only to the extent that the contents concern the same class of property as that involved in the appeal. The taxpayer may file, within 45 days of the decision of the County Board of Equalization, a written appeal of the assessment, requesting a hearing before the State Board of Tax Appeals sitting as a State Board of Equalization. The appeal must furnish the grounds on which the appeal is being filed and a copy of the appeal must be given to the clerk of the County Board of Equalization.

If the taxpayer isn't satisfied with the decision of the State Board of Tax Appeals, an appeal may be filed with the District Court of the county in which the property is located. No appeal may be taken to the district court unless the assessment is unreasonable, arbitrary and capricious. If the decision of the district court on certain matters isn't to the taxpayer's satisfaction, an appeal may be filed with the State Supreme Court.

REFER TO STATE LAW IMPOSED BY:
Chapter 79 of the Kansas Statutes Annotated, 1963, as amended.

CHANGES:
1. 6/1/76 - Required certification of county appraisers.

2. 12/31/80 - Division of Property Valuation authority to reappraise classes/subclasses.

3. 7/1/85 - Required quarterly reports to Division Property Valuation.

4. 11/5/86 - Referendum will decide if proposed assessment classification system will be allowed - see Assessment Level, proposed classification system.

ADDRESS (STATE):
Kansas Department of Revenue
Division of Property Valuation
John Littjohnn, Director
Robert B. Docking State Office Building
Topeka, Kansas 66612-1585

TELEPHONE:
(913) 296-2365

VERIFIED BY THIS OFFICE:
Yes.

COMMENTS:
This State has a very open appeal process with equity of assessments, sales ratio studies and overevaluations all being grounds for appeal.

KENTUCKY

NAME OF TAX:
Property Taxes.

VALUATION STANDARD:
Fair Cash Value, defined as being "established at the price the property would bring at fair, voluntary sale, except the following: real property qualifying for an assessment moratorium shall not have its fair cash value assessment changed while under the assessment moratorium unless the assessment moratorium expires or is otherwise cancelled or revoked."

REVALUATION CYCLE:
Physical inspection is required at least every two years.

ASSESSMENT LEVEL:
100% of fair market value.

HOMEOWNERS EXEMPTIONS:
1. Real property owned and maintained by a person 65 or older or who's classified as totally disabled under a program authorized or administered by an agency of the U.S. government or by the railroad retirement system as his home is exempt, except for special assessments, up the assessed value of $6,500 (adjusted for inflation) on the home and contiguous realty.

ASSESSMENT DATES:
January 1.

LEVEL OF GOVERNMENT RESPONSIBLE FOR ASSESSMENT:
County.

EQUALIZATION:
Performed between counties. Department of Revenue annually equalizes county/district assessed values by percentage adjustments to (1) the aggregate assessed value, (2) property classes or (3) individual parcel values.

ASSESSORS:
Elected to four-year term, certification required.

STATE ISSUED MANUALS:
Assessment manuals.

PROPERTY OWNERSHIP MAPS REQUIRED:
Yes.

PERMIT REAL PROPERTY TO BE VALUED IN CURRENT USE RATHER THAN IN A FINANCIALLY BETTER USE:
No.

MEDIAN AREA ASSESSMENT TO SALES:
85.10.

FREQUENCY OF STATE RATIO STUDIES:
Annual.

STATE RATIO STUDY AVAILABLE TO PUBLIC:
Yes.

ADMINISTRATION OF ASSESSMENTS AND TAX LAWS:
All assessments of real property and personal property are determined at the county level, but are administered and approved by the Kentucky Revenue Cabinet to ensure equalized assessments among the counties. The Revenue Cabinet is required to provide property valuation administrators with up-to-date appraisal manuals and to conduct a biennial audit of each property valuation administrator's office.

APPEALS AND PROTESTS:
The Property Tax Administrator of each county shall complete the tax roll on the first Monday in May and open these rolls for inspection for twelve (12) days commencing on the fourth Monday in May. Any taxpayer aggrieved by the assessment may appeal it by filing a written petition with the County Clerk within the 12-day inspection period requesting a hearing before the County Board of Assessment Appeals. The decision of the County Board may be appealed to the Kentucky Board of Tax Appeals within 30 days of the decision of the County Board. The taxpayer may appeal any unfavorable decision of the Kentucky Board of Tax Appeals by filing with the Circuit Court.

If a taxpayer is falsely taxed on property not owned, an appeal may be made to the County Judge/Executor within 30 days of receipt of the bill. Further appeal may be made to the Circuit Court.

If the Department of Revenue exacts an equalization rate to the assessments of a county, the taxpayer may file an appeal with the County Clerk for exoneration on the basis of the value being above its fair cash value within 10 days of publication of the rate increase. The appeal will be heard by the County Board of Assessment Appeals and can be appealed to the Kentucky Board of Tax Appeals and the Circuit Court.

REFER TO STATE LAW IMPOSED BY:
Title IX and XI of the Kentucky Revised Statutes, as amended, cover revenue and taxation including the taxation of property.

CHANGES:
1.   1982 - Established qualifications for assessment moratoriums.

ADDRESS (STATE):
Commonwealth of Kentucky
Department of Property Tax, Revenue Cabinet
Billy Whittaker, Director of Real Estate
592 East Main Street
Frankfort, Kentucky 40620

TELEPHONE:
(502) 564-6730

VERIFIED BY THIS OFFICE:
No.

COMMENTS:
A survey of property record cards in the assessor's records in this State have been found to contain little valuation information. It appears to be more of a "carrying forward" of old calculations with some annual equalization update.

LOUISIANA

NAME OF TAX:
The State Ad Valorem Tax was repealed effective 1/1/73 and municipalities, parishes were authorized under Title 33 of the Louisiana Revised Statutes of 1950, as amended to levy property taxes on real property, tangible personal property and intangible personal property.

VALUATION STANDARD:
Fair Market Value, defined as "the price for property which would be agreed upon between a willing and informed buyer and a willing and informed seller under usual and ordinary circumstances; it shall be the highest price estimated in terms of money which property will bring if exposed for sale on the open market with reasonable time allowed to find a purchaser who is buying with knowledge of all the uses and purposes to which the property is best adapted and for which it can be legally used."

REVALUATION CYCLE:
Not greater than every four years.

ASSESSMENT LEVEL:
Class 1:	Land - 10%.
Class 2:	Residential improvements - 10%.
Class 3:	Electric cooperative properties, excluding land - 15%.
Class 4:	Public service properties, excluding land - 25%.
Class 5:	All other property - 15%.

HOMEOWNERS EXEMPTIONS:
1. Homesteads not exceeding 160 acres to the extent of $7,500 of assessed value (the homestead exemption doesn't extend to municipal taxes except (1) in Orleans Parish to state, general city, school, levee and levee district taxes and (2) to any municipal taxes levied for school purposes).

2. With approval of the local governing authority, the State Board of Commerce and Industry may grant to a property owner, who proposes the expansion, restoration, improvement or development of an existing structure or structures in a downtown, historic or economic development district, the right for five years after completing the work to pay taxes based upon the assessed value of the property for the year before the project's beginning.

ASSESSMENT DATES:
January 1.

LEVEL OF GOVERNMENT RESPONSIBLE FOR ASSESSMENT:
Parish.

EQUALIZATION:
Performed between parishes. State Tax Commission performs annual assessment ratio study for each property class on a revolving basis.

ASSESSORS:
Elected to four year term, certification not required.

STATE ISSUED MANUALS:
Assessment manuals.

PROPERTY OWNERSHIP MAPS REQUIRED:
Yes.

PERMIT REAL PROPERTY TO BE VALUED IN CURRENT USE RATHER THAN IN A FINANCIALLY BETTER USE:
No.

MEDIAN AREA ASSESSMENT TO SALES PRICE RATIOS:
6.60.

FREQUENCY OF STATE RATIO STUDIES:
Annual.

STATE RATIO STUDY AVAILABLE TO PUBLIC:
Yes.

ADMINISTRATION OF ASSESSMENTS AND TAX LAWS:
The Louisiana State Tax Commission is responsible for the administration and approval of assessments to ensure that property is being equitably assessed among the parishes and municipalities.

APPEALS AND PROTESTS:
Each assessor shall publish the time and place of the public exposure of the assessment lists of both real and personal property for 15 days between August 15 and September 15, during which time the taxpayer may request the assessment be reviewed. If the taxpayer isn't satisfied with the assessor's decision, an appeal may be filed seven days prior to the hearing, either by appearing in person at the Board's office or by filing the complaints by certified mail, requesting a hearing with the Board of Review. (In Orleans Parish the assessor's review is August 1-15 and the Board of Review hearing must be requested within three days after August 15.)

Taxpayers dissatisfied with the Board of Review's decision may file an appeal with the Louisiana Tax Commission within 10 days of the Board of Review's decision or such determination will be final. The Tax Commission will notify the taxpayer of its decision, in writing, within 30 days following the hearing.

The decision of the Louisiana Tax Commission can be appealed to the District Court of the parish where the tax commission is domiciled or the parish where the property is located if at least 25% of the parishes in which the property is located are named in the suit. Where less than 25% of the parishes are named in the suit, the suit must be filed in the parish in which the property is located.

REFER TO STATE LAW IMPOSED BY:

Title 33 of the Louisiana Revised Statutes of 1950, as amended, authorizes the levy of property taxes by municipalities and parishes.

CHANGES:

1.   11/30/79 - Assessment class VI created.

ADDRESS (STATE):

Louisiana Tax Commission
Property Tax Division
Donald Strain, Director
923 Executive Park Avenue Suite 12 (P.O. Box 66788)
Baton Rouge, Louisiana 70896

TELEPHONE:

(504) 925-7830

VERIFIED BY THIS OFFICE:

Yes.

MAINE

NAME OF TAX:
Property Tax.

VALUATION STANDARD:
Just Value, defined as "that value arising from presently possible alternatives to which the particular parcel of land may be placed. The just value of land is deemed to arise from and is attributable to legally permissible uses or uses only."

REVALUATION CYCLE:
Not greater than every four years.

ASSESSMENT LEVEL:
100% of just value or a uniform percentage thereof that's at least 70% of just value.

HOMEOWNERS EXEMPTIONS:
1. Property of aged or disabled veterans, their unremarried widows and mothers or minor children, to the value of $4,000 ($40,000 for paraplegic veterans or unremarried widows of such veterans).

2. Residents age 62 or older, unmarried persons 55 or older receiving federal disability payments and married persons 55 or older if both are receiving federal disability payments who own or rent a home in Maine are eligible for the following benefit amounts. "Benefit base" is the property taxes paid or rent constituting property taxes paid (25% of gross rent paid).

3. For claimants representing non-elderly households, the benefit base is 33.3% (50% effective July 1, 1989) of the amount by which the benefit base exceeds 4.5% of income to a maximum payment of $250 ($400, effective July 1, 1989). Claimants with household incomes over $28,000 aren't eligible for a benefit. "Benefit base" means property taxes paid or rent constituting property taxes paid.

ASSESSMENT DATES:
April 1.

LEVEL OF GOVERNMENT RESPONSIBLE FOR ASSESSMENT:
Municipal.

EQUALIZATION:
Performed between counties. Bureau of Taxation equalizes assessed values among towns and equalizes state and county taxes among towns.

ASSESSORS:
Elected and appointed for indefinite term, certification is required.

STATE ISSUED MANUALS:
Appraisal manuals.

PROPERTY OWNERSHIP MAPS REQUIRED:
Yes.

PERMIT REAL PROPERTY TO BE VALUED IN CURRENT USE RATHER THAN IN A FINANCIALLY BETTER USE:
No.

MEDIAN AREA ASSESSMENT TO SALES PRICE RATIOS:
75.80.

FREQUENCY OF STATE RATIO STUDIES:
Bureau of Taxation, Property Tax Division performs annual ratio study to determine if minimum 70% assessment level is being met by localities. Provides recommendation for reappraisal order to State Tax Assessor (head of Bureau of Taxation) for those localities failing to meet this requirement.

STATE RATIO STUDY AVAILABLE TO PUBLIC:
Yes.

ADMINISTRATION OF ASSESSMENTS AND TAX LAWS:
The administration of property taxes is handled by the local assessor in incorporated cities and towns. The administration of property taxes in unincorporated townships is handled by the State Tax Assessor. Effective 7/16/86, the State Tax Assessor shall maintain and periodically update a state assessment manual, which shall identify accepted and preferred methods of assessing property. Any municipality performing or contracting the performance of a revaluation after 1/1/87 shall use or require the use of the state assessment manual or another professionally accepted manual or procedure.

Bureau of Taxation can order revaluation/reassessment of any property not assessed in accordance with law.

APPEALS AND PROTESTS:
Taxpayers in incorporated cities and towns may appeal an assessment to the local assessor and taxpayers in unincorporated townships may appeal to the State Tax Assessor in writing requesting abatement of tax for up to one year from the date of commitment (date assessor submits tax list to the tax collector usually in July or August as determined by the voters at a town meeting). The assessor will send notice of his decision within 10 days after its made, and if no decision is made within 60 days of application the taxpayer may consider his appeal as being denied. In municipalities having a Board of Assessment Review, the taxpayer may apply to the Board in writing requesting a review if done within 60 days of the assessor's decision. In primary assessing areas, the assessor's decision will be appealed to the State Board of Property Tax Review or County Commissioner to the Supreme Court of the State of Maine. The State Board of Property Tax Review may hear, at the property owner's option, appeals for nonresidential property exceeding $500,000 equalized valuation.

REFER TO STATE LAW IMPOSED BY:
Title 36, Part 2 of the Maine Revised Statutes Annotated, 1964, as amended.

CHANGES:
1. 1979 - Established current minimum assessment level requirement (1977 and before was 50%, 1978 was 60%).

2. 1980 - Changes revaluation cycle from three years to current four-year cycle.

3. 7/1/80 - Required certification of full-time assessors and private contractors.

ADDRESS (STATE):
State Tax Assessor
Property Tax Division
Bureau of Taxation
Augusta, Maine 04330

TELEPHONE:
(207) 289-2011

VERIFIED BY THIS OFFICE:
No.

MARYLAND

NAME OF TAX:
Property Tax.

VALUATION STANDARD:
Full Cash Value, defined as "current value" or "fair market value."

REVALUATION CYCLE:
Three year cycle requires review of all county and city of Baltimore property at least once during the cycle, increased value is phased in over the next three years.

ASSESSMENT LEVEL:
Full cash value adjusted by "growth factor" established by State Department of Assessments and Taxation. The "growth factor" declines as full cash values state-wide increase by more than 6% per year.

1981 - .468252
1982 - .456343
1983 - .442617
1984 - .434925
1985 - .434750
    etc. (check for current rate)

HOMEOWNERS EXEMPTIONS:
1.   Homes and lots owned by residents who are 100% permanently disabled veterans or owned by the unmarried widow of such a veteran.

2.   Homes and lots to $6,000 in value of a permanently blind individual or his unremarried surviving spouse.

3.   Realty tax credits are allowed to homeowners who reside in a dwelling in which the person has a legal interest or home purchasers who occupy or expect to occupy a home occupied by not more than two families. The credit may not exceed $1,500 ($2,000, effective July 1, 1990) and is to equal the realty taxes in excess of a percentage of combined income of the homeowner.

      For home purchasers, the credit is the amount calculated by the number of days in the year that the home purchaser occupies or expects to occupy the home. The credit isn't available if the homeowner's combined net worth is over $200,000.

4.   Maryland counties and cities may provide a tax credit against any local property taxes on a structure for using solar or geothermal energy devices or a qualifying energy conservation device for heating or cooling.

5. Counties may defer realty taxes on dwellings occupied by the owner if he resided in the home for a least five years, is at least 65 years old, is permanently and totally disabled and meets local income eligibility requirements.

6. Counties, municipal corporations or Baltimore City may provide a credit against tax for the following:

   a. Expenditures by a private owner-taxpayer for restoration, preservation and construction of property having historic or architectural value. Credit may be in an amount up 10% of the owner's expenses for restoration and preservation and up to 5% of the owner's expenses for costs of construction of architecturally compatible new structures in an historic district.

   b. Unsold or unrented newly constructed or substantially rehabilitated single dwelling units or commercial property, or both, in an amount not exceeding 100% of the local property taxes on the dwelling or property, excluding land, for the period the unit or property remains unsold or unrented.

   c. Residential real property damaged by flood conditions.

ASSESSMENT DATES:
January 1.

LEVEL OF GOVERNMENT RESPONSIBLE FOR ASSESSMENT:
State.

EQUALIZATION:
None.

ASSESSORS:
Appointed (state civil service), certification required.

STATE ISSUED MANUALS:
Appraisal manuals.

PROPERTY OWNERSHIP MAPS REQUIRED:
Yes.

PERMIT REAL PROPERTY TO BE VALUED IN CURRENT USE RATHER THAN IN A FINANCIALLY BETTER USE:
No.

MEDIAN AREA ASSESSMENT TO SALES PRICE RATIOS:
34.50.

FREQUENCY OF STATE RATIO STUDIES:
Annual.

STATE RATIO STUDY AVAILABLE TO PUBLIC:
Yes.

ADMINISTRATION OF ASSESSMENTS AND TAX LAWS:
The State Department of Assessments and Taxation is responsible for establishing all assessments and advising each county and incorporated city, town or village of the assessment established for each taxpayer in its jurisdiction. The State Comptroller will collect all state taxes and each county and incorporated city, town or village will administer the billing and collecting of the tax from each taxpayer within its jurisdiction.

APPEALS AND PROTESTS:
The taxpayer must file a written request for a hearing with the Maryland Department of Assessment and Taxation within 30 days of issuing the notice of tentative assessment or the assessment will become final. When an assessment appeal is filed with a supervisor and the proposed property value is more than $500,000, the Department of Assessments and Taxation must notify the appropriate county legal officer of the filing. After the hearing the department will issue a final assessment. For the assessment made by the Supervisors of Assessments, the Department of Assessment of Baltimore City or the assessing authorities of any other city, appeal lies to the property tax assessment appeal board where the property is located. Any appeals filed with a property tax assessment appeal board in which the value of property is at issue on or after July 1, 1989, requires that the Department of Assessments and Taxation and the taxpayer exchange any written appraisals to be used for placing a value on the property at least 10 days before a hearing on the appeal. If, after a hearing, the taxpayer disagrees with the final assessment issued, an appeal of the assessment can be filed with the Maryland Tax Court within 30 days of issuing the final notice by the Department. On any appeal to the Maryland Tax Court, the Department and the taxpayer must exchange written appraisals to be used for placing a value on the property in question at least 10 days before the hearing. The decision of the Tax Court may be appealed by applying for a review by the Circuit Court of the County in which the property is located or in the Baltimore City Court. Appeals may be taken to the Court of Special Appeals if dissatisfied with the final judgement of the Circuit Court. Appeals to the Court of Special Appeals must be filed within 30 days of the issuance of the Circuit Court's final judgment.

REFER TO STATE LAW IMPOSED BY:
Article 81 of the Annotated Code of Maryland, 1957, as amended.

CHANGES:
1.   7/1/79 - Beginning of state assumption of assessment functions.

2.   1979 -   a. Established current assessment level standard previously was "current value less an allowance for inflation of 50%."

   b. Began the use of growth factors - see Assessment Level.

   c. Three-year revaluation cycles established - previously required annual reassessment.

ADDRESS (STATE):
State Department of Assessment and Taxation
Gene Bruner, Director
301 West Preston Street
Baltimore, Maryland   21201

TELEPHONE:
(301) 225-1191

VERIFIED BY THIS OFFICE:
No.

COMMENTS:
The best approach to prove current "full cash value" and then have the State-issued local assessment sales ratio for that current year applied.

MASSACHUSETTS

NAME OF TAX:
Ad Valorem Property Tax.

VALUATION STANDARD:
Full and Fair Cash Value (not defined by statute).

REVALUATION CYCLE:
Chapter 40 Section 56 of the General Laws provides that "the commissioner shall triennially certify as to whether the board of assessors is assessing property at full and fair cash valuation."

ASSESSMENT LEVEL
100% of fair cash value. The standard to be used in determining "fair cash value" for taxation purpose is the "fair market value", which is the price an owner willing but not under compulsion to sell ought to receive from one willing but not under compulsion to buy. Boston Gas Co. v. Assessors of Boston, 334 Mass.549, 137 N.E.2d 462 (1956).

Note: For tax rate purposes, property is classified either residential, open space, commercial or industrial.

HOMEOWNERS EXEMPTIONS:
NOTE: Although the following statutes still recite the valuation method, due to the full and fair cash value method, the assessors only use the flat rate for exemption purposes.

1. Real property to the value of $2,000 or the sum of $175, whichever abates the greater amount of tax due, occupied by a surviving spouse or minor whose parent is deceased or a person over age 70 who has owned and occupied the house for not less than 10 years, provided the value of the total estate does not exceed $20,000 exclusive of any mortgage interest in property (G.L. Ch. 59 S5 Cl.17). By local option (G.L. Ch. 59 S5 Cl. 17C) the total estate test is less stringent since real and personal property cannot exceed $40,000 exclusive of any mortgage interest and exclusive of the first $60,000 of value in the domicile. Under another local option statute (G.L. Ch.59 S5 Cl.17-1/2) the total estate cannot exceed $40,000 exclusive of any mortgage and exclusive of the first $150,000 of value in the domicile. There is another local option statute (G.L. Ch.59 S5 Cl.17D) and under its provisions a $175 exemption is granted to a surviving spouse or minor child with parent deceased or to a person over 70 who has owned and occupied the property as a domicile for not less than five years. The total estate cannot exceed $40,000 exclusive of any mortgage interest and exclusive of the total value of the domicile except so much of the domicile as produces income and exceeds two dwelling units.

2. For real estate owned by a blind person there is an exemption to the value of $5,000 or the sum of $437.50, whichever is greater (G.L. Ch.59 S5 Cl.37). By local option (G.L. Ch.59 S5 Cl.37A) a blind person would receive a $500 exemption on his home.

3. There is an exemption (G.L. Ch.59 S5 Cl.41) for persons 70 years of age or over in the amount of $4,000 valuation or $500 in taxes, whichever will exempt the greater amount of

taxes due, if the person (1) has had gross income of less than $6,000 ($7,000 if married) for the preceding year, (2) had a whole estate, real and personal, not over $17,000 ($20,000 if married) not including the realty occupied as a domicile except that portion which produces income or not over $40,000 ($45,000 if married) if such real estate is included. The statute's domiciliary and ownership requirements were declared unconstitutional in a Superior Court decision. By local option (G.L. Ch.59 S5 Cl.41B) the statutory requirements have been broadened. The property must be owned and occupied by a person at least 70 years of age who has been domiciled in Massachusetts for the 10 receding years and has owned and occupied such property or other property in the commonwealth for five years or is a surviving spouse who inherits the property and has occupied such real property for five years. The taxpayer must have gross receipts in the preceding year of less than $10,000 ($12,000 if married) and a whole estate not exceeding $20,000 ($23,000 if married). The value of the domicile is excluded from the total estate except that portion which produces income. Under another local option (G.L. Ch.59 S5 Cl.41C) the ownership and occupancy requirements are the same as in Clause 41B. However, the gross receipts must be less than $13,000 ($15,000 if married) and the whole estate must not exceed $28,000 ($30,000 if married). The value of the domicile is excluded from the total worth except so much of the domicile as produces income and exceeds two dwelling-units.

4. Real estate owned and occupied by surviving spouse or surviving minor children of a police officer or fire fighter killed in the line of duty is totally exempt from real estate taxes. (G.L. Ch.59 S5 Cl.42 & 43).

5. A taxpayer who is at least 65 years of age who meets ownership and domiciliary requirements may defer real estate taxes provided the gross receipts for the preceding year didn't exceed $20,000 (G.L. Ch.59 S5 Cl.41A).

6. Real estate of Massachusetts veterans, their spouses, unremarried surviving spouses and fathers and mothers of veterans killed in such war times who served in the U.S. armed forces between February 15, 1898, and July 4, 1902; between April 6, 1917, and November 11, 1918, or who received the WW I Victory Medal; between September 16, 1940, and December 31, 1946; between June 25, 1950 and January 31, 1955; or in Viet Nam between August 5, 1964, and the termination of the Viet Nam emergency (or veterans serving at least 180 days active service between February 1, 1955, and August 4, 1964), when occupied at least in part as a domicile, to the amount of $2,000 or the sum of $175, whichever abates the greater amount of tax due. The exemption applies to veterans (and their spouses) who have a wartime disability ration of 10% or more, veterans awarded the Purple Heart, and surviving spouses of World War I veteran or veterans who were awarded the World War I Victory Medal who have not remarried and whose whole estate does not exceed $20,000 in value. An exemption to the amount of $4,000 or the sum of $350, whichever abates the greater amount of tax due, is allowed veterans (and their spouse) who have lost, or lost the use of one foot, hand or one eye, or have been awarded the Congressional Medal of Honor, Distinguished Service Cross, Navy Cross or the Air Force Cross. An exemption to the amount of $8,000 or the sum of $700, whichever abates the greater amount of tax due, is allowed veterans (and their spouses) who have lost, or lost the use of both feet, both hands or one foot and one hand, or both eyes. An exemption for "specially adapted housing" is allowed to the amount of $10,000 or the sum of $875, whichever abates the greater amount of tax due, for permanent or totally disabled veterans (and their spouses). A homestead

exemption to the amount of $6,000 in value or the sum of $525, whichever abates the greater amount of tax due, is allowed veterans who are 100% disabled due to a wartime injury and are incapable of working. A total exemption is granted to veterans who have been certified by the VA as being "paraplegic." The surviving spouse so long as she remains unmarried will be entitled to the same exemption.

7. Cities and towns certified to be assessing all property at its full and fair market value may grant the above taxpayers an additional exemption (in the year in which full and fair cash value is first certified) not to exceed 100% of the above exemption. The total additional exemption granted to any individual cannot reduce the taxable value of the property after all exemptions below 10% of full and fair cash value. The additional exemption cannot result in a taxpayer paying less than the taxes paid the preceding fiscal year.

8. A 20-year exemption is allowed for solar or wind powered devices used to heat or supply energy for taxable property.

9. Realty classified as Class I residential may, with city or town approval be exempt from tax in an amount equal to not more than 20% of the average assessed value of all Class I parcels in the city or town. The exemption is limited to the principal residence of the taxpayer. This exemption is in addition to any other available exemptions but the taxable value of the property, after application of all available exemptions, may not be reduced below 10% of its full and fair cash value (exempt through application of exemptions for property of the aged, infirm or poverty stricken).

ASSESSMENT DATE:
January 1 preceding the fiscal year which runs July 1st to June 30th.

LEVEL OF GOVERNMENT RESPONSIBLE FOR ASSESSMENT:
City and towns.

EQUALIZATION:
Established between counties.

ASSESSORS:
Elected for three-year term or appointed. Certification is required by Chapter 58, Section 3 of the General Laws.

STATE ISSUED MANUALS:
Assessment manual (use optional).

PROPERTY OWNERSHIP MAPS REQUIRED:
Yes, required by regulation.

PERMIT REAL PROPERTY TO BE VALUED IN CURRENT USE RATHER THAN IN A FINANCIALLY BETTER USE:
No.

MEDIAN AREA ASSESSMENT TO SALES PRICE RATIOS:
59.60.

FREQUENCY OF STATE RATIO STUDIES:
Biennial.

STATE RATIO STUDY AVAILABLE TO PUBLIC:
Yes.

ADMINISTRATION OF ASSESSMENTS AND TAX LAWS:
The administering of the assessment and collecting of all real and tangible personal property taxes in the Commonwealth of Massachusetts is handled by the city and town assessor and collected in the jurisdiction where the property is located.

APPEALS AND PROTESTS:
The taxpayer may file an abatement application to appeal the assessment of real or tangible personal property. The form must be approved by the Commissioner of Revenue. It must be filed with the assessor by October 1 of the tax year or within 30 days of the mailing of the tax bill if sent after September 1, whichever is later. A taxpayer can appeal the assessors' decision to the Appellate Tax Board or the County Commissioners. If the appeal concerns personal property tax, one-half of the tax must be paid in order to appeal the decision. If the appeal concerns real estate tax, and the tax is more than two-thousand dollars, an abatement cannot be granted on appeal unless the tax has been paid without incurring interest. A decision of the Appellate Tax Board can be appealed to the Appeals Count and from there to the Supreme Judicial Court.

REFER TO STATE LAW IMPOSED BY:
Chapter 59 Section 11 of the General Laws. Chapters 58, 59, 60, 61, 61A and 61B of the Massachusetts General Laws, as amended are relevant.

CHANGES:
1.   1978 - Amended constitution to authorize the classification and taxation of real property according to use.

2.   1979 -   a. Expanded Department of Revenue supervisory and enforcement authority.

       b. Established statutory framework and property tax classification first applicable for taxes assessed as of January 1, 1980, for fiscal year 1981.

3.   1980 - Established limitations on property tax levy of 2.5% of community's full and fair cash value.

ADDRESS (STATE):
Commonwealth of Massachusetts
Department of Revenue
Division of Local Services
Harry M. Grossman, Chief
Property Tax Bureau
200 Portland Street (P.O. Box 7015)
Boston, Massachusetts 02204-1715

TELEPHONE:
(617) 727-2300

VERIFIED BY THIS OFFICE:
Yes.

MICHIGAN

NAME OF TAX:
Taxation--Real and Personal Property.

VALUATION STANDARD:
True Cash Value, defined as "the usual selling price at the place where the property which the term is applied at the time of assessment, being the price which could be obtained for the property at private sale and not at forced or auction sale."

REVALUATION CYCLE:
Not specified by statute.

ASSESSMENT LEVEL:
50% of the true cash value.

HOMEOWNERS EXEMPTIONS:
1.   All realty owned and used as a homestead by a disabled veteran receiving pecuniary assistance due to the disability for specially adapted housing or by the unremarried surviving spouse.

2.   Solar, wind or water energy conservation devices are exempt if installed before 1984.

3.   Persons 65 or older to totally and permanently disabled persons are allowed to defer collecting of special assessments on homestead properties of not less than $300. To be eligible, the person must be a U.S. citizen, a resident of Michigan for five or more years, the sole owner of the homestead for five or more years, and have household income of no more than $10,000 as indexed for inflation.

4.   Unqualified circuit breakers.

ASSESSMENT DATES:
December 31.

LEVEL OF GOVERNMENT RESPONSIBLE FOR ASSESSMENT:
Township and municipal.

EQUALIZATION:
State Tax Commission equalizes county assessed values by Adjustments to property classes.

ASSESSORS:
Elected and appointed (township - four-years; city assessors and county equalization directors are indefinite).

STATE ISSUED MANUALS:
Assessment manual.

PROPERTY OWNERSHIP MAPS REQUIRED:
No.

PERMIT REAL PROPERTY TO BE VALUED IN CURRENT USE RATHER THAN IN A FINANCIALLY BETTER USE:
No.

MEDIAN AREA ASSESSMENT TO SALES PRICE RATIOS:
44.30.

FREQUENCY OF STATE RATIO STUDIES:
Annual.

STATE RATIO STUDY AVAILABLE TO PUBLIC:
Yes.

ADMINISTRATION OF ASSESSMENTS AND TAX LAWS:
The State Tax commission supervises the administration of property taxes, and shall assist and give such advice and counsel to the assessing officers of the state as they deem necessary and essential to managing of laws governing assessments and levying of property taxes. This would include an assessor's manual to establish guidelines for determining value.

APPEALS AND PROTESTS:
Township and city boards of review meet annually on the first Tuesday after the first Monday in March, unless otherwise provided by the city's charter for the reviewing the assessments prepared by the Supervisor or Assessor. At this time any taxpayer not satisfied with his assessment may request that it be corrected. The Board of Review and the Supervisor or Assessor meet again on the second Monday of March (can vary slightly as the result of the charter provisions in some jurisdictions) to review the assessment rolls of taxpayers who requested corrections of their assessments. Notice of any changes will be issued and any objections will be reviewed promptly. Boards of Review are required to complete the review of all assessments by the first Monday of April.

Any further objections to an assessment by the taxpayer must be made by filing an appeal with the State Tax Tribunal. The Tribunal was established to resolve all disputes regarding property tax assessments. Applications for appeal of an assessment must be filed with the Tribunal prior to June 30 of the tax year or within 60 days of mailing of the tax bill in order to correct an error on the tax bill. If the date set by law for paying taxes has passed, a final decision on the entire proceeding won't be made by the Tribunal until the taxes are paid, unless this requirement is waived at the Tribunal's discretion. The State Tax Commission is responsible for correcting assessments and certifying the correct amount of taxes when notified that property liable for taxation has been omitted or incorrectly reported.

REFER TO STATE LAW IMPOSED BY:
Property taxes are imposed under Chapter 211 of the Michigan Compiled Laws, 1979, as amended. Property of certain public utilities is imposed under Chapter 207.

CHANGES:

1. 1981 - Legislated authority for property class equalization, previous equalizations were accomplished by adjustments to aggregate assessment roll.

2. 1982 - Instituted Truth in Assessing provisions.

ADDRESS (STATE):

State of Michigan
Department of Treasury
State Tax Commission
John Person, Director
4th Floor - Treasury Building
Lansing, Michigan 48922.

TELEPHONE:

(517) 373-0500

VERIFIED BY THIS OFFICE:

No.

COMMENTS:

Testing residential assessments as to their relationship to true value specifically in the large metropolitan areas - the assessments have been found to be consistently below the 50% of true value. However, sales ratio studies and comparable assessments are considered grounds for appeal in this State and would be the best method in reducing an assessment.

MINNESOTA

NAME OF TAX:
Property Tax.

VALUATION STANDARD:
Market Value, defined as "the usual selling price at the place where the property to which the term is applied shall be at the time of assessment; being the price which would be obtained at a private sale or an auction sale, if it's determined by the assessor that the price from the auction sale represents an arm's length transaction, the price obtained at a forced sale shall not be considered."

REVALUATION CYCLE:
Every four years by the annual appraisal of 25% of all property.

ASSESSMENT LEVEL:
The Minnesota system has five classes and 24 subdivision assessment levels range. Check with the local assessors office for your properties class and assessment level.

HOMEOWNERS EXEMPTIONS:
1.   Property tax refund qualified for age, income, disability, etc.

2. $68,000 base value on each homestead is assessed at lower rate.

ASSESSMENT DATES:
January 2.

LEVEL OF GOVERNMENT RESPONSIBLE FOR ASSESSMENT:
County, township and municipal.

EQUALIZATION:
Yes, by local Boards of Reviews, County Boards of Equalization and State Board of Equalization. Commissioner of Revenue equalizes assessed values in counties, cities, towns and districts statewide by adjusting assessment rolls.

ASSESSORS:
Appointed four-year terms, certification required.

STATE ISSUED MANUALS:
None.

PROPERTY OWNERSHIP MAPS REQUIRED:
No.

PERMIT REAL PROPERTY TO BE VALUED IN CURRENT USE RATHER THAN IN FINANCIALLY BETTER USE:
Yes.

MEDIAN AREA ASSESSMENT TO SALES PRICE RATIOS:
15.80.

FREQUENCY OF STATE RATIO STUDIES:
Annual.

STATE RATIO STUDY AVAILABLE TO PUBLIC:
Yes.

ADMINISTRATION OF ASSESSMENTS AND TAX LAWS:
The Commissioner of Revenue supervise's the administration of the assessment and taxation laws of the state, the assessors, town, county and city boards of review and equalization and all other assessing officers in performing their duties and ensure the assessment of property is just and equitable in compliance with the state laws.

Commissioner of Revenue can increase or decrease individual parcel values to market value after the assessment has gone to a county board of equalization.

APPEALS AND PROTESTS:
Any taxpayer who is dissatisfied with his assessment should appeal to the county or city assessor for a review. Should the taxpayer not be satisfied with the outcome of the informal meeting with the assessor, he may file an appeal with the Local Board of Review. The Local Board meets between April 1 and May 31 each year. Appeal of the decision of the Local Board of Review may be made to the County Board of Review. The County Board will meet the last two weeks in June that contain ten meeting days excluding Saturday and Sunday. Should the taxpayer not obtain relief from the County Board he may file an appeal with the Minnesota Tax Court by May 16 of the year following the year of assessment protesting the decision of the County Board of Equalization. The tax court filing deadline for personal property taxes is before July 1 of the year in which the tax is due.

Appeals to the tax court may be filed in one of two divisions:

Small Claims Division - hears appeals on homestead properties or any other class of property on which the assessor's estimated market value is less than $100,000. Decisions of the small claims division are final.

Regular Division - hears any arising from the state tax laws. Decisions made in the regular division may be appealed.

REFER TO STATE LAW IMPOSED BY:
Chapters 270 through 275 of the Minnesota Statutes, as amended.

CHANGES:
1.   1975 - Established current revaluation cycle for taxes paid in 1976.

2.   1983 - a. Amended "market value" definition to include underlined wording - see Valuation Standard.
           b. Established provision for funding of special assessors.

ADDRESS (STATE):
State of Minnesota
Department of Revenue
Michael P. Wandmacher, Director
Local Government Services Division
Mail Station 3340
St. Paul, Minnesota 55146-3340

TELEPHONE:
(612) 296-2286

VERIFIED BY THIS OFFICE:
Yes.

COMMENTS:
Sales ratio, inequity of assessments, and overevaluation are all considered to be acceptable appeals in this State. Grounds for appeal include classification, valuation and unequal assessment.

MISSISSIPPI

NAME OF TAX:
Property Tax or Ad Valorem Taxes.

VALUATION STANDARD:
True Value, generally "shall mean and include, but shall not be limited to market value, cash value, actual cash value, proper value and value for the purposes of appraisal for ad valorem taxation."

Class I and II property:	"The appraisal shall be made according to its current use, regardless of its location." (Residential property in this Class).
Class III and IV property:	"Must consider location factors, (e.g., access to transportation facilities, proximity to municipalities, etc.) and any other circumstances that tend to affect its value and not what it might bring at forced or auction sale, but what the owner would be willing to accept and would expect to receive for it if he were disposed to sell it to another able and willing to buyer."

REVALUATION CYCLE:
True value of each class of property shall be determined annually.

ASSESSMENT LEVEL:

Class I:	Real property not in Class IV (Residential property in this Class) - 10%.
Class II:	Real Property not single family owner occupied - 15%.
Note:	Class III property relates to personal property - 15%.
Class IV:	State-appraised public utility property other than airlines or railroads - 30%.

HOMEOWNERS EXEMPTIONS:
1. Exemptions for persons not yet 65 and not totally disabled are allowed a homestead exemption if assessed value is over $7,350. The maximum exemption is $258 for claims filed in 1987 if assessed value is over $6,300, persons 65 or older and totally disabled persons are exempt from taxes not in excess of $6,000 of assessed homestead value.

ASSESSMENT DATES:
January 1.

LEVEL OF GOVERNMENT RESPONSIBLE FOR ASSESSMENT:
County.

EQUALIZATION:
Performed between counties. State Tax Commission equalizes assessed values within a county by ordering county boards of supervisors to make fixed percentage adjustments to property classes.

ASSESSORS:
Elected to four-year term, certification required.

STATE ISSUED MANUALS:
Appraisal manual.

PROPERTY OWNERSHIP MAPS REQUIRED:
Yes.

PERMIT REAL PROPERTY TO BE VALUED IN CURRENT USE RATHER THAN IN A FINANCIALLY BETTER USE:
Yes.

MEDIAN AREA ASSESSMENT TO SALES PRICE RATIOS:
8.10. The acceptable limits around a median ratio shall not exceed 20%, plus or minus, on Class I property, and not exceed 25%, plus or minus, on Class II and III properties. Further, counties which are ordered to adjust shall meet a ratio of not more than 15%, plus or minus, on Class I property, and 20%, plus or minus, on Class II and Class III properties after adjustments.

FREQUENCY OF STATE RATIO STUDIES:
Annually.

STATE RATIO STUDY AVAILABLE TO PUBLIC:
No.

ADMINISTRATION OF ASSESSMENTS AND TAX LAWS:
Although assessment and collection of property taxes are handled by the county assessors and collectors, the State Tax Commission issues property assessment rules and regulations in an administration manual as advice to assessors, boards of supervisors, collectors, etc.

APPEALS AND PROTESTS:
The taxpayer should request an informal hearing with the assessor upon receipt of an assessment that's considered excessive. The failure to obtain the relief requested from the assessor gives the taxpayer the right to file an objection in writing with the County Board of Supervisors furnishing the clerk with the grounds for the request for hearing so it can be docketed and preserved with the assessment rolls. The appeal should be filed in July and the hearings of the Board of Supervisors begin on the first Monday in August. Should the taxpayer fail to file objections, he will be precluded from questioning the validity of the assessment after it has been approved by the Board of Supervisors.

Any taxpayer aggrieved at the action of the Board of Supervisors in equalization of assessments may appeal to the circuit court, within 10 days after the adjournment of the meeting of the Board of Supervisors, at which approval of the roll by the State Tax Commission is entered. There is no provision for a hearing by the State Tax Commission regarding its equalization and approval of the assessment roll. Relief must be sought through the County Circuit Court. The decision of the County Circuit Court may be appealed to the State Supreme Court.

REFER TO STATE LAW IMPOSED BY:
Title 1, Chapter 3; Title 21, Chapter 33; Title 27, Chapters 3 and 29 through 53; Title 37, Chapter 57; and Title 81, Chapter 3 of Mississippi Code 1972, as amended.

CHANGES:

1.   11/2/82 - Established assessment classifications.

2.   1983 - Established current revaluation cycles.

3.   7/1/83 - Specified current valuation standards - see Valuation Standard.

4.   1984 - Established assessment ratios for each property class.

ADDRESS (STATE):
Robert M. Megginson, Director
Property Tax Bureau
Mississippi State Tax Commission (P.O. Box 960)
Jackson, Mississippi 39205-0960

TELEPHONE:
(601) 359-1076

VERIFIED BY THIS OFFICE:
Yes.

MISSOURI

NAME OF TAX:
Property Taxes.

VALUATION STANDARD:
True Value in Money (not defined by statute).

REVALUATION CYCLE:
Not specified by statute.

ASSESSMENT LEVEL
Class I: Real property.
   Subclass I: Residential property - 19%.
   Subclass II: Agricultural property - 12%.
   Subclass III: Utility, industrial, commercial, railroad and all other real property not in
                    Subclass I or II - 32%.

HOMEOWNERS EXEMPTION:
Circuit breaker qualified by age, income, disability, etc.

ASSESSMENT DATE:
January 1.

LEVEL OF GOVERNMENT RESPONSIBLE FOR ASSESSMENT:
County.

EQUALIZATION:
State Tax Commission equalizes county assessed values by percentage adjustments to property classes.

ASSESSORS:
Elected four-year term, certification required.

STATE ISSUED MANUALS:
Assessment manuals.

PROPERTY OWNERSHIP MAPS REQUIRED:
No.

PERMIT REAL PROPERTY TO BE VALUED IN CURRENT USE RATHER THAN IN A FINANCIALLY BETTER USE:
No.

MEDIAN AREA ASSESSMENT TO SALES PRICE RATIOS:
12.60.

FREQUENCY OF STATE RATIO STUDIES:
Annual.

STATE RATIO STUDY AVAILABLE TO PUBLIC:
Yes.

ADMINISTRATION OF ASSESSMENTS AND TAX LAWS:
The county assessors and, in some cases, the city assessors are responsible for assessing of property within their jurisdiction. The State Tax Commission administers over all these jurisdictions, issues assessor's manuals changes in the law or procedures required, and revises assessments where it's needed to equalize assessment throughout the state.

APPEALS AND PROTESTS:
Although there is no statutory provision for appealing an assessment with the local assessor, any taxpayer aggrieved of his assessment should contact the local assessor before to following the appeal procedure. It's possible any differences can be resolved at an informal meeting with the assessor.

The first step to follow in the appeal procedure is to file a written appeal to the County Board of Equalization or City Board of Equalization if appropriate. These boards meet at varying times (depending on the county or city) commencing after May 31 and terminating on the first Monday in July. If the taxpayer isn't satisfied with the decision of the county or city board, he may appeal to the State Tax Commission. Final decisions of the Board of Equalization concerning all questions and disputes involving the exclusion or exemption of property from assessment pursuant to the U.S. Constitution or the state constitution or the taxable situs of the property, should be appealed directly to the state circuit court in the county where the property is located.

Decisions of the State Tax Commission regarding assessment of property may be appealed to the state circuit court for the county where the property is located. A taxpayer failing to use any administrative remedy loses the right to further appeal.

REFER TO STATE LAW IMPOSED BY:
Title VII and Title X of the Revised Statutes of Missouri.

CHANGES:
1. 1/1/78 - Established assessor salary and costs reimbursement program for counties and cities not within counties.

2. 1/1/83 - a. Assessor reimbursement extended to townships.

      b. Revaluation costs reimbursement program established.

3. 1984 - Extended statewide revaluation completion date from 12/31/84 to 12/31/85.

4. 1985 - Established subclass assessment ratios roughly preserving class shares of 1984 tax rolls. Previous assessment level was 33-1/3% of true value in money for all property.

ADDRESS (STATE):
State Tax Commission of Missouri
Bruce Davis, Administrative Secretary
623 East Capitol Avenue (P.O. Box 146)
Jefferson City, Missouri 65102-0146

TELEPHONE:
(314) 751-2414

VERIFIED BY THIS OFFICE:
No.

COMMENTS:
Most commonly used and accepted method for assessment reduction is sales/ratio study. You must determine current County level, prove current value of your property and request reduction to current ratio level.

MONTANA

NAME OF TAX:
Property Taxes.

VALUATION STANDARD:
Market Value, defined as "the value at which property would change hands between a willing buyer and a willing seller, neither being under any compulsion to buy nor sell and both having reasonable knowledge of reasonable facts."

REVALUATION CYCLE:
Every five years.

ASSESSMENT LEVEL:

Class 3:   Agricultural property - 30% of productive capacity.

Class 4:   Lands and improvements not elsewhere classified (includes residential property) - 3.86%.

Class 11:   Centrally-assessed public utility companies - 12%.

While Montana requires property to be assessed at 100% of market value, taxes are paid on a value established by adjusting the assessment level as described. The Montana system has 18 classes with taxable levels ranging from 3% to 12% of market value.

HOMEOWNERS EXEMPTIONS:

1.   Residence, including the lot, owned and occupied by a veteran killed in service or who dies from service-connected disability or by a totally disabled veteran or his unremarried surviving spouse having an annual adjusted gross income of not more than $15,000 ($18,000 or a married couple).

2.   A property tax reduction is allowed for realty or mobile homes destroyed by natural disasters.

3.   The following portions of the appraised value of non-fossil fuel energy generation equipment are exempt for a period of 10 years following installation: $20,000 in the case of a single family residence; and $100,000 in the case of a multi-family residential dwelling or a non-residential structure.

4.   A reduction in property taxes is allowed for the first $80,000 or less of the market value of any improvement on real property and land not exceeding five acres owned or under contract for deed and actually occupied for at least 10 months a year as the primary residential dwelling of any person whose total income from all sources including otherwise tax-exempt income of all types isn't more than $10,000 for a single person or $12,000 for a married couple. The income limit is adjusted each year for cost of living. The amount of adjustment received is based on the income. The taxpayers that have the most income receive the smallest tax adjustment.

ASSESSMENT DATES:
January 1.

LEVEL OF GOVERNMENT RESPONSIBLE FOR ASSESSMENT:
County Appraisers and Assessors are State employees. The State Department of Revenue is responsible for the tax roll each year.

EQUALIZATION:
The purpose of the periodic reappraisal is to ensure all properties in the state are at market value. This is the equalization process.

ASSESSORS:
Elected for four-year term, certification required.

STATE ISSUED MANUALS:
Appraisal manuals and Assessment Manuals for Personal Property.

PROPERTY OWNERSHIP MAPS REQUIRED:
Each County Appraisal Office keeps county ownership maps up-to-date.

PERMIT REAL PROPERTY TO BE VALUED IN CURRENT USE RATHER THAN IN A FINANCIALLY BETTER USE:
Yes.

MEDIAN AREA ASSESSMENT TO SALES PRICE RATIOS:
3.70. The state has been divided into areas. Sales ratio studies are done in those areas each year. If an adjustment to the market value in an area for residential and commercial property is indicated, the values are adjusted.

FREQUENCY OF STATE RATIO STUDIES:
Annual.

STATE RATIO STUDY AVAILABLE TO PUBLIC:
Yes.

ADMINISTRATION OF ASSESSMENTS AND TAX LAWS:
The assessment of property, other than that which is centrally assessed and industrial property, is administered at the county level, but is subject to review by the Montana Department of Revenue, which has the ultimate responsibility of equalizing assessments throughout the state. Real property is scheduled for revaluation of the property tax assessment on a five-year cycle with the current cycle that was due to end on December 31, 1990, being extended for an additional two years until December 31, 1992, and the new revaluation cycle commencing on January 1, 1993.

Department of Revenue:

1.   Appraises all privately-owned taxable property.

2.   Maintains assessment records and tax maps for all areas in the State.

APPEALS AND PROTESTS:

A taxpayer dissatisfied with an assessment may file, by first monday in June or within 15 days after receiving a notice of classification and appraisal (whichever is later), an appeal with the County Tax Appeal Board in the county where the property is located. Any deliberation of the county tax appeal board concerning an application for a reduction of a property tax assessment must be open to the public under the State Constitution, unless the presiding officer of the hearing determines that the deliberation involves matters of individual privacy. Should the taxpayer be dissatisfied with the county's decision, he has 30 days to appeal the decision to the State Tax Appeal Board. An unfavorable decision by the State Board can be appealed to the District Court by the taxpayer within 60 days.

REFER TO STATE LAW IMPOSED BY:

Title 15, Chapters 1 through 24, of the Montana Code Annotated, as amended.

CHANGES:

1.   7/1/80 - Appraiser certification program established.

2.   1981 - Extended current revaluation from 12/31/83 to 12/31/85.

ADDRESS (STATE):

State of Montana
Department of Revenue
Property Assessment Division
Mitchell Building
Helena, Montana 59620

TELEPHONE:

(406) 443-0811

VERIFIED BY THIS OFFICE:

Yes.

NEBRASKA

NAME OF TAX:
Property Taxes.

VALUATION STANDARD:
Actual Value, defined as "the market value of the property in the ordinary course of trade. Actual value may be determined using professionally accepted mass appraisal techniques, including but not limited to: (1) earning capacity of the property; (2) relative location; (3) desirability and functional use; (4) reproduction cost less depreciation; (5) comparison with other properties of known or recognized values; (6) market value in the ordinary course of trade; and (7) existing zoning property."

REVALUATION CYCLE:
Not specified by statute.

ASSESSMENT LEVEL:
100% of actual value.

HOMEOWNERS EXEMPTIONS:
1. Circuit breakers qualified for age, income, disability etc.

2. The value of a home substantially contributed by the U.S. Veterans' Administration for a paraplegic or multiple amputee veteran.

3. Mobile homes and one motor vehicle of disabled or blind veterans.

4. All homesteads in Nebraska are assessed the same as other property except that no tax applies to a percentage of the first $35,000 of the actual value of any homestead of any veteran totally disabled by:

    - a non-service connected accident or illness.
    - individuals who are paralyzed in both legs.
    - individuals who have undergone amputation of both legs.
    - individuals with progressive neuromuscular or neurological disease.
    - individuals who have permanently lost the use of control of both arms.
    - individuals who have undergone amputation of both arms above the elbow.

    The homestead of any totally disabled veteran (or his or her unmarried widow or widower) who is not eligible for total exemption, or of any veteran (or his or her unremarried widow or widower) who dies from a service-connected disability, house percent of income relief is exempt from tax determined as follows:

0 to $15,000	100%	$17,001 to $18,000	40%
$15,001 to $16,000	80%	$18,001 to $19,000	20%
$16,001 to $17,000	60%		

Senior citizens (65 or older) are allowed a homestead exemption equal to a percentage of the first $35,000 of the actual value of the homestead based on the income of the homeowner. The percentage of relief allowed is similiar as above except the whose household income limit for 100% is not over $10,400.

ASSESSMENT DATES:
January 1.

LEVEL OF GOVERNMENT RESPONSIBLE FOR ASSESSMENT:
County.

EQUALIZATION:
Performed both within and between counties. State Board of Equalization equalizes assessed values of property classes by fixed percentage adjustments.

ASSESSORS:
Elected for four-year term, certification is required.

STATE ISSUED MANUALS:
Appraisal manuals.

PROPERTY OWNERSHIP MAPS REQUIRED:
Yes.

PERMIT REAL PROPERTY TO BE VALUED IN CURRENT USE RATHER THAN IN A FINANCIALLY BETTER USE:
No.

MEDIAN AREA ASSESSMENT TO SALES PRICE RATIO:
92, currently.

FREQUENCY OF STATE RATIO STUDIES:
Annual.
STATE RATIO STUDY AVAILABLE TO PUBLIC:
Yes.

ADMINISTRATION OF ASSESSMENT AND TAX LAWS:
The county assessors compute the assessment of property within their jurisdiction but are subject to the supervision of the Tax Commissioner. The Tax Commissioner has the responsibility to administer all the revenue laws of the state, which includes the formulating and promulgating of rules and regulations pertaining to the valuation and assessment of property.

APPEALS AND PROTESTS:
A taxpayer dissatisfied with the assessment may meet with the county assessor at any time between January 1 and April 1 to try to resolve the problem. If the taxpayer is dissatisfied with the results of the meeting with the county assessor, he may file an appeal with the County Board of Equalization. The board meets starting 4/1 until 5/30. Should the taxpayer not obtain relief from the board, an appeal can be filed with the District Court within 45 days after the adjournment of

the county board. (Effective 7/17/86, a bond of not more than $200 but not less than $50, as determined by the district court, is required to be filed with the petition to the District Court.

Assessments determined by the Tax Commissioner may be protested by filing an administrative appeal with the Tax Commissioner in writing stating that the taxpayer claims that the valuation is unjust and inequitable, giving the valuation the taxpayer feels is correct and requesting an adjustment. After a review and final order is furnished to the taxpayer by the Tax Commissioner, the taxpayer may appeal such order to the district court.

REFER TO STATE LAW IMPOSED BY:
Chapter 77, Articles 1 through 6, 8, 10 and 12 through 19, 28, 35, 37, 41, and 42 of the Revised Statutes of Nebraska, 1943, as amended. The city of Lincoln as well as Omaha, property taxes are imposed under Article IX of the Charter of the city of Lincoln.

CHANGES:
1. 1/1/81 - Assessment level changed from 35% of actual value to current 100%.

2. 1/1/84 - Provided for Department of Revenue authority to bring assessed values into compliance.

3. 7/10/84 - Provided for Department of Revenue authority or order complete reappraisal.

4. 1/1/85 - Repealed laws requiring revaluation in odd-numbered years after 1981.

5. 1989 - LB361, passed in 1989 Legislature, requires agricultural land values to be based on the market value. It also requires the correlation of values of all classes of property.

ADDRESS (STATE):
State of Nebraska, Department of Revenue
Larry D. Worth, CAE - Administrator
Property Tax Division
P.O. Box 94818
Lincoln, Nebraska 68509

TELEPHONE:
(402) 471-2971

VERIFIED BY THIS OFFICE:
Yes.

NEVADA

NAME OF TAX:
Property Taxes.

VALUATION STANDARD:
Taxable value, defined as "(a) the full cash value of the land, based on the use to which the improvements are being put and (b) the value of any improvements made on the land determined by subtracting from the cost of replacement of the improvements all applicable (i.e., straight-line) depreciation and obsolescence. The computed taxable value of any property may not exceed its full cash value".

REVALUATION CYCLE:
At least every five years.

ASSESSMENT LEVEL:
35% of full "taxable value", values for years in which physical revaluation has not occurred must be adjusted using State Tax Commission factors.

Note: Most counties are on the five year cycle, but a few have elected a three or four-year cycle.

HOMEOWNERS EXEMPTIONS:
1. Circuit breaker qualified by age, income, disability, etc.

2. Property of widows and orphan children to the extent of $1,000 assessed value per family; property of totally blind persons to the extent of $3,000 assessed value.

3. Improvements made to property owned and occupied by a handicapped person, designed to remove architectural barriers to the movement of the handicapped person.

4. Residential property to the extent of $1,000 assessed value if owned and occupied by a resident and if it contains a qualified fallout shelter.

5. Persons 62 or older on or before the last day in June immediately succeeding the filing period whose homes are placed upon the secured or unsecured tax roll, who have owned and maintained the home as their primary residence for at least six months immediately preceding the filing of their claim, and whose household incomes aren't over $15,100, are entitled to an allowance against the property tax accrued against their homes.

6. Any value added to property by any residential, commercial or industrial system, method, construction, installation, machinery, equipment, device or appliance to heat or cool the building, or water used in the building, or to provide electricity in the building via solar or wind energy, geothermal energy, energy derived from solid waste conservation or water power is exempt from tax.

7. Honorably discharged veterans with a permanent service-connected disability are entitled to an exemption based on the total percentage of disability. The maximum exemption for total

permanent disability is the first $10,000 assessed valuation. A person with a permanent service-connected disability of 80% to 99%, is entitled to a $7,500 assessed value exemption; 60% to 79%, a $5,000 assessed value exemption.

ASSESSMENT DATES:
July 1.

LEVEL OF GOVERNMENT RESPONSIBLE FOR ASSESSMENT:
County.

EQUALIZATION:
Performed by within and between counties. State Board of Equalization reviews county assessment rolls and equalizes property values.

ASSESSORS:
Elected for four-year terms, certification is required.

STATE ISSUED MANUALS:
Appraisal manuals.

PROPERTY OWNERSHIP MAPS REQUIRED:
Yes.

PERMIT REAL PROPERTY TO BE VALUED IN CURRENT USE RATHER THAN IN A FINANCIALLY BETTER USE:
No.

MEDIAN AREA ASSESSMENT TO SALES PRICE RATIOS:
22.30.

FREQUENCY OF STATE RATIO STUDIES:
Annual.

STATE RATIO STUDY AVAILABLE TO PUBLIC:
Yes.

APPEALS AND PROTESTS:
A taxpayer dissatisfied with his assessment must file an appeal with the County Board of Equalization prior to January 15. The Board will hold its hearings in January and February and conclude them on or before February 20. If the taxpayer isn't satisfied with the decision, he may appeal to the State Board of Equalization if such appeal is filed by the first Monday in March. The State Board will meet from the third Monday in March and will complete its business before October 1. Any appeals heard by the State Board must have been heard first by the County Board unless the assessment notice was received by the taxpayer after the County Board's adjournment. A taxpayer dissatisfied with his assessment on unsecured personal property assessed between December 15 and April 30 may file an appeal on or before May 15 with the State Board. The State Board will complete these hearings by May 31.

Taxpayers who, after administrative review by the County and State Boards of Equalization, still believe their assessment is excessive may further appeal, within three months after full payment of the last installment of taxes, to whichever court has jurisdiction in the county where the property is located. Each installment payment of the tax must be made "under protest." The statement of protest must be prepared in triplicate and must accompany the payment. Any recovery realized by the taxpayer as the result of the decision of the court will bear interest.

REFER TO STATE LAW IMPOSED BY:
Title 32, Chapter 361, of the Nevada Revised Statutes 1957, as amended.

ADMINISTRATION OF ASSESSMENTS AND TAX LAWS:
The assessment and collection of property taxes is administered at the county level except for centrally assessed public utilities, but the Nevada Tax Commission has the responsibility of supervising the general administration of the assessment of property by the county assessors.

CHANGES:
1.	1981 - Mandated the use of factors for properties which aren't physically reappraised.

2.	1982 - Changed previous assessment level of 35% of adjusted cash value to current 35% of taxable value.

ADDRESS (STATE):
Nevada Department of Taxation
Division of Assessment Standards
John P. Comeux, Director
Capitol Complex
1340 S. Curry Street
Carson City, Nevada 89710-0003

TELEPHONE:
(702) 885-4840.

VERIFIED BY THIS STATE:
No.

COMMENTS:
Assessors aren't required to furnish copies of comparable properties, and this limits the preparation of evidence in attempting to prove unequal treatment in the assessment process which is still grounds for appeal.

NEW HAMPSHIRE

NAME OF TAX:
Property Tax.

VALUATION STANDARD:
Full and True Value in Money, defined as "the same in payment of a just debt due from a solvent debtor, considering all evidence that may be submitted relative to the property value, the value of which cannot be determined by personal examination."

REVALUATION CYCLE:
Not specified by statute, other than to require that property must be examined each April 1 and reappraised if a change in value has occurred.

ASSESSMENT LEVEL:
Uniform percentage of full and true value.

HOMEOWNERS EXEMPTIONS:
1. Resident veterans (or their spouses or surviving spouses), residents (or their widows) whose services were terminated for a service-connected disability, and widows of a resident who suffered a service-connected death are eligible for a homestead exemption amounting to $50 in taxes*; widows of veterans who died while on active duty are exempt from tax on their property, whether residential or not, amounting to $700 in taxes; totally disabled veterans, double amputees or paraplegics, or a surviving spouse, whose disability is service-connected are exempt from $700 in taxes on their homesteads**.

    * Option of $100, if voted by town.
    ** Option of $1,400 if voted by town.

2. Specially adapted homesteads of totally and permanently disabled veterans or their unremarried surviving spouse, if the disability is service connected.

3. Residential real estate of totally blind persons to the value of $15,000.

4. The value of improvement to residential realty, made by the owner who resides there, to assist physically handicapped persons residing there (the value of such improvements are deducted from assessed value of the realty before determining the tax).

5. Municipalities may adopt, if voters approve, an exemption for persons with realty equipped with a wind-powered energy system, a solar energy heating or cooling system or a wood-heating energy system.

6. Residential realty to the assessed value of $5,000 is exempt from taxation if owned by the following qualified persons:

Standard Exemption:
-68 years of age on or before April 1.

Income limit of $5,000 if single, $6,000 if married.
Assets not in excess of $35,000.

Expanded Exemption:
-65 years of age on or before April 1.
Income limit of $7,000 if single, $9,000 if married.
Assets not in excess of $50,000.

65-74 years old receive $5,000 exemption.
75-79 years old receive $10,000 exemption.
80+ years old receive $20,000 exemption.
Adjusted Exemption -Same as expanded exemption except:

Income limit of $10,000 if single, $12,000 if married.
Assets not in excess of $30,000 excluding the value of any residential real estate.

ASSESSMENT DATES:
April 1.

LEVEL OF GOVERNMENT RESPONSIBLE FOR ASSESSMENT:
Township and municipal.

EQUALIZATION:
Performed for each individual municipality. Department of Revenue Administration equalizes assessed values of cities, towns and unincorporated places by adding or subtracting the total assessed value of the locality.

ASSESSORS:
Elected and appointed indefinitely, certification is not required.

STATE ISSUED MANUALS:
Appraisal manuals.

PROPERTY OWNERSHIP MAPS REQUIRED:
No.

PERMIT REAL PROPERTY TO BE VALUED IN CURRENT USE RATHER THAN IN A FINANCIALLY BETTER USE:
Yes.

MEDIAN AREA ASSESSMENT TO SALES PRICE RATIOS:
54.00.

FREQUENCY OF STATE RATIO STUDIES:
Annual.

STATE RATIO STUDY AVAILABLE TO PUBLIC:
Yes.

ADMINISTRATION OF ASSESSMENT AND TAX LAWS:

The administration of property taxes is handled by the municipal assessors and collectors under the supervision of the Commissioner of Revenue Administration of the Department of Revenue Administration. The Coos County Commissioner will list all polls and take inventory of all taxable property in unincorporated or unorganized areas each April.

State Board of Tax and Land Appeals can order reassessment of particular parcels of property if property owner files a written complaint or upon discovery of improperly assessed or omitted property.

APPEALS AND PROTESTS:

First, within four months after the receipt of the tax bill, an appeal may be entered with the Board of Selectmen or other assessing officials. Then, if dissatisfied with that decision or none is received within a reasonable length of time, the taxpayer may select within six months of receipt of the tax bill to either: (1) enter a written appeal with the New Hampshire Board of Tax and Land Appeals if an Inventory of Taxable Property has been filed with the Board of Selectmen prior to April 15. Filing fee of $40.00 must accompany appeal. Appeals should be addressed to:

> State of New Hampshire
> Board of Tax and Land Appeals
> State Office Park South
> 107 Pleasant Street
> Concord, New Hampshire 03301

or, (2) if no appeal has been filed with the State Board of Tax and Land Appeals, a petition may be entered with the appropriate county's Superior Court.

Note: No form of appeal excuses paying the tax; interest will accrue on any unpaid balance. However, if an appeal warrants an adjustment, the Board of Taxation will refund the excess taxes paid plus interest at the rate of 6% per annum for the period between the date of tax payment and date of refund.

REFER TO STATE LAW IMPOSED BY:

Chapters 71 through 76, 79 through 82, 84 and 85 of the Revised Statutes Annotated of New Hampshire, 1955, as amended.

CHANGES:

1. 1973 - Provided Board of Tax and Land Appeals with authority to order reassessment.

2. 7/1/85 - Allowed Department of Revenue Administration to provide technical assistance to local governments.

ADDRESS (STATE):
Richard M. Young, Director
Property Appraisal Division
State of New Hampshire
Department of Revenue Administration
61 South Spring Street (P.O. Box 457)
Concord, New Hampshire 03301

TELEPHONE:
(603) 271-2191

VERIFIED BY THIS OFFICE:
Yes.

NEW JERSEY

NAME OF TAX:
Property Tax.

VALUATION STANDARD:
Full and Fair Value, defined as "such a price as it would sell for at a fair and bona fide sale by private contract on October 1 of the pre-tax year."

REVALUATION CYCLE:
Not specified by statute.

ASSESSMENT LEVEL:
Uniform percentage of full and fair value, in multiples of 10% from 20% to 100%, as determined by county boards of taxation - 50% of full and fair value if county fails to determine the level. However, once a county selects a percentage it must remain in effect for not less than three years.

Note: Presently all 21 counties have declared a 100% assessment level.

HOMEOWNERS EXEMPTIONS:
1. In addition to other exemptions granted on his real or personal property, the dwelling house and lot of an honorable discharged veteran having a service-connected disability from paraplegia, sarcoidosis, osteochondritis resulting in permanent loss of the use of both legs, or permanent paralysis of both legs and lower parts of the body, or from hemiplegia and permanent paralysis of one leg and one arm on either side of the body resulting from injury to the spinal cord, skeletal structure, brain or from disease of the spinal cord, total blindness or from the amputation of both arms or both legs, or both hands or both feet, or the combination of a hand and a foot or from other service-connected disability declared by the Veterans Administration to be a total or 100% permanent disability; this exemption applies to the widow of a qualified veteran during her widowhood.

2. Property of veterans honorably discharged or released from active service in time of war or their surviving spouses in the amount of $50 from their final property tax bills; residents age 65 or older, or who are under 65 but permanently and totally disabled, whose annual income isn't over $10,000 and who live in a home they own are allowed a deduction against realty taxes equal to the amount of tax or $250, whichever is less. The surviving spouse of a decedent who received this deduction is entitled to it if he or she remains unmarried and resides in the same dwelling provided such surviving spouse was 55 or older when the decedent died. "Income" doesn't include gain from the sale of a home on which this deduction was allowed, Social Security benefits or benefits received under other federal programs or state and local pension, disability or retirement programs.

3. Value of fallout shelters erected on residential property.

4. Historic lands, buildings and contents.

5. A homestead rebate* is available to all taxpayers, including the owner of a house situated on land owned by another person, a life tenant, a tenant under a lease of 99 years or more, and a person who takes possession of land and a dwelling house under an executory contract or under an agreement with a lending institution that holds title as security for a loan. The rebate is calculated at $1.50 per $100 of equalized value, whichever is less, plus 12.5% of the effective tax rate in the municipality where the rebate is claimed, multiplied by $10,000 of equalized value or two-thirds of equalized value, whichever is less. The rebate is limited to 50% of the net property tax otherwise due for the pre-tax year. Senior citizens, totally disabled persons under 65 and surviving spouses are allowed a $50 additional homestead rebate.

6. Cities in which residential neighborhoods have been declared to be rehabilitated may deem up to $4,000, $10,000 or $15,000, as may be specified by general ordinance, in home improvements per dwelling unit over 20 years old as not increasing the property's value for five years and may allow an abatement of some portion of the assessed value of property receiving such exemption as it existed prior to the improvement for not to exceed five years and for not to exceed 30% of the annual amount of the exemption. Municipalities qualified for state aid may exempt, for five years, improvements to property in need of rehabilitation, whether commercial, industrial or residential property.

*The homestead rebate is constitutional. Rubin v. Glaser ('80).

ASSESSMENT DATES:
October 1.

LEVEL OF GOVERNMENT RESPONSIBLE FOR ASSESSMENT:
Townships and municipalities.

EQUALIZATION:
Performed between counties.

ASSESSORS:
Elected and appointed indefinitely, certification required.

STATE ISSUED MANUALS:
Assessor's law manual or handbook.

PROPERTY OWNERSHIP MAPS REQUIRED:
Yes.

PERMIT REAL PROPERTY TO BE VALUED IN CURRENT USE RATHER THAN IN A FINANCIALLY BETTER USE:
No.

MEDIAN AREA ASSESSMENT TO SALES PRICE RATIOS:
58.50.

FREQUENCY OF STATE RATIO STUDIES:
Annual.

STATE RATIO STUDY AVAILABLE TO PUBLIC:
Yes.

ADMINISTRATION OF ASSESSMENTS AND TAX LAWS:
Real property taxes are assessed and collected by the assessors and collectors of the respective cities and townships, but are subject to supervision and review by the county boards of taxation.

APPEALS AND PROTESTS:
Since real property assessments are handled at the local level, the taxpayer should first arrange an informal meeting with the city or township assessor to discuss his dissatisfaction with the assessment. If the taxpayer isn't satisfied after meeting with the assessor, an appeal may be filed with the County Board of Taxation on or before August 15 of the year following assessment. When a petition of appeal is filed within 19 days preceding August 15, respondents have 20 days from the date of service to file a cross-petition of appeal with the county board of taxation. Upon filing an appeal with the County Board, a copy thereof must be furnished to the local taxing jurisdiction. Where an assessment is increased or added to the tax rolls after January 1 following the assessment date, aggrieved taxpayers may file an appeal with the County Board on or before December 1. The taxpayer or the taxing district has the option of appealing directly with the State Tax Court on or before August 15. Any party who's dissatisfied with the ruling by the County Board may file an appeal with the State Tax Curt within 45 days of the County Board's decision. The appeal must be submitted in accordance with the rules established by the court and, at the time filed, all taxes or any installments thereof due and payable for the year for which review is sought must have been paid. There is a generally accepted guideline that the Tax Court will not, in most cases, hear appeals wherein the difference between the assessor's and the owner's values differ by less than 15% unless the matter involves a large assessment. Appeals should be addressed to Tax Court of New Jersey, P.O. Box 290, Trenton, NJ 08625. Dissatisfaction with the decision of the Tax Court can be appealed to the Superior Court of the State of New Jersey.

REFER TO STATE LAW IMPOSED BY:
Titles 1, 40 and 54 of the Revised Statutes of New Jersey, 1937, as amended.

CHANGES:
None found.

ADDRESS (STATE):
State of New Jersey
Division of Taxation
Department of the Treasury
Appraisal Section
John R. Baldwin, Director
50 Barrack Street
Trenton, New Jersey 08646

TELEPHONE:
(609) 292-7974

VERIFIED BY THIS OFFICE:
Yes.

COMMENTS:
Generally, residential properties are assessed substantially below 100% of value. In many instances, comparing assessments of neighboring properties can help in preparing a good case, however statutorily, assessors aren't required to furnish property record cards for any property other than that owned by the taxpayer. This makes it difficult to prepare evidence for an appeal unless you can obtain information such as square footage from other sources.

NEW MEXICO

NAME OF TAX:
Property Taxes.

VALUATION STANDARD:
Market Value, "as determined by sales of comparable property or, if that method cannot be used due to lack of comparable sales date for the property being valued, then its value shall be determined using an income method or cost method of valuation. In using any method of valuation authorized by this subsection, the valuation authority shall apply generally accepted appraisal techniques."

REVALUATION CYCLE:
Not specified by statute.

ASSESSMENT LEVEL:
Locally assessed property - 33-1/3% of market value.
Centrally assessed property - special methods are applied.

Note: Upon completion of statewide reappraisal, there will be a two-year lag in market values, e.g, 1988 assessed values will use 1986 market values.

HOMEOWNERS EXEMPTIONS:
1. Property to $2,000 in value, including the community or joint property of a husband and wife, owned by a veteran or his unmarried surviving spouse if the veteran or his spouse are New Mexico residents.

ASSESSMENT DATES:
January 1.

LEVEL OF GOVERNMENT RESPONSIBLE FOR ASSESSMENT:
County.

EQUALIZATION:
None.

ASSESSOR:
Elected for two-year term, certification is not required.

STATE ISSUED MANUALS:
Appraisal manuals.

PROPERTY OWNERSHIP MAPS REQUIRED:
Yes.

PERMIT REAL PROPERTY TO BE VALUED IN CURRENT USE RATHER THAN IN A FINANCIALLY BETTER USE:
No.

MEDIAN AREA ASSESSMENT TO SALES PRICE RATIOS:
10.40.

FREQUENCY OF STATE RATIO STUDIES:
Annual.

STATE RATIO STUDY AVAILABLE TO PUBLIC:
Yes.

ADMINISTRATION OF ASSESSMENTS AND TAX LAWS:
The county assessor determines the assessed value of property that isn't centrally assessed by the State Taxation and Revenue Department, which determines the centrally assessed property. However, the State Taxation and Revenue Department, property Tax Division, is responsible for administering all property taxes and issuing regulations and rulings.

APPEALS AND PROTESTS:
Assessment notices must be mailed to the taxpayer on or before April 1 each year. The taxpayer has 30 days from the mailing of the assessment notice to elect to either appeal any assessment that he's dissatisfied with or pay the tax and file a claim for refund. Once a taxpayer files a petition of protest, he waives the right to file a claim for refund. Appeals of an assessment of centrally assessed property by the state must be filed with the State Property Tax Department, and appeals of assessments determined by the county assessor must be filed with the county assessor or the County Valuation Protest Board. The claim for refund is filed with the District Court in the county where the property is located and must be filed by no later than the 60th day after the first installment of the property tax for which a claim for refund is made is due.

Claims for refund of tax paid on centrally assessed property must be filed with the District Court for Santa Fe County.

If the taxpayer is dissatisfied with the decision of an appeal filed with either the State Property Tax Department or the County Valuation Protest Board or the decision of the District Court concerning a claim for refund, the taxpayer may appeal to the State Court of Appeals.

REFER TO STATE LAW IMPOSED BY:
Chapter 7, Articles 35 through 38, of the New Mexico Statutes Annotated, 1978 Compilation, as amended.

CHANGES:
1.   1/1/75 - Property tax code was rewritten, only 5 sections were kept verbatim from previous code.

2.   1982 - Legislature required statewide reappraisal to be completed by 12/31/86.

ADDRESS (STATE):
State of New Mexico
Taxation and Revenue Department
Property Tax Division (P.O. Box 630)
Santa Fe, New Mexico 87509-0630

TELEPHONE:
(505) 827-0700

VERIFIED BY THIS OFFICE:
No.

NEW YORK

NAME OF TAX:
Real Property Tax.

VALUATION STANDARD:
Value (not defined by statute).

REVALUATION CYCLE:
Not specified by statute.

ASSESSMENT LEVEL:
Uniform percentage of value of 100%.

Note: Classified systems of taxation exist in certain jurisdictions. If a classified system exists, different tax rates are applied to different classes of property based on the proportion of each class's taxable assessed value to the total, taxable assessed value in the assessing unit. Two types of classified systems are allowed:

Mandatory classified systems in assessing units with a population of one million or more (New York City and Nassau County);

Class I:	Residential property with not more than 3 units, excluding condominiums more than three stories in height, cooperatives and certain mobile homes and certain vacant land.
Class II:	Residential property other than Class I, excluding hotels, motels and similar commercial property.
Class III:	Public utility property.
Class IV:	All property other than Classes I, II and III (includes railroads and other carriers).

Optional classified system in approved (full-value) assessing units:

Homestead:	Residential property containing not more than three dwelling units and any farm dwellings, excluding certain mobile homes.
Non-Homestead:	All property other than Class I.

HOMEOWNERS EXEMPTIONS:
1. Circuit breakers programs qualified by age, income, disability, etc.

2. Property to the extent of $5,000 of a veteran, his wife or survivor, purchased with funds granted by the U.S. or New York for military service or as a prisoner of war; an additional exemption is allowed to seriously disabled veterans (or their widows) from taxes on their

primary residence if the veteran has applied for and received federal assistance to purchase suitable housing. Veterans are allowed a 10-year exemption from county, city, town or village (but not school) taxes equal to the lesser of 15% of assessed homestead value or $12,000, $9,000 or $6,000 as set locally plus, if the veteran served in a combat zone, a ten-year exemption equal to the lesser of 10% of assessed homestead value or $8,000, $6,000 or $4,000 as set locally plus, if the veteran has a service-connected disability, an indefinite exemption equal to the lesser of 50% of the veteran's disability rating or $40,000, $30,000 or $20,000 as set locally.

3. Property of a resident priest, minister or rabbi or unremarried surviving spouse, up to $1,500;

4. A 15-year exemption is provided for realty containing solar or wind energy systems constructed before July 1, 1988, but only due to any increase in value due to the system.

5. Fallout shelters to the extent of $100 multiplied by the number of persons the shelter accommodates.

6. Insulation and other energy conservation measures added to qualified one-, two-, three- or four-family homes.

7. Localities may exempt improvements to one, two or three family residences made for the purpose of accommodating household members who are physically disabled.

ASSESSMENT DATES:
March 1.

LEVEL OF GOVERNMENT RESPONSIBLE FOR ASSESSMENT:
Township and municipal.

EQUALIZATION:
Performed both within and between counties. State Board of Equalization and Assessment establishes equalization rates for counties, cities, towns and villages to apportion State school aid and local property taxes.

ASSESSORS:
Elected (four-year term) and appointed (six years or indefinite), certification is required.

STATE ISSUED MANUALS:
Assessor's manual.

PROPERTY OWNERSHIP MAPS REQUIRED:
Yes.

PERMIT REAL PROPERTY TO BE VALUED IN CURRENT USE RATHER THAN IN A FINANCIALLY BETTER USE:
No, generally, highest and best use.

MEDIAN AREA ASSESSMENT TO SALES PRICE RATIOS:
14.60.

FREQUENCY OF STATE RATIO STUDIES:
Annual.

STATE RATIO STUDY AVAILABLE TO PUBLIC:
Yes.

ADMINISTRATION OF ASSESSMENTS AND TAX LAWS:
Real property taxes are assessed and collected by the assessors and collectors of the respective cities, towns and villages, but the State of New York Board of Equalization and Assessment is responsible for administering of the taxes on real property.

APPEALS AND PROTESTS:
Taxpayers who aren't satisfied with an assessment may arrange an informal meeting with the assessor. However, if not satisfied with the results of meeting with the assessor, the taxpayer may complain to the local board of assessment review. In New York City, the assessing is the responsibility of the City Tax Commissioner.

Note: If the appeal is filed by other than the taxpayer or corporate officer, a power of attorney may have to accompany the filing.

Courts: Taxpayers dissatisfied with the decision of the Board of Assessment Review may appeal to the Supreme Court in the appropriate judicial district while in special term to hear property tax appeals which shall commence within 30 days after the final completion and filing of the assessment roll containing such assessment. Taxpayers must file for an appeal before the this special term of the court ends.

In New York City such appeals of the final decision of the City Tax Commission must be filed prior to the October 25 commencement of such judicial sessions.

Note: There may be additional administrative solutions available to taxpayers other than direct appeal of the decisions of the Board of Assessment Review to the Supreme Court. These options vary in availability depending on the taxing jurisdiction involved, the type of property, the nature of the grievance or other unique circumstances and include review and assessment by the governing body, County Board of Supervisors or the State Board of Equalization.

In general, the dates relating to the appeals before the local Board of Assessment Review and other administrative and judicial bodies are as follows:

Tentative completion of the tax roll - May 1.
Grievance day or the first grievance day - 3rd Tuesday of May.

Final Filing of Tax Roll - July 1.

REFER TO STATE LAW IMPOSED BY:
Chapter 50 - a. of the Consolidated Laws of the State of New York, as amended. Cited as Real
Property Tax Law.

CHANGES:
1.   1981 -   a.   Changed valuation standard from "full value" to "value" both of which are
undefined.

b.   Established classified tax rate systems - see Assessment Level, Note.

c.   Required elected assessors to be certified, previously was only required of
appointed assessors.

ADDRESS (STATE):
State of New York
Executive Department
Division of Equalization and Assessment
Robert L. Beebe
16 Sheridan Ave.
Albany, New York 12210-2714

TELEPHONE:
(518) 474-8821

VERIFIED BY THIS OFFICE:
Yes.

COMMENTS:
In New York City and the burroughs the assessments are relatively low. Other counties accept
evidence based on unequal treatment in the assessment process.

NORTH CAROLINA

NAME OF TAX:
Property Tax or Ad Valorem Tax.

VALUATION STANDARD:
True Value in Money (Market Value), defined as "The price estimated in terms of money at which the property would change hands between a willing and financially able buyer and a willing seller, neither being under any compulsion to buy or to sell and both having reasonable knowledge of all the uses to which the property is adapted and for which it is capable of being used."

REVALUATION CYCLE:
Eight-year cycle is accomplished by counties being assigned into one of eight groups and requiring revaluation on one group per year.

ASSESSMENT LEVEL:
100% of true value in money (in year of last revaluation).

Note: Boards of county commissioners may order revaluation sooner than required, but must adhere to eight year requirement.

HOMEOWNERS EXEMPTION:
1. Historic property exemption credit.

2. The first $36,000 in assessed value of the residence and land of a disabled veteran.

3. The first $12,000 in assessed value of realty or of a mobile home owned and occupied as a permanent residence is exempt if owned by a resident aged 65 or older or permanently and totally disabled provided his disposable income for the previous year was not over $11,000.

ASSESSMENT DATES:
January 1.

LEVEL OF GOVERNMENT RESPONSIBLE FOR ASSESSMENT:
County and townships.

EQUALIZATION:
Only in cases of public utilities, railroads, etc.

ASSESSORS:
Appointed to two-year term, certification is required.

STATE ISSUED MANUALS:
None.

PROPERTY OWNERSHIP MAPS REQUIRED:
No.

PERMIT REAL PROPERTY TO BE VALUED IN CURRENT USE RATHER THAN IN A FINANCIALLY BETTER USE:
Yes, for agricultural, horticultural and forest land.

MEDIAN AREA ASSESSMENT TO SALES:
57.50.

FREQUENCY OF STATE RATIO STUDIES:
Annual.

STATE RATIO STUDY AVAILABLE TO PUBLIC:
No.

ADMINISTRATION OF ASSESSMENTS AND TAX LAWS:
The assessment of property is handled by the counties, but the Ad Valorem Section of the State Property Tax Division has the responsibility of serving as technical advisor to the counties and assists in the education and certification of the county assessment personnel in addition to investigating appeals made to the Property Tax Commission, which sits as the State Board of Equalization and Review.

APPEALS AND PROTESTS:
Any taxpayer dissatisfied with the assessment made by the County Assessor should arrange immediately for an informal meeting with the assessor to explain why he thinks the assessment is excessive. If a satisfactory conclusion cannot be reached, the taxpayer should file an appeal with the County Board of Equalization and Review (Board of County Commissioners) requesting a hearing during the Board's session to examine the disputed assessment.

A taxpayer dissatisfied with the decision of the County Board may file an appeal with the State Property Tax Commission within 30 days of the mailing of the decision by the County Board. The appeal form and a written statement concerning the basis of the appeal is to be filed with the County Assessor and the State Property Tax Commission.

The decision of the Property Tax Commission may be appealed to the Court of Appeals and to the North Carolina Supreme Court.

REFER TO STATE LAW IMPOSED BY:
Property taxes on tangible property are imposed by the "Machinery Act of North Carolina" which is codified as Subchapter II of Chapter 105 of the General Statutes of North Carolina, 1943, as amended, and property taxes on intangible personal property are imposed by Article 7, Subchapter I of Chapter 105 of the General Statutes of North Carolina.

CHANGES:
1. 1/1/74 - Established current assessment level, previously was uniform percentage of true value in money.

2. 1983 - a. Required examination of private appraisers.

    b. Required training for local appraisers.

3. 1/1/87 - Non-business (household) personal property classified as exempt from taxation.

ADDRESS (STATE):
North Carolina Department of Revenue
Property Tax
Frank S. Goodrum, Director
P.O. Box 871
Raleigh, North Carolina 27602

TELEPHONE:
(919) 733-7711

VERIFIED BY THIS OFFICE:
Yes.

NORTH DAKOTA

NAME OF TAX:
Property Taxes.

VALUATION STANDARD:
True and Full Value, defined as "the value determined by considering the earning or productive capacity if any, the market value, if any, and all matters that affect the actual value of the property to be assessed.

REVALUATION CYCLE:
North Dakota Century Code Section 57-02-11 provides that all real property subject to taxation shall be listed and assessed every year with reference to its value on February 1 of that year.

ASSESSMENT LEVEL:
Net assessment level as a percentage of 50% of true and full value, as follows:

Class I: Residential property - 9%.
Class II: Agricultural property - 10%.
Class III: Commercial, air carrier and railroad property - 10%.
Class IV: Centrally-assessed property - 10% (1/1/85).

HOMEOWNERS EXEMPTIONS:
1. Indian property inalienable without the consent of the United States Secretary of the Interior.

2. Homesteads up to a taxable value of $10,000 owned and occupied by a paraplegic disabled veteran, or his unremarried spouse, or any veteran who has been awarded specially adapted housing by the Veterans Administration, or unmarried surviving spouse; up to $5,000 reduction of taxable value on a homestead owned and occupied by veterans with a service connected disability of 50% or more, or their unmarried surviving spouses, if their income for the prior year didn't exceed the maximum income provided for the senior citizens' and disabled persons' homestead exemption exclusive of federal disability compensation; a $5,000 reduction in taxable value is allowed on homesteads of permanently and totally disabled persons who are confined to a wheelchair or to the unremarried surviving spouse.

3. Up to $75,000 of the true and full value of a qualified new single-family residential property, exclusive of land, is exempt for two tax years subsequent to the tax year in which construction is begun, or up to $75,000 of the true and full value of each unit of qualified new condominium and townhouse residential property, exclusive of land, is exempt for two tax years subsequent to the tax year in which construction is begun.

4. Persons aged 65 or older or persons totally and permanently disabled whose annual incomes are $13,000 or less (with a deduction for medical expenses) from all sources, including that of any dependents, and the value of whose assets, excluding their homesteads, doesn't exceed $50,000, are eligible to reduce their homestead assessment. In addition, these homeowners may qualify for a special assessment credit which becomes a lien on the real property and must be repaid when the property is sold.

5. A three-year exemption is available on residential property for the value added by rehabilitation or remodeling to property which is 25 years old or older.

ASSESSMENT DATES:
February 1.

LEVEL OF GOVERNMENT RESPONSIBLE FOR ASSESSMENT:
Township and municipal.

EQUALIZATION:
Performed both within and between counties. State Board of Equalization equalizes county and tax district assessed values by whole number percentage adjustments to aggregate assessed values.

ASSESSORS:
Elected and appointed (township elected two-or appointed four-year term; city appointed indefinitely), certification required.

STATE ISSUED MANUALS:
Assessment manuals.

PROPERTY OWNERSHIP MAPS REQUIRED:
No.

PERMIT REAL PROPERTY TO BE VALUED IN CURRENT USE RATHER THAN IN A FINANCIALLY BETTER USE:
No, except agricultural property.

MEDIAN AREA ASSESSMENT TO SALES PRICE RATIOS:
100.4. Residential true and full value/sales price (1988 assessment/1988 sales price).

FREQUENCY OF STATE RATIO STUDIES:
Annually.

STATE RATIO STUDY AVAILABLE TO PUBLIC:
Yes.

ADMINISTRATION OF ASSESSMENTS AND TAX LAWS:
The county, township, city and district assessors generally determine the assessment on the real property within their jurisdiction with all assessments subject to review and equalization by the local County and State Board of Equalization. The tax commissioner appoints a State Supervisor of Assessments to furnish advice to the assessors and supply them with methods and procedures of property assessment to ensure uniform and equitable assessment of property throughout the state. Railroad and utility property is assessed by the State Board of Equalization.

APPEALS AND PROTESTS:
The taxpayer should start with informal appeals by appearing at the local Boards of Equalization (either city or township). City Boards meet on the second Tuesday in April and Township Boards meet on the second Monday in April. Should the taxpayer not obtain the relief requested, he may

forward informal appeals to the County Board of Equalization, which meets on the first Tuesday in June. Appeals from the County Board of Equalization may be forwarded by any taxpayer not satisfied with the decision received to the State Board of Equalization, which meets the second Tuesday in August.

If the taxpayer is dissatisfied with the State Board of Equalization's decision, he can begin a formal appeal by completing and filing an application for abatement and refund of taxes with the county auditor of the county where the property is located. After filing the application, a hearing at the local governing body and at the County Board of Commissioners is convened. Applications for abatement must be filed on or before November 1 of the year following the year in which the tax becomes delinquent.

Appeals of the decision of the County Board of Commissioners on the applications for abatement may be filed with the district court and continued to the Supreme Court.

Appeals of public utility and railroad assessments made by the State Board of Equalization may be filed with the district court and continued to the Supreme Court.

REFER TO STATE LAW IMPOSED BY:
Chapter 57-01 through 57-35 of the North Dakota Century Code, as amended.

CHANGES:
1.   1977 - Required certification of county directors of tax equalization and city/township assessors.

2.   1981 - Established classified assessment system.

3.   Provided state payments in lieu of taxes on state land obtained by the Bank of North Dakota through foreclosure.

ADDRESS (STATE):
State of North Dakota
Office of State Tax Commissioner
Charles S. Krueger
Deputy State Supervisor of Assessments
State Capital
Bismark, North Dakota 58505

TELEPHONE:
(701) 224-3127

VERIFIED BY THIS OFFICE:
Yes.

COMMENTS:
Grounds for reduction.

1. When an error has been made in any identifying entry or property description, in entering the valuation thereof, or in the extension of the tax, to the injury of the complainant.

2. When improvements on any real property were considered or included in the valuation thereof which didn't exist at the time fixed by law for making the assessment.

3. When the complainant had no taxable interest in the property assessed against him at the time fixed by law for making the assessment.

4. When taxes have been erroneously paid, or errors made in noting payment, or in issuing receipts there of.

5. When the same property has been assessed against the complainant more than once in the same year, and the complainant produces satisfactory evidence that the tax thereon for such year has been paid.

6. When any building, mobile home, structure or other improvement has been destroyed or injured by fire, flood or tornado; the abatement or refund shall be granted only for that year remaining after the property was damaged or destroyed.

OHIO

NAME OF TAX:
Property Taxes.

VALUATION STANDARD:
True Value in Money, defined as the sale price of property which "has been the subject of an arm's length sale between a willing seller and a willing buyer within a reasonable length of time, either before or after the tax lien date. However, the sale price in an arm's length transaction between a willing seller and a willing buyer shall not be considered the true value of the property subsequent to the sale (a) the property loses value due to some casualty or (b) an improvement is added to the property."

REVALUATION CYCLE:
Every six years.

ASSESSMENT LEVEL:
Established by rule, not to exceed 35% of true value in money.

HOMEOWNERS EXEMPTIONS:

1. Circuit breakers program qualified by age, income, disability, etc.

2. Historic buildings and lands.

3. Solar, wind or hydrothermal energy system on which construction or installation is completed during August 14, 1979 through December 31, 1985.

4. Persons aged 65 or older or who are permanently and totally disabled are allowed realty tax relief on a homestead owned and occupied by them if federal adjusted gross income of the owner and his spouse for the preceding year, minus disability benefits doesn't exceed $5,200, plus certain social security benefits, retirement payments not included in federal adjusted gross income, railroad retirement act payments and interest from government bonds, is not more than $16,500. The reduction in taxable value is graduated from lesser of $5,000 or 75% where such total income is $6,500. Or the lesser of $1,000 or 25% where the total income ranges from $11,500 to $16,500. An additional real property tax reduction is allowed on a homestead equal to 2 1/2% of the taxes charged and payable on the homestead are reduced for the year.

5. The assessable value of a manufactured home that's owned and occupied as a home by an individual whose domicile is in Ohio and who's age 65 or older or permanently and totally disabled is reduced for any tax year for which the owner obtains a certificate of reduction from the county auditor provided that the individual didn't acquire ownership for the purpose of qualifying for the reduction. The reduction in taxable value is graduated from the lesser of $5,000 or 75% where the total income is $6,500. Or the lesser of $1,000 or 25% where the total income ranges from $11,500 to $16,500.

6. Owners of real property in rehabilitation areas may apply for tax exclusions for new structures or remodeling completed after November 27, 1969. Exclusions are available for qualified property as follows: (1) for dwellings containing not more than two-family units if the cost of remodeling is at least $2,500, five years; (2) for a dwelling containing more than two units and commercial properties if the cost of remodeling is at least $5,000 and equivalent to 25% of the assessed value of the property, five years; and (3) for construction of new dwellings, commercial or industrial buildings, 10 years.

ASSESSMENT DATES:
January 1.

LEVEL OF GOVERNMENT RESPONSIBLE FOR ASSESSMENT:
County.

EQUALIZATION:
Performed both within and between counties. Department of Taxation equalizes assessed values between tax districts by adjustments to property classes or total assessed values.

ASSESSORS:
Elected to four-year term, certification is not required.

STATE ISSUED MANUALS:
None.

PROPERTY OWNERSHIP MAPS REQUIRED:
No.

PERMIT REAL PROPERTY TO BE VALUED IN CURRENT USE RATHER THAN IN A FINANCIALLY BETTER USE:

No.

MEDIAN AREA ASSESSMENT TO SALES PRICE RATIO:
30.20.

FREQUENCY OF STATE RATIO STUDIES:
Annual.

STATE RATIO STUDY AVAILABLE TO PUBLIC:
Yes.

ADMINISTRATION OF ASSESSMENTS AND TAX LAWS:
The Tax Commissioner has the administrative duty to adopt, prescribe and promulgate rules for determining true value and taxable value of real property by uniform rule for such values.

APPEALS AND PROTESTS:
A taxpayer dissatisfied with his real property tax assessment upon receipt of the final assessment may file an appeal with the county auditor by March 31 of ensuing tax year, requesting a hearing

before the County Board of Revision. Such hearings are generally concluded within 90 days of filing the appeal. The next appeal procedure, should the taxpayer not be pleased with the decision of the County Board of Revision, is the alternative of appealing within 30 days of the mailing of the decision to either the Board of Tax Appeals or the Court of Common Pleas, specifying exactly what the grounds are for the dispute. If the taxpayer is dissatisfied with the decision of the Board of Tax Appeals or the Court of Common Pleas, an appeal for review of the decision may be filed with the District Court of Appeals. The decision of the District Court of Appeals may be appealed by the taxpayer to the Ohio Supreme Court.

On Preliminary or Amended Preliminary Assessment Certificates, the following appeals procedure should be followed:

Objection to assessed penalty only: The taxpayer may request abatement of the penalty by filing a Petition for Abatement with the Tax Commissioner within 30 days after mailing the assessment. The petition may be accompanied by, and refer to, a true copy of the assessment certificate and must indicate that the taxpayer's only objection is to the penalty and the reason for the objection. The taxpayer is required to pay the full amount of tax due except the penalty. The taxpayer may pay the penalty as well, subject to refund if his petition is approved.

Objection to increase in taxable value: The taxpayer may request a review of the increased assessment by making an Application for Review and Redetermination with the Tax Commissioner within 30 days after mailing the assessment. The application may include, and refer to, a true copy of the assessment certificate and must indicate the taxpayer's objections. The taxpayer may pay all the undisputed portion of the tax to avoid interest charges.

Objection to both late-filing penalty and increase in taxable value: The taxpayer may request a review by making the Application for Review and Redetermination with the Tax Commissioner within 30 days after the mailing of the assessment. The application may include, and refer to, a true copy of the assessment certificate and must indicate the taxpayer's objections, including the objections to the penalty. The taxpayer may pay all of the undisputed portion of the tax to avoid interest charges.

No special form is required for requesting the abatement or review, but the request must be in writing to the Tax Commissioner and must meet the requirements set forth above.

On all final determinations of the Tax Commissioner, the taxpayer appeals directly to the Board of Tax Appeals. The taxpayer may appeal the decision of the Board of Tax Appeals to the District Court of Appeals or to the Ohio Supreme Court.

REFER TO STATE LAW IMPOSED BY:
Title LVII, Chapters 5701 through 5725 of the Ohio Revised.

CHANGES:
None.

ADDRESS (STATE):
State of Ohio
Department of Taxation
David Stone, Assistant Administrator
Tax Equalization Tax Division
State Office Tower (P.O. Box 530)
Columbus, Ohio 43266-0030

TELEPHONE:
(614) 466-5744

VERIFIED BY THIS OFFICE:
Yes.

COMMENTS:
Another State that appears to substantially "underassess" residential properties in the major metropolitan areas. Assessing officials, in general, aren't receptive to appeals based on equity of assessments even though it appears to be a statutory basis for appeal.

OKLAHOMA

NAME OF TAX:
Ad Valorem Tax.

VALUATION STANDARD:
Fair Cash Value, defined as being "estimated at the price the property would bring at a fair, voluntary sale for (1) the highest and best use for which the property was actually used during the preceding calendar year; or (2) the highest and best use for which the property was last classified for if not actually used during the preceding calendar year."

REVALUATION CYCLE:
Every five years (every four years beginning in 1992).

ASSESSMENT LEVEL:
Not to Exceed 35% of fair cash value real property, assessment level must be between 11% and 14%.

HOMEOWNERS EXEMPTION:
1.   Homesteads to the extent of $1,000 of assessed value, plus an additional exemption of $1,000 of assessed value on homesteads of heads of households whose gross income for the preceding year didn't exceed $10,000.

ASSESSMENT DATES:
January 1.

LEVEL OF GOVERNMENT RESPONSIBLE FOR ASSESSMENT:
County.

EQUALIZATION:
Performed within the county. State Board of Equalization equalizes assessed values between counties by adjustments to property classes.

ASSESSORS:
Elected for four-year term, certification is required beginning January 1, 1991.

STATE ISSUED MANUALS:
Appraisal manual.

PROPERTY OWNERSHIP MAPS REQUIRED:
No.

PERMIT REAL PROPERTY TO BE VALUED IN CURRENT USE RATHER THAN IN A FINANCIALLY BETTER USE:
No.

MEDIAN AREA ASSESSMENT TO SALES PRICE RATIOS:
11.07.

FREQUENCY OF STATE RATIO STUDIES:
Annual.

STATE RATIO STUDY AVAILABLE TO PUBLIC:
Yes.

ADMINISTRATION OF ASSESSMENTS AND TAX LAWS:
The county is responsible for assessing and collecting of taxes on property. However, the Oklahoma Tax Commission has the authority and the duty to confer with and assist the county assessors and County Board of Equalization in performing of their duties to ensure uniform and equitable assessments among the counties.

APPEALS AND PROTESTS:
Prior to 1/1/92, any taxpayer aggrieved of the assessment received must file a complaint with the County Board of Equalization by the first Monday of May. If the complaint concerns an assessment increase, the taxpayer has 20 days after mailing the notice of increase to file the complaint. The County Board holds sessions commencing on April 1 and ending no later than May 31 unless extended for extraordinary circumstances. Commencing on 7/1/86, the full amount of the taxes assessed against the property of any taxpayer who has appealed from the State Board of Equalization or any County Board of Equalization shall be paid at the time provided by law, and of taxes that may be protested and paid under protest pending an appeal from the Board of Equalization is limited to the taxes for the year in question less the amount that would be payable by the taxpayer for that year if the valuation claimed by the taxpayer was determined to be correct. The taxes paid under protest will be held in a protest fund and the amount not contested is apportioned as provided by law.

The decision of the County Board of Equalization may be appealed by filing the protest with the Clerk of the County District Court within 10 days after final adjournment of the County Board of Equalization. A further appeal may be made to the State Supreme Court, but only after the appeal has been presented to the District Court.

Effective 1/1/92, any taxpayer aggrieved of the assessment received must file a written complaint with the county assessor within 20 days from the date of the assessment notice. Following the filing of the written complaint, an informal hearing will be held with the county assessor. If the taxpayer isn't satisfied with the results of the informal hearing, he has 15 days from the date of notice of the assessor's final action to file a written complaint with the County Board of Equalization. The taxpayer has 10 days from the date of the decision of the county board of equalization to protest an unfavorable decision by filing an appeal with the Board of Property Tax Review. Within 10 days of the decision of the Board of Property Tax Review, the taxpayer may file an appeal with the district court. The decision of the district court may be appealed to the State Supreme Court in the manner provided for appeals from civil judgment.

REFER TO STATE LAW IMPOSED BY:

Title 68, Article 24 of the Oklahoma Statutes, 1981, as amended. Effective 1/1/92, the Ad Valorem Code has been recodified as Title 68, Articles 28 and 29 of the Oklahoma Statutes, and is substantially the same a

CHANGES:

1. 5/30/75 - Valuatio   "highest and best use" provisions - see Valuation Standar

2. 3/30/76 - State Bo   es to achieve 12% assessment level, with 3% deviation   least 1/3 of the movement occurring each year.

3. 10/1/84 - State Boa   conduce county-wide reappraisal by 1/1/87 and to ac   e in assessed values to the tax roll between 1984 and

4. 1/1/85 - State Tax   ation program.

ADDRESS (STATE):
Oklahoma Tax Commission
Ad Valorem Tax Division
Robert L. Hartman, Director
M.C. Connors Building
2501 N. Lincoln Boulevard
Oklahoma City, Oklahoma 73194

TELEPHONE:
(405) 521-3178

VERIFIED BY THIS OFFICE:
Yes.

COMMENTS:
The majority of residential properties are substantially underassessed, thus equity approach and sales ratio studies would be the most successful reduction methods.

OREGON

NAME OF TAX:
Property Taxes.

VALUATION STANDARD:
True Cash Value, defined as "the market value of the property, determined by methods and procedures in accordance to with rules adopted by the Department of Revenue and in accordance with the following: if the property has no immediate market value, its true cash value is the amount of money that would justly compensate the owner for the loss of the property; if the property is subject to governmental restriction as to the use on the assessment date under applicable law or regulation, its true cash value shall not be based upon a sale that reflects for the property a market value that the property would have if the use of the property were not subject to the restriction unless adjustments in value are made reflecting the effect of the restrictions.

REVALUATION CYCLE:
Not greater than every six years.

ASSESSMENT LEVEL:
100% of true cash value.

Note: Although 100% standard isn't required until 1/1/86, tax districts have practiced this standard since 1/1/85.

HOMEOWNERS EXEMPTIONS:
1. Property not exceeding $7,500 in assessed value of any resident honorably discharged, veteran of the Spanish-American War, the Philippine insurrection or the Boxer Rebellion, any resident veteran officially certified by the Veterans Administration having disability of 40% or more and any resident veteran who served in the armed forces who has a disability of 40% or more if the veteran's total income for the first year from the government for such service is not more than $4,960 if the veteran is without a dependent or spouse, $6,499 if the veteran has one dependent or $6,499 plus $840 for each additional dependent if over one (the exemption is also available to the veteran's surviving spouse); property not exceeding $10,000 in assessed value of a resident veteran certified by the Veterans Administration as having a service connected disability of 40% or more (the exemption is also available to the veteran's unremarried surviving spouse if the veteran died as the result of service connected injury or illness or if the veteran received the maximum exemption for at least one year).

2. $2,000 of the taxable value of a homestead actually resided in by a pensioned, unremarried widow of any honorably discharged veteran of the Civil or Spanish Wars.

3. For assessment years beginning on or after January 1, 1976, and before January 1, 1998, property equipped with solar, geothermal, wind, water, or methane gas energy systems is exempt from tax in an amount equal to the difference in the value of the property with and without the system.

4.   Refunds of property tax based on household income up to $17,500 annual. Persons 62 years or older may defer payment of real property tax.

ASSESSMENT DATES:
January 1.

LEVEL OF GOVERNMENT RESPONSIBLE FOR ASSESSMENT:
County.

EQUALIZATION:
Performed both within and between counties. Department of Revenue equalizes county assessed values by adjustments to total, local taxable value.

ASSESSORS:
Elected for four-year term, certification is required.

STATE ISSUED MANUALS:
Assessment manuals.

PROPERTY OWNERSHIP MAPS REQUIRED:
Yes.

PERMIT REAL PROPERTY TO BE VALUED IN CURRENT USE RATHER THAN IN A FINANCIALLY BETTER USE:
No.

MEDIAN AREA ASSESSMENT TO SALES PRICE RATIOS:
79.20.

FREQUENCY OF STATE RATIO STUDIES:
Annual.

STATE RATIO STUDY AVAILABLE TO PUBLIC:
Yes.

ADMINISTRATION OF ASSESSMENTS AND TAX LAWS:
The Oregon Department of Revenue determines the assessed property value of public utilities and industrial plants of chemical, food processing, metal and wood products over $5 million in value for local tax purposes. In addition, the department has full administrative power to supervise local assessments to ensure statewide uniformity of assessments.

APPEALS AND PROTESTS:
Assessment notices are generally mailed to the taxpayer by the first Monday in May. The taxpayer should contact the assessor as soon as possible with respect to any assessment that he's dissatisfied with, requesting that the assessment be reviewed. Should the taxpayer still be dissatisfied after the assessor has reviewed the assessment, he may file an appeal with the County Board of Equalization on or before May 31. However, if the assessment notice was mailed after the first Monday in May, the period in which the taxpayer may appeal is extended by the difference

between the normal deadline (the first Monday in May) and the mailing date of the assessment notice. In no case shall a petition be filed later than July 1.

Any taxpayer dissatisfied with the decision of the County Board of Equalization may further appeal, within 30 days, depending on the assessment, to the Department of Revenue or the Small Claims Division of the Oregon Tax Court. Where it was determined that the parcel of land has a true cash value of not more than $35,000, or that the total improvements on the parcel of land have a true cash value of not more than $50,000, or that the tangible personal property has a true cash value of not more than $15,000, the appeal would be to the Small Claims Division of the Oregon Tax Court. All true cash values, including those in excess of these amounts may be appealed to the Department of Revenue.

If the original assessment notice was mailed on or after June 1, thereby depriving the taxpayer of the proper opportunity to file an appeal before the County Board of Equalization, the taxpayer may file an appeal directly with either the Small Claims Division of the Oregon Tax Court or the Department of Revenue based on the true cash values noted above. Any appeal by the taxpayer to the Small Claims Division of the Oregon Tax Court is considered as the final administrative remedy and cannot be further appealed.

A Taxpayer dissatisfied with the decision of the Department of Revenue may appeal that decision within 60 days to the Oregon Tax Court. The decision of the Oregon Tax Court (not including Small Claims Division) may be further appealed to the Oregon Supreme Court.

REFER TO STATE LAW IMPOSED BY:
Title 29, Chapters 306 through 312, of the Oregon Revised Statutes, as amended.

CHANGES:
1. 1/1/80 - Property classified either homestead or non-homestead for Department of Revenue Assessment factors.

2. 9/84 - Abolished homestead classifications.

3. 1985 - a. Abolished previous practice of determining factors to limit the increases in market values from one year to the next, e.g., 1981 factors: homestead - 81.6%; non-homestead - 84.4%.

      b. Required assessments to be performed at 100% of true and cash value as of 1/1/86.

ADDRESS (STATE):
Oregon Department of Revenue
Property Tax Division
George Weber, Administrator
Revenue Building
955 Center Street, N.E.
Salem, Oregon 97310

TELEPHONE:
(503) 378-3022

VERIFIED BY THIS OFFICE:
Yes.

COMMENTS:
This is a State where the assessors attempt to value all properties as close as possible to 100% of true cash value. Homeowners have been particularly successful in appealing raw land value and comparative "per acre" assessments for nearly similar properties.

PENNSYLVANIA

NAME OF TAX:
Property Tax.

VALUATION STANDARD:
Actual Value, defined as "the price at which any property may have actually been sold either in the base year or in the current year must be considered, but it is not to be controlling. Instead, the selling price, estimated or actual, is subject to revision to accomplish equalization with other similar property within the tax district. In arriving at actual value, all three methods; namely, cost (reproduction or replacement, as applicable, less depreciation and all forms of obsolescence), comparable sales and income approaches must be considered in conjunction with one another."

REVALUATION CYCLE:
Not specified by statute.

ASSESSMENT LEVEL:
Locally determined by boards of county commissioners, but limited to 75% of actual value (fourth - eighth class counties) or 100% of actual value (first - third class counties).

HOMEOWNERS EXEMPTION:
1.   Veterans with 100% permanent service-oriented disability receive full exemption at a maximum of $10,000 of improvement per unit in certain deteriorated neighborhoods and new residential homes in deteriorated neighborhoods receive a 100% exemption for three years.

2.   Veterans 65 years or older or widow/widowers over 50 years of age and permanent disabled veterans 18 years or older, receive a rebate in taxes graduated based on income less than $15,000 at a percentage of taxes and dividends.

ASSESSMENT DATES:
Varies with assessment revisions.

LEVEL OF GOVERNMENT RESPONSIBLE FOR ASSESSMENT:
County.

EQUALIZATION:
Performed between counties.

ASSESSORS:
Elected terms vary, certification isn't required.

STATE ISSUED MANUALS:
Appraisal manuals.

PROPERTY OWNERSHIP MAPS REQUIRED:
Yes.

PERMIT REAL PROPERTY TO BE VALUED IN CURRENT USE RATHER THAN IN A FINANCIALLY BETTER USE:
No.

MEDIAN AREA ASSESSMENT TO SALES PRICE RATIOS:
13.10.

FREQUENCY OF STATE RATIO STUDIES:
Triennial.

STATE RATIO STUDY AVAILABLE TO PUBLIC:
No.

ADMINISTRATION OF ASSESSMENTS AND TAX LAWS:
Real property taxes are assessed and collected by the assessors and collectors of the respective counties, cities, boroughs, townships and school districts. The Commonwealth of Pennsylvania has no supervision over assessing of real property and only gets involved through the court system when a taxpayer files an appeal.

APPEALS AND PROTESTS:
Taxpayers dissatisfied with an assessment should contact the assessor for an informal meeting to discuss it prior to the closing of the tax rolls. Should the meeting not resolve the matter, the taxpayer would have to appeal to the Board of Revision of Taxes and then, if not satisfied, seek relief through the courts. The procedure that the taxpayer would follow because of the various dates of hearings by the County and City Boards of Revision of taxes is as follows:

Board of Revision of Taxes:

First Class County/City (Philadelphia): Board must complete revisions to the tax rolls on or before the third Monday in September. Taxpayers will be notified of changes at least 10 days before the first Monday in October. Taxpayers dissatisfied with an assessment must file an appeal on or before the first Monday in October.

Second Class County: Taxpayers dissatisfied with an assessment may file an appeal on or before the last day in February.

Second Class City (Pittsburgh): by Allegheny County assessor.

Second Class A and Third Class County: Taxpayers dissatisfied with an assessment may file an appeal by September 1. All appeals should be acted upon by the last day in October.

Second Class A City (Scranton): by Lackawanna County Assessor.

Third Class City: May adopt county assessment.

or

Board of Revision of Taxes and Appeals: Taxpayers will be notified by the assessor of alternations in the assessment. Taxpayers dissatisfied with an assessment must file for an appeal no later than 30 days after mailing the assessment notice.

Fourth - Eighth Class County: Board will notify property owners of changes in the assessment on or before August 15. Taxpayers dissatisfied with an assessment may file an appeal by September 1.

Court of Common Pleas:

Taxpayers dissatisfied with the decision of the Board of Revision (or similar body) may, within 60 days of the decision, appeal to the Court of Common Pleas of the county in which the property is located. Effective 5/26/88, the Court of Common Pleas may refer any appeal to Boards of Arbitrators or Boards of Reviewers.

Supreme Court or Superior Court:

Taxpayers dissatisfied with the decision of the Court of Common Pleas may appeal to the Supreme Court or Superior Court.

REFER TO STATE LAW IMPOSED BY:
The General County Assessment Law (Act of May 22, 1933), as amended. The Commonwealth of Pennsylvania doesn't impose a tax upon real property. Real property taxes are imposed by counties, cities, boroughs, townships or school districts and the General County Assessment law is applicable in all counties of the Commonwealth, unless the law of a smaller taxing district applies.

CHANGES:
1. 12/31/82 - a. Valuation standard amended to include references to current and base year - see Valuation Standard.

b. Established maximum county assessment levels - see Assessment Level.

c. Required common level ratios for counties.

ADDRESS (STATE):
The Commonwealth of Pennsylvania has no supervisory power over the county or local assessment or collection of taxes on real property. The Commonwealth does not get involved except through the court system when the taxpayer pursues relief through the courts for an alleged overassessment.

TELEPHONE:
Not applicable.

VERIFIED BY THIS OFFICE:
Not applicable.

RHODE ISLAND

NAME OF TAX:
Property Tax.

VALUATION STANDARD:
Full and fair cash value or a locally determined uniform percentage of full and fair cash value (not defined by statute).

REVALUATION CYCLE:
Each 10th year following last revaluation.

Note: Towns and cities were required to complete a revaluation by 12/31/83: (1) unless they had previously completed a revaluation within seven years of that date; and (2) except for the city of Woonsocket and the town of Cumberland which had until 12/31/86 and 12/31/84, respectively, to complete a revaluation.

ASSESSMENT LEVEL:
Not greater than 100% of full and fair cash value, locally determined.

HOMEOWNERS EXEMPTION:
1. Veterans and unmarried widow or widowers receive exemptions of $1,000 plus an additional $1,000 if they served during World War I or II, in Korea, Vietnam, Grenada or Lebanon and $10,000 if disabled and unmarried. Municipalities may grant $15,000 if the veteran was a Prisoner of War and $10,000 if the veteran is totally disabled. Parents of persons who have died as a war casualty receive up to $13,000. Blind veterans receive $6,000 (cities and towns may increase up to $18,000).

2. Historic residences receive 20% up to five years. Cities and towns may freeze tax rates and valuation for totally disabled and low income veterans 65 years old or older.

ASSESSMENT DATES:
December 31.

LEVEL OF GOVERNMENT RESPONSIBLE FOR ASSESSMENT:
Township and municipal.

EQUALIZATION:
Performed within counties.

ASSESSORS:
Elected and appointed (term by local option).

STATE ISSUED MANUALS:
Assessment manuals.

PROPERTY OWNERSHIP MAPS REQUIRED:
No.

PERMIT REAL PROPERTY TO BE VALUED IN CURRENT USE RATHER THAN IN A FINANCIALLY BETTER USE:
No.

MEDIAN AREA ASSESSMENT TO SALES PRICE RATIOS:
28.

FREQUENCY OF STATE RATIO STUDIES:
Annual.

STATE RATIO STUDY AVAILABLE TO PUBLIC:
Yes.

ADMINISTRATION OF ASSESSMENTS AND TAX LAWS:
The administration of the assessment and collection of all real and tangible personal property taxes in Rhode Island is handled by the municipal assessor and collector in the jurisdiction where the property is located.

APPEALS AND PROTESTS:
A taxpayer aggrieved by a property tax assessment in any town or city may file an appeal with the local assessor within three months after the last day appointed for payment of tax without penalty, or payment of the first installment. If the appeal with the local assessor isn't filed on time and the decision isn't favorable, the taxpayer may file an appeal with the Superior Court within 30 days of the assessor's decision.

REFER TO STATE LAW IMPOSED BY:
Title 44, Chapters 1 through 9 of the General Laws of Rhode Island, 1956, as amended.

CHANGES:
1. 1/1/85 - Allowed city of Pawtucket to adopt classified assessment system upon satisfaction of certain conditions - see Assessment Level, City of Pawtucket classified assessment system and State Control.

ADDRESS (STATE):
Mr. Charles Munsch
Supervisor of Tax Equalization
Department of Administration
275 Westminster Mall
Providence, Rhode Island 02903

TELEPHONE:
(401) 277-2885

VERIFIED BY THIS OFFICE:
No.

SOUTH CAROLINA

NAME OF TAX:
Property Tax.

VALUATION STANDARD:
True Value in Money, defined as "the price which property would bring following reasonable exposure to the market, where both the seller and the buyer are not acting under compulsion, and are reasonably well informed as to the uses and purposes for which it is adapted and for which it is capable of being used."

REVALUATION CYCLE:
Not specified by statute.

ASSESSMENT LEVEL:

Class I:	Manufacturing and public utility property other than transportation companies - 10.5%.
Class III:	Residential property not exceeding five acres - 4%.
Class IV:	Agricultural property: Private ownership - 4%.
	Corporate ownership - 6%.
Class V:	Property not elsewhere classified - 6%.
Class VII:	Transportation company property - 9.5%.

Note: Classes II and VI relate to personal property.

HOMEOWNERS EXEMPTION:
Veterans that are totally disabled from service-connected injuries, widows or widowers of veterans killed in action, paraplegics, and homesteads of veterans 65 years old or older that are totally or permanently disabled or blind are exempt up to $20,000 of the fair market price.

ASSESSMENT DATES:
December 31.

LEVEL OF GOVERNMENT RESPONSIBLE FOR ASSESSMENT:
County.

EQUALIZATION:
State Tax Commission equalizes assessed values among counties, cities, towns and districts.

ASSESSORS:
Appointed for an indefinite term, certification is not required.

STATE ISSUED MANUALS:
Assessment manuals.

PROPERTY OWNERSHIP MAPS REQUIRED:
Yes.

PERMIT REAL PROPERTY TO BE VALUED IN CURRENT USE RATHER THAN IN A FINANCIALLY BETTER USE:
No.

MEDIAN AREA ASSESSMENT TO SALES PRICE RATIOS:
2.10.

FREQUENCY OF STATE RATIO STUDIES:
Annual.

STATE RATIO STUDY AVAILABLE TO PUBLIC:
Yes.

ADMINISTRATION OF ASSESSMENTS AND TAX LAWS:
The assessments of property are made by the County Auditor who must use assessment guides furnished by the South Carolina Tax Commission to ensure that assessments are equitable among the counties.

APPEALS AND PROTESTS:
Appeals of assessments on property assessed by County Auditors differ in the initial steps for appeals of assessments on property assessed by the South Carolina Tax Commission. The taxpayer may appeal real property assessments made by the County Assessor by filing a written notice of protest with the County Assessor within 30 days of the mailing of the assessment outlining the objections. The County Auditor will schedule a conference within 20 days, and within 30 days thereafter give written notice of any action taken upon the taxpayer's objections. Within 10 days of the decision of the County Assessor the taxpayer may file a written appeal to the County Board of Equalization containing all grounds for appeal and the taxpayer's valuation of fair market value. A hearing will be set to hear all evidence and arguments.

All decisions of the County Board of Equalization that a taxpayer may object to may be appealed to the South Carolina Tax Commission by giving written notice of appeal within 10 days of the decision containing all grounds for the appeal and the taxpayer's valuation of fair market value, which will be presented at the hearing before the Commission. The taxpayer may appeal through the Civil Courts with regard to legal questions but not on a matter of value.

Assessments on property assessed by the South Carolina Tax Commission may be appealed by the taxpayer by submitting written notification of the intent to appeal within 20 days of receipt of mailing the proposed assessment, which must contain all grounds for the appeal and the taxpayer's valuation of fair market value. Any appeals of the decision by the Tax Commission of the intent to appeal within 10 days after mailing the proposed assessment placed by the Tax Commission as a result of the appeal before that body. The notice must contain all grounds for appeal and the taxpayer's valuation of fair market value. Further appeal may be made to the Civil Courts but it must be based on a legal question, and not on a matter of value.

REFER TO STATE LAW IMPOSED BY:
Title 12 of the Code of Laws of South Carolina, 1976, as amended.

CHANGES:

1. 1975 - Statewide revaluation of property began.

2. 1976 - Required uniform assessments within property classes.

3. 1982 - Statewide revaluation completed.

ADDRESS (STATE):

South Carolina Tax Commission
Property Division
James L. Brodie, Director (P.O. Box 125)
Columbia, South Carolina 29214

TELEPHONE:

(803) 737-4485

VERIFIED BY THIS OFFICE:

Yes.

COMMENTS:

Resort area along the coast and the larger metropolitan jurisdictions tend to attempt to value properties as close as possible to 100%.

SOUTH DAKOTA

NAME OF TAX:
Ad Valorem Tax.

VALUATION STANDARD:
True and Full Value in Money, defined as "the usual selling price at the place where the property to which the term is applied shall be at the time of assessment."

REVALUATION CYCLE:
Not specified by statute.

ASSESSMENT LEVEL:
Property is required to be assessed at 100% of true and full value in money, taxes are levied against the same.

HOMEOWNERS EXEMPTIONS:
1. Dwellings owned and occupied by a paraplegic veteran.

2. Heads of households aged 65 or older, or who are disabled before January 1 of the assessment year may apply for a refund of realty taxes on their dwellings if they have owned the property at least three years or resided in the state at least five years. Persons receiving this refund aren't eligible for a sales and service tax refund. Refunds for single-member households are based on income up to 35% of taxes.

3. Low-income persons age 65 or older or disabled persons may apply for a reduction in municipal realty taxes on their homes if they have resided in the dwelling for at least five years. This tax reduction will not be denied because the homeowner received a property tax refund or a realty assessment freeze.

4. A credit is allowed for including a renewable resource energy system as part of an improvement to realty. The credit for a residential application is a sum equal to the assessed value of the realty with the system minus the assessed value of the realty without the system. However, the credit shall not be less than the actual installed cost of the system.

5. Tax assessments on single-family dwellings owned by qualified heads of households who are 65 or older or disabled may be frozen if the dwelling's market value is less than $80,000 and household income is less than $9,000 in the case of a single-member household or $11,000 in the case of a multiple-member household.

ASSESSMENT DATES:
January 1.

LEVEL OF GOVERNMENT RESPONSIBLE FOR ASSESSMENT:
County.

EQUALIZATION:
Performed within county. State Board of Equalization equalizes assessed values between counties or, upon request, of municipalities or school districts overlapping county boundaries, by whole number percentage adjustments to total assessed values.

ASSESSORS:
Appointed to five year term, certification is required.

STATE ISSUED MANUALS:
Appraisal manuals.

PROPERTY OWNERSHIP MAPS REQUIRED:
Yes.

PERMIT REAL PROPERTY TO BE VALUED IN CURRENT USE RATHER THAN IN A FINANCIALLY BETTER USE:
No.

MEDIAN AREA ASSESSMENT TO SALES PRICE RATIOS:
77.30.

FREQUENCY OF STATE RATIO STUDIES:
Annual.

STATE RATIO STUDY AVAILABLE TO PUBLIC:
Yes.

ADMINISTRATION OF ASSESSMENTS AND TAX LAWS:
The Secretary of Revenue is directly responsible for the general supervision over the administration of assessments to ensure equitable assessments throughout the State.

APPEALS AND PROTESTS:
A taxpayer dissatisfied with an assessment may appeal to the local board of equalization of the township, town or city where the property is located requesting a correction. The local board meets from the third through the fourth Monday in April. The Director of Equalization is required to mail a notice of assessment to each property owner at least 14 days before the meeting of the Local Board of Equalization. The decision of the local board may be contested by filing a written notice with the local board at the time it's in session, stating the reason for the appeal. The appeal should also be delivered to the County Auditor within 10 calendar days before or after the convening of the county board of equalization. The county board of equalization is comprised of the county commissioners and the County Auditor who meet from the first Tuesday in May through the third Tuesday in May.

If the taxpayer is dissatisfied with the county board's decision, he may file, within 30 days after receiving notice of the decision, an appeal with the State Tax Appeal Board. The State Board will commence these hearings on the third Monday in July and continue until all appeals are heard. The decision of the State Board of Equalization may be appealed to the Circuit Court.

REFER TO STATE LAW IMPOSED BY:
Title 10, Chapters 10-1 through 10-38 of the South Dakota Codified Laws.

CHANGES:
1.   1974 - Assessor certification program established - see State Control.

ADDRESS (STATE):
South Dakota Department of Revenue
Division of Property Taxes
Linda Osberg, Director
700 Governors Drive
Pierre, South Dakota 57501-2276

TELEPHONE:
(605) 773-3311

COMMENTS:
The 60% "taxable value" tends to confuse many taxpayers. Generally, assessors seem to undervalue properties considerably and not many appeals are filed historically.

TENNESSEE

NAME OF TAX:
Property taxes.

VALUATION STANDARD:
Value, determined from "the evidences of its sound, intrinsic, and immediate value for purposes of sale between a willing seller and a willing buyer without consideration of speculative values."

REVALUATION CYCLE:
Every five years.

ASSESSMENT LEVEL:

Class I	(a): Public utility property - 55%.
Class I	(b): Industrial and commercial property - 40%.
Class I	(c): Residential property - 25%.
Class I	(d): Agricultural property - 25%.

HOMEOWNERS EXEMPTIONS:

1. Taxpayers age 65 or older, or who are permanently and totally disabled, whose annual income isn't over $6,000 will be reimbursed for all or part of the property taxes paid on their residence. The refund is paid on the first $15,000 of the full market value of the property. Qualified disabled veterans are eligible for reimbursement from the State equal to all or part of local taxes on the first $120,000 worth of the full market value of property owned and used as a home by the veteran. Counties and municipalities may authorize persons age 65 or older who own their residence and whose total or combined annual income doesn't exceed $12,000 to pay taxes not to exceed the maximum tax on the property imposed on May 31, 1979, or the year in which they become 65, whichever is later.

2. Counties and cities are authorized to defer payment of all real property taxes on residences owned and occupied by any single person age 65 or older, any married couple both age 65 or older, or any person who's totally and permanently disabled, if combined gross income doesn't exceed $12,000 per year. The deferral applies to no more than $60,000 of the appraised fair market value and applies only to the principal residence and no more than one acre of land. Deferred taxes will be subject to interest at the rate of 10% a year.

3. Counties and cities are authorized to provide any taxpayer or spouse who is age 65 or older, totally and permanently disabled, or a disabled veteran and who owns residential property as his principal place of residence may defer property taxes that exceeds his or her property tax for the year 1979. The tax deferment isn't available to taxpayers whose incomes exceed $12,000 annually and only applies to the principal residence and not in excess of one acre of ground. The value of the principal place of residence must be under $50,000. Deferred taxes are subject to interest.

ASSESSMENT DATES:
January 1.

LEVEL OF GOVERNMENT RESPONSIBLE FOR ASSESSMENT:
County.

EQUALIZATION:
None.

ASSESSORS:
Elected to four-year term, certification is not required.

STATE ISSUE MANUALS:
Appraisal manuals.

PROPERTY OWNERSHIP MAPS REQUIRED:
Yes.

PERMIT REAL PROPERTY TO BE VALUED IN CURRENT USE RATHER THAN IN A FINANCIALLY BETTER USE:
No.

MEDIAN AREA ASSESSMENT TO SALES PRICE RATIOS:
12.10.

FREQUENCY OF STATE RATIO STUDIES:
Irregular.

STATE RATIO STUDY AVAILABLE TO PUBLIC:
Yes.

ADMINISTRATION OF ASSESSMENTS AND TAX LAWS:
The assessment and collection of property taxes is handled at the county level, but the property tax is administered at the State level by the State Board of Equalization. The State has jurisdiction over the valuation, classification and assessment of all property in the State, and it is responsible for the equalization of assessments in all taxing jurisdictions.

APPEALS AND PROTESTS:
The first administrative remedy against an assessment that's considered excessive is through filing an appeal with the County Board of Equalization. If the taxpayer fails to protest the assessment to the County Board of Equalization while it is in session, the assessment becomes final and the taxpayer cannot challenge it. The decision of the County Board may be appealed to the State Board of Equalization if filed prior to August 1 or within 30 days after a change of assessment made after July 1. Appeal may be made directly to the State Board if the taxpayer was deprived of a hearing before the County Board because an assessment notice wasn't sent. The decision of the State Board is final on all matters subject to judicial review, as the taxpayer may appeal to the Circuit Court in matters of law after paying the tax involved under protest.

REFER TO STATE LAW IMPOSED BY:
Title 67, Chapter 5 of the Tennessee Code, as amended.

CHANGES:

1. 1973 - Provided for Division of Property Assessment authority to supervise revaluations.

2. 1980 - Required ongoing statewide revaluation of all property and established state fund to assist localities.

ADDRESS (STATE):
State Board of Equalization
Division of Property Assessment
Tom Flemming, Director
505 Beaderick Suite 1400
Nashville, TN 37243

TELEPHONE:
(615) 741-4883

VERIFIED BY OFFICE:
No.

COMMENTS:
Larger metropolitan counties, as is typical nationally, tend to value commercial properties as close as possible to 100%. Residential properties appear to be substantially underassessed in relation to true value.

TEXAS

NAME OF TAX:
Property Tax or Ad Valorem Tax.

VALUATION STANDARD:
Market Value, defined as "tThe price at which a property would transfer for cash or its equivalent under prevailing market conditions if: (a) exposed for sale in the open market with a reasonable time for the seller to find a purchaser; (b) both the seller and the purchaser know all the uses and purposes to which the property is adapted and for which it is capable of being used and of the enforceable restrictions on its use; and (c) both the seller and the purchaser seek to maximize their gains and neither is in a position to take advantage of the exigencies of the other."

REVALUATION CYCLE:
At least once every three years.

ASSESSMENT LEVEL:
100% of market value (appraised value).

HOMEOWNER EXEMPTIONS:
1. Homestead exemptions:
    a. $5,000 homestead exemption for school taxes.
    b. $3,000 homestead exemption for special county taxes.
    c. optional taxing unit offered not to exceed 20% of market value but not less than $5,000.

2. Homeowners over 65 years of age:
    a. $10,000 homestead exemption for school taxes in addition to $5,000 for all homeowners.
    b. optional taxing unit for an additional $3,000.
    c. tax ceiling for school taxes.
    d. tax deferral.

3. Homeowners and disabled veterans:
    a. $10,000 exemption for school taxes in addition to $5,000 for all homeowners.
    b. disabled veterans and their surviving family receive an additional exemption ranging from $1,500 to $3,000.

4. Exemption for solar or wind-powered energy devices.

ASSESSMENT DATES:
January 1.

LEVEL OF GOVERNMENT RESPONSIBLE FOR ASSESSMENT:
County Appraisal District.

EQUALIZATION:
Performed within counties.

ASSESSORS:
Appointed to an indefinite term, certification required by the Board of Tax Professional Examiners

STATE ISSUED MANUALS:
Assessment manual.

PROPERTY OWNERSHIP MAPS REQUIRED:
No.

PERMIT REAL PROPERTY TO BE VALUED IN CURRENT USE RATHER IN A FINANCIALLY BETTER USE:
No.

FREQUENCY OF STATE RATIO STUDIES:
Yearly.

STATE RATIO STUDY AVAILABLE TO PUBLIC:
Yes.

ADMINISTRATION OF ASSESSMENTS AND TAX LAWS:
The property assessment in each appraisal district is determined by the chief appraiser for the appraisal district, and the tax is collected by the individual taxing units unless they have an agreement for the district is in their behalf. The State Property Tax Board serves in an advisory capacity and has no enforcement or authoritative powers.

APPEALS AND PROTESTS:
A taxpayer, if dissatisfied with his assessment, may file an appeal with the Appraisal Review Board before 7/1 (6/1 effective 1/1/88) within 30 days after the appraisal district delivered the notice of appraisal value, whichever date is later. If the Appraisal Review Board has ordered a change in the taxpayer's property appraisal records, the taxpayer must file a notice of protest within 10 days of the date on which the Appraisal Review Board delivered the notice. If the taxpayer doesn't file a notice of protest before the Appraisal Review Board approves the appraisal records, he loses to protest and the right to file a lawsuit with the court about the taxable value.

A taxpayer who's dissatisfied with the decision of the Appraisal Review Board has the right to appeal that decision to the State District Court in the taxpayer's county. A written notice of appeal must be filed with the Appraisal Review Board, if the property is appraised at more than $1 million, within 15 days of the date the written order of the Appraisal Review Board was received. Within 45 days of receiving the written order, the taxpayer must file a petition for review with the district court. The taxpayer is also required to pay at least the tax that isn't in dispute before the delinquency date.

Effective 9/1/89, a property owner may appoint the lessee or any other person, even a person not in possession of the property owner's property, as the property owner' agent in relation to property tax matters relating to the property or the property owner. The appointment must be in writing and remains in effect until revoked by the owner.

REFER TO STATE LAW IMPOSED BY:
Title 1 of the Texas Tax Code.

CHANGES:

1. 1/1/80 - Established countywide appraisal districts with responsibility for appraising property for all tax entities in the district.

2. 1981 - Established current valuation standard.

3. 1/1/82 - Established assessment limits.

4. 8/29/82 - Discontinued assessing at less than 100% of market value.

5. 9/1/89 - a. Changed previous five-year revaluation cycle to a current four-year cycle and to three-year reappraisal.
   b. Required completion of first biennial assessment ratio study (since changed to an annual study).

ADDRESS (STATE):
The State of Texas
State Property Tax Board
Jim Robinson, Director
4301 W. Bank Dr. Suite 100
Austin, Texas 78746

TELEPHONE:
(512) 329-7901

VERIFIED BY THIS OFFICE:
Yes.

COMMENTS:
Topsy-turvy real estate market resulting from the State's oil industry problems, has created significant sources of tax appeals. Properties such as condominiums have been over-built and over-sold to the point that the foreclosure sale has become "the market" for this type of property. Assessor's had to set-up special formulas for valuing income property that may be 80% to 100% vacant. Residential properties appear to be given special consideration and are generally "under-assessed." An appeal based on comparable assessments are given little consideration by the various appraisal districts. Best chance for a successful appeal is where a local economic condition has created a value depreciation such as a glut of properties, local industry closings, etc.

UTAH

NAME OF TAX:
Property Taxes.

VALUATION STANDARD:
Reasonable Fair Cash Value (not specifically defined by statute, but "value" and "full cash value" are defined as "the amount at which the property would be taken of a just debt due from a solvent debtor").

Note: After 1/1/88, tax commission will generate comparable sales and cost approach formulas that exclude dollar amount of sale not related to property value, e.g., closing costs, fees, service, etc.

REVALUATION CYCLE:
Not specified by statute.

ASSESSMENT LEVEL:
100% of reasonable fair cash value.

HOMEOWNERS EXEMPTIONS:
1. Up to $30,000 of the real and tangible personal property of disabled veterans and unmarried surviving spouses and minor orphans of the unremarried surviving spouse and minor children of a person who died as a result of military service if annual income does not exceed $24,000.

2. Real and tangible personal property of blind persons, their unremarried surviving spouses, or minor orphans, to the taxable value of $11,500.

3. Residents who are 65 or older, exempt otherwise qualified surviving spouses regardless of age, may claim a homeowner's credit against property tax bill, but not to exceed property taxes accrued up to $300 based on income.

ASSESSMENT DATE:
January 1.

LEVEL OF GOVERNMENT RESPONSIBLE FOR ASSESSMENT:
County or state for centrally assessed property.

EQUALIZATION:
Performed within counties.

ASSESSORS:
Elected for four-year term, certification not required.

STATE ISSUED MANUALS:
No manuals.

PROPERTY OWNERSHIP MAPS REQUIRED:
Yes.

PERMIT REAL PROPERTY TO BE VALUED IN CURRENT USE RATHER THAN IN A FINANCIALLY BETTER USE:
No.

MEDIAN AREA ASSESSMENT TO SALES PRICE RATIOS:
10.50.

FREQUENCY OF STATE RATIO STUDIES:
Annual.

STATE RATIO STUDY AVAILABLE TO PUBLIC:
Yes.

ADMINISTRATION OF ASSESSMENTS AND TAX LAWS:
The State Tax Commission supervises over property tax assessment by the Utah Constitution. The Commission administers the property tax law and issues guidelines to the County Assessors for their use in determining assessed values to ensure uniform assessment of property throughout the state.

Commencing in 1990 (extended to 1991), the State Tax Commission must order County Assessors to use the comparable sales and cost appraisal methods implemented by the Commission in valuing taxable property for assessment purposes which provide that intangible expenses related to the sales price of the property are excluded from such comparable values. Until 1990 (extended to 1991), County Assessors may take 80% of comparable sales and appraisal values to reflect the cost of expenses incurred in a sale of the property, thereby eliminating the 20% considered as intangible costs in arriving at fair market value.

APPEALS AND PROTESTS:
The taxpayer should first contact the County Assessor to resolve any dissatisfaction with the assessment of locally assessed property. If the taxpayer isn't satisfied with the decision of the assessor, he may file a written application for revision by the County Board of Equalization with the County Auditor complete with all the facts pertinent to the claim for reduction. The County Board of Equalization will meet and hold public hearings as early as August 2 and will continue until no later than October 1, except as otherwise specifically provided. The Board will make and issue written decisions on all appeals by October 1, unless more time is granted by the State Tax Commission.

A taxpayer dissatisfied with the decision of the County Board regarding the assessment of real or personal property may appeal that decision to the State Tax Commission by filing with the county auditor a notice of appeal within 30 days after the final action of the County Board specifying the grounds of complaint. The auditor will transmit the notice of appeal to the commission. The commission must render all decisions on real property appeals by March 1, and personal property appeals within 90 days after receipt of the appeal, and every decision made by the commission upon the appeal shall be final.

If the assessment with which the taxpayer is dissatisfied is centrally-assessed property assessed by the commission, the taxpayer must file an appeal with the commission by June 1 requesting a hearing. Such hearings must be held and a decision rendered no later than October 1, and the decision of the commission is final.

Although the decision of the State Tax Commission is generally considered as final, the taxpayer may pay the tax "under protest" and file a suit in the State District Court to recover the tax claimed to be excessive if the court action is taken within six months of paying the tax.

REFER TO STATE LAW IMPOSED BY:
Title 59, Chapter 2, of the Utah Code Annotated, as amended.

CHANGES:
1. 5/12/81 - Locally assessed realty values rolled back to 1/1/78 price levels.

2. 1984 - Utah Supreme Court ruled 1/1/78 valuation approach unconstitutional.

3. 1/1/84 - Tax Commission order effective through 12/31/84 required counties to increase the value of all locally assessed property by an index of 1.12 to equalize counties, unless a lower index was ordered for a specific county.

4. 11/1/84 - Tax Commission responsibility and authority to perform biennial ratio studies and order corrective actions.

ADDRESS (STATE):
Utah State Tax Commission
Property Tax Division
Mike Monson, Director
Heber M. Wells Building
160 East 300 South
Salt Lake City, Utah 84134

TELEPHONE:
(801) 530-6297

VERIFIED BY THIS OFFICE:
Yes.

COMMENTS:
You seldom find assessments reflective of 100% of value. The only approach to use in appeal would be comparing assessments of similar properties.

VERMONT

NAME OF TAX:
Property Tax.

VALUATION STANDARD:
Appraisal Value (estimated market value), defined as "the price which the property will bring in the market when offered for sale and purchased by another, taking into consideration all the elements of the availability of the property, its use both potential and prospective, any functional deficiencies, and all other elements such as age and condition which combine to give property a market value."

REVALUATION CYCLE:
Not specified by statute.

ASSESSMENT LEVEL:
1% of appraisal value.

HOMEOWNERS EXEMPTIONS:
1. Dwelling houses used as a home and owned by Civil War veterans and Spanish War veterans and widows entitled to federal pensions; real and personal property to the value of $10,000, owned and occupied by a veteran, his or her spouse, widow, widower or child, if one or more of them is receiving compensation for at least 50% disability, death or dependency and indemnity, or pension for disability paid through any federal military department or the veterans administration. Unremarried widows or widowers of a veteran who was qualified at the time of death are entitled to the exemption whether they receive government compensation or pension.

2. The first $15,000 of appraised value of farm buildings, homes and dwelling houses used and occupied as such started or completed during the 12 months following or preceding the annual town meeting may be exempted up to three years, if the town so votes.

3. Buildings which have been improved and occupied on pasture lands are exempt for five years if the town so votes.

ASSESSMENT DATES:
April 1.

LEVEL OF GOVERNMENT RESPONSIBLE FOR ASSESSMENT:
Township and municipal.

EQUALIZATION:
None.

ASSESSOR:
Elected to a three-year term, certification is not required.

STATE ISSUED MANUALS:
Assessment manual.

PROPERTY OWNERSHIP MAPS REQUIRED:
Yes.

PERMIT REAL PROPERTY TO BE VALUED IN CURRENT USE RATHER THAN IN A FINANCIALLY BETTER USE:
No.

MEDIAN AREA ASSESSMENT TO SALES PRICE RATIOS:
.60.

FREQUENCY OF STATE RATIO STUDIES:
Biennial.

STATE RATIO STUDY AVAILABLE TO PUBLIC:
Yes.

ADMINISTRATION OF ASSESSMENTS AND TAX LAWS:
The administration of property tax in Vermont is handled by the city, town assessors and collectors. The assessment and collection of tax for these two entities is administered by the Director, Division of Property Valuation and Review. The Commissioner of Taxes is responsible for the security of information required by law to be kept confidential, coordinating the work of the Department of Taxes and its agencies, advising the Secretary of Administration and the General Assembly regarding matters of tax policy, providing assistance to taxpayers and preparers, establishing procedures for handling appeals and maintaining records of tax returns and other data furnished to the Department of Taxes.

APPEALS AND PROTESTS:
The taxpayer must file a written grievance with the Board of Listers (assessors) within 14 days of completion of the Grand List. The date set for the completion of the Grand List is set by the Listers or Assessors (the tax rate is set by Selectmen Aldermen) based on the population of the city or town as follows:

Population Grand List Completion Date

0-1,999	May 15
2,000-2,999	May 25
3,000-3,999	June 4
4,000-7,499	June 9
7,500-9,999	June 19
10,000 and over	June 24

If the taxpayer is dissatisfied with the decision of the Board of Listers, an appeal must be filed with the Board of Civil Authority within 14 days of the mailing of the results of the grievance by the Board of Listers. The decision of the Board of Civil Authority can be appealed either to the Director of Property Valuation or the Superior Court within 21 days of the decision of the Board of Civil Authority. In cases involving real property, the value will remain the same for that year and the next two years unless the property is materially altered or a townwide reappraisal has been completed.

REFER TO STATE LAW IMPOSED BY:
Titles 1, 16, 20, 24 and 32 of the Vermont Statutes Annotated, as amended.

CHANGES:
4/19/82 - Began practice of decreasing education aid for excess listing deviation.

ADDRESS (STATE):
State of Vermont
Department of Taxes
Division of Property Valuation and Review
43 Randall Street
Waterbury, Vermont 05676

TELEPHONE:
(802) 241-3500

VERIFIED BY THIS OFFICE:
No.

VIRGINIA

NAME OF TAX:
Property Tax.

VALUATION STANDARD:
Fair Market Value (not specifically defined by statute, other than state constitutional requirement of having "to be ascertained as described by law").

REVALUATION CYCLE:
Counties-Generally every four years, unless (1) county has a population of 50,000 or less and elects a five-or six-year cycle through a local law, (2) county elects an annual assessment cycle through a local law, or (3) a biennial reassessment program is elected - see Biennial General Reassessment below.

Cities - Generally every two years, unless (1) city has a population of 30,000 or less and elects a 4-year cycle through a local law, (2) city elects an annual assessment cycle through a local law, or (3) a biennial reassessment program is elected - see Biennial General Reassessment below.

Biennial General Reassessments -

1. Counties or cities may elect a two-year reassessment cycle if they have a certified appraiser/assessor.

2. Biennial reassessment can take two years to be completed.

3. Reassessment can be performed in any year if governing body elects to do so, but two- or four-year requirement must be met thereafter.

ASSESSMENT LEVEL:
100% of fair market value.

HOMEOWNERS EXEMPTIONS:
1. Counties, cities or towns are authorized to provide exemption from, and/or deferral of, realty taxes on dwellings owned and occupied by persons aged 65 or older, or persons who are permanently and totally disabled, whose annual income isn't over $22,000 (localities may exclude the first $7,500 of income of an owner who's permanently disabled), excluding the first $6,500 of any relative of the owner other than his spouse, and whose combined net worth excluding the value of the dwelling and lot, isn't over $75,000. Localities may enact a combination program of exemptions and deferrals, in which case they may increase the income limitation to $22,000 if they have a program providing for a deferral of realty taxes on any person or persons whose total combined income levels exceed $18,000.

2. Localities may exempt for up to 10 years real estate rehabilitated for residential, commercial or industrial use.

3.   Counties, cities or towns may provide for the special assessment and valuation of all real property within its jurisdiction that's encumbered by a recorded perpetual easement permitting the inundation of such property by water.

ASSESSMENT DATES:
January 1.

LEVEL OF GOVERNMENT RESPONSIBLE FOR ASSESSMENT:
County and city.

EQUALIZATION:
Performed within county or city.

ASSESSORS:
Appointed indefinite term, certification is required.

STATE ISSUED MANUALS:
Assessment manual.

PROPERTY OWNERSHIP MAPS REQUIRED:
No.

PERMIT REAL PROPERTY TO BE VALUED IN CURRENT USE RATHER THAN IN A FINANCIALLY BETTER USE:
Certain agricultural, forest and open space land only.

MEDIAN AREA ASSESSMENT TO SALES PRICE RATIOS:
84.70.

FREQUENCY OF STATE RATIO STUDIES:
Annual.

STATE RATIO STUDY AVAILABLE TO PUBLIC:
Yes.

ADMINISTRATION OF ASSESSMENTS AND TAX LAWS:
Although property taxes are covered in the Virginia Code, the actual administration of assessing and collecting the property tax is handled at the local level.

APPEALS AND PROTESTS:
If the taxpayer is dissatisfied with the assessment of real property or personal property, the following administrative steps may be taken starting before the completion of 3 years from the last day (December 31) of the tax year:

A taxpayer dissatisfied with an assessment may apply for correction of the assessment with the County or City Real Estate Assessor. Assessment notices following a general reappraisal will usually indicate dates and times the Assessor will be available to discuss the assessment. In counties or cities having a permanent Board of Equalization and in those counties or cities in which a temporary Board of Equalization is used following a general reappraisal, such Board will convene to hear taxpayers' complaints. Notice will be given to the taxpayers at least 10 days in advance giving them the time, place and duration of the hearings and will usually specify the deadline for filing an application.

Any taxpayer dissatisfied with the results of the local hearing may appeal to the County or City Circuit Court wherein the original assessment was rendered. The appeal to the court can be filed even though the taxpayer did not avail himself of the right to apply for a correction of the assessment locally first. A claim for refund may be made within three years (five years effective 7/1/89) from the last day of the year in which the assessment was made.

If the county or city in which the appeal is heard has an appropriate ordinance, the taxpayer may be due interest on any refunded tax at a percentage not to exceed the interest charged for delinquent tax payments.

REFER TO STATE LAW IMPOSED BY:
Code of Virginia, 1950, as amended. The law furnishes the detail provisions to be followed by the local authorities, but the actual procedures for the assessment and collection of the tax is left to the local assessors and tax collectors.

CHANGES:
1.   1976 - Established Biennial General Reassessment Program - see Revaluation Cycle.

ADDRESS (STATE):
State of Virginia
Department of Taxation
Property Tax Division
Otho C.W. Fraher, Director
P.O. Box 6-L
Richmond, Virginia 23282

TELEPHONE:
(804) 367-8020

VERIFIED BY THIS OFFICE:
Yes.

COMMENTS:
Assessors do attempt to keep abreast with rapidly escalating real estate value in the State's metropolitan districts. In a mass appraisal system, many overevaluations are made. Current sales data is the best source for preparing a case for appeal.

WASHINGTON

NAME OF TAX:
Property Taxes.

VALUATION STANDARD:
True and Fair Value (not defined by statute).

REVALUATION CYCLE:
Four-year physical inspection and valuation cycle is required, unless county elects a six-year plan which must include an annual statistical update of values. Two-year cycle also permitted.

ASSESSMENT LEVEL:
100% of true and fair value.

HOMEOWNERS EXEMPTIONS:

1. Persons age 61 or older or disabled or the surviving spouse of a claimant who is age 57 or older are exempt from regular and excess levies on their residences, including the land, not to exceed one acre, and permanently attached mobile homes, as follows; if combined disposable income is $18,000 or less, a full exemption is allowed from all excess levies; a qualified person who has a combined disposable income of $14,000 or less but greater than $12,000 is exempt from regular property taxes on the greater of $24,000 or 30% of the value of the residence, or a qualified person who has a combined disposable income of $12,000 or less is exempt from all regular property taxes on the greater of $28,000 or 50% of the value of the residence.

2. Physical improvements to existing single family dwellings are exempt for the three assessment years after completion of the improvement to the extent that the improvement represents 30% or less of the value of the original structure. The exemption cannot be claimed more than once in a five-year period.

3. The true cash value of property destroyed in whole or in part, or reduced in value by more than 20% as the result of a natural disaster, must be reduced and an amount of tax abated or refunded.

4. Residents 61 or older and disabled persons and the surviving spouse age 57 or older of a claimant may defer payment of special assessments and/or realty taxes up to 80% of their equity value in their homes that are exempt from tax.

ASSESSMENT DATE:
January 1.

LEVEL OF GOVERNMENT RESPONSIBLE FOR ASSESSMENT:
County.

EQUALIZATION:

Performed both within and between counties. Department of Revenue equalizes values between counties by adjusting property type or geographic area values for state tax purposes.

ASSESSORS:

Elected to four-year term, certification not required.

STATE ISSUED MANUALS:

County Assessor's procedure manual.

PROPERTY OWNERSHIP MAPS REQUIRED:

Yes.

PERMIT REAL PROPERTY TO BE VALUED IN CURRENT USE RATHER THAN IN A FINANCIALLY BETTER USE:

Open space, farm, agricultural and timberlands are valued at their current use, forest lands are valued according to a legislatively mandated schedule.

MEDIAN AREA ASSESSMENT TO SALES PRICE RATIOS:

90.50.

FREQUENCY OF STATE RATIO STUDIES:

Annual.

STATE RATIO STUDY AVAILABLE TO PUBLIC:

Yes.

ADMINISTRATION OF ASSESSMENTS AND TAX LAWS:

The County Assessor directly administers the assessment of all property except centrally assessed property, which is determined by the Department of Revenue. The county treasurer has administrative power in the collecting the tax.

The Department of Revenue is responsible for maintaining a uniform procedure for the County Assessors to follow through the issuance of prescribed forms, publishing an assessor's manual and supplying the assessors with schedules for use in valuing taxable property.

APPEALS AND PROTESTS:

The assessment roll is generally completed by the County Assessor by May 31, but if the assessments are delayed in being completed there's usually an extension of time within which the taxpayer may appeal assessment to the County Board of Equalization.

Should the taxpayer not obtain the desired relief from the County Assessor, he may appeal to the County Board of Equalization prior to the hearings on July 15. The board will hear appeals for a period from three days to four weeks depending on the demand, but may be extended into special session if necessary. If the taxpayer is late in filing an appeal, he may request that the Board reconvene.

Centrally-assessed property, which is assessed by the State Department of Revenue, that the taxpayer thinks is overassessed should be reviewed with the Department of Revenue.

Taxpayers who are dissatisfied with the decision of the County Board of Equalization and taxpayers owning centrally assessed property who don't obtain relief from the State Department of Revenue should file an appeal with the State Tax Appeals Board. The appeal; should be filed with the County Auditor within 30 days after the issuing of the decision being appealed in duplicate, specifying the actions complained of, and the auditor will transmit one copy to the State Board of Tax Appeals.

Taxpayers dissatisfied with the decision of the State Tax Appeals Board may appeal to the State Superior Court if all taxes, penalty and interest have been paid. Taxpayers may appeal directly to the State Superior Court, eliminating any other administrative remedies, if it can be shown that the assessor refused to follow the constitutional requirements that all property be taxed equally.

REFER TO STATE LAW IMPOSED BY:
Title 84 of the Revised Code of Washington, as amended.

CHANGES:
1. 1/1/74 - Changed previous assessment level of 50% of true and fair value to current 100% level.

2. 4/20/82 - Permitted six-year revaluation cycle - see Revaluation cycle.

ADDRESS (STATE):
State of Washington
Department of Revenue
Property Tax Division
Will Rice, Director
General Administration Building
Olympia, Washington 98504-0090

TELEPHONE:
(206) 753-5503

VERIFIED BY THIS OFFICE:
Yes.

COMMENTS:
One of the more liberal States as to an open system and encouragement to appeal if dissatisfied. In some instances, assessments for prior tax years may even be appealed, if just cause can be shown as to the reason for overevaluation. Seattle area assessors seem to be more cooperative and willing to adjust assessments based on taxpayers evidence than other States' metropolitan areas.

WEST VIRGINIA

NAME OF TAX:
Property Tax.

VALUATION STANDARD:
True and Actual Value, defined as "the price for which such property would sell if voluntarily offered for sale by the owner upon such terms as such property, the value of which is sought to be ascertained, is usually sold, and not the price which might be realized if such property were sold at a forced sale."

REVALUATION CYCLE:
Not specified by statute, but State Tax Commission must recommend a revaluation cycle to the legislature 3/31/95.

ASSESSMENT LEVEL:
60% of true and actual value, but the full value standard (100% of true and actual value) must be retained until the completion of the statewide reappraisal of property (excepted completion date of 3/31/85).

Notes:

1. Values established from statewide reappraisal will be uniformly phased-in from 1986 - 1995, i.e., 10% per year.

2. For tax rate purposes, property is classified as follows:

Class II	Intangible personal property, agricultural personal property.
Class II	Agricultural and owner-occupied residential real property.
Class III	All property outside municipalities, other than Class I or II.
Class IV	All property inside municipalities, other than Class I or II.

HOMEOWNERS EXEMPTIONS:
1. The first $20,000 of assessed value of any residential realty or mobile home owned and occupied by a West Virginia resident aged 65 or older or permanently and totally disabled.

2. Persons aged 65 or older who were domiciled in the state during any part of the year preceding that in which a homeowner files for tax relief, and whose gross household income isn't over $5,000 for such year, are eligible for tax relief according to a percentage ranging from 75% to 30% of the amount of real property tax, which is in excess of a percentage of gross household income ranging from 0.5% if such income is over $500 but not over $1,000 to 4.5% if such income is over $4,500 but not over $5,000. If property taxes exceed $125, the amount for tax relief purposes is limited to $125. Claims for relief must be filed with the State Tax Commissioner between July 1 and September 30.

3. Persons 65 or older and permanently and totally disabled persons are allowed an exemption equal to $20,000 of assessed value of a homestead owned, occupied and used by them exclusively for residential purposes.

ASSESSMENT DATE:
July 1.

LEVEL OF GOVERNMENT RESPONSIBLE FOR ASSESSMENT:
County.

EQUALIZATION:
None.

ASSESSORS:
Elected to four-year term, certification is not required.

STATE ISSUED MANUALS:
Assessment manual.

PROPERTY OWNERSHIP MAPS REQUIRED:
Yes.

PERMIT REAL PROPERTY TO BE VALUED IN CURRENT USE RATHER THAN IN A FINANCIALLY BETTER USE:
No.

MEDIAN AREA ASSESSMENT TO SALES PRICE RATIOS:
21.

FREQUENCY OF STATE RATIO STUDIES:
Annual.

STATE RATIO STUDY AVAILABLE TO PUBLIC:
Yes.

ADMINISTRATION OF ASSESSMENTS AND TAX LAWS:
The County Assessors value the property within their county and the county collects its own taxes. It's the duty of the State Tax Commission to meet with the county assessors and administer over the assessments for the purpose of securing a uniform valuation of property within the State.

APPEALS AND PROTESTS:
The assessor prepares the assessment rolls but isn't required to notify taxpayers of any increase in value. However, valuations must be completed by January 30 and the assessments must be presented to the County Court by February 1 for review and equalization. The County Court may only rule in a matter of value with any matters of the classification or taxability being the duty and responsibility of the State Tax Commissioners. The County Court must complete its review by February 28 and advise the taxpayer of any intended increase in value at least five days in advance in writing.

Since the protest of matters involving the classification or taxability of property is handled differently than matters of valuation, such procedures are described separately below:

Classification and Taxability of Property:

If a taxpayer thinks that part or all his property has been misclassified or that such property shouldn't be taxable, a written protest should be filed with the assessor explaining the basis which the taxpayer's conclusion. The assessor will review the appeal with the taxpayer and advise the taxpayer of the decision in writing. Any taxpayer who is not satisfied with the county assessor's decision may request that the Tax Commissioner certify the protest.

The decision of the State Tax Commissioner may be appealed to the Circuit Court within 30 days of the court adjournment. The Circuit Court generally has jurisdiction only over matters concerning mistakes and errors. Should the taxpayer be dissatisfied with the decision of the State Tax Commissioner or the County Circuit Court, an appeal may be made to the Supreme Court of Appeals if the matter involves property valued at $50,000 or more.

Valuation of Property:

The taxpayer, upon learning of the assessment, may review the matter with the assessor or bring it before the County Court, which meets annually starting no later than February 1 to review and to equalize of assessments. If not satisfied with the assessment, the taxpayer may file an appeal with the County Circuit Court within 30 days of its adjournment (the State Tax Commissioner doesn't resolve matters of valuation). The decision of the County Circuit Court may be appealed to the Supreme Court of Appeal if the matter involves property valued at $50,000 or more.

REFER TO STATE LAW IMPOSED BY:
Chapter 11 and 11-A of the West Virginia Code of 1931, as amended.

CHANGES:
1.   11/2/82 - Assessment level changed from previous 100% of true and actual to current 60% level, but see Assessment Level.

2.   1983 - First statewide reappraisal of property started.

ADDRESS (STATE):
State of West Virginia
State Tax Department (P.O. Drawer 2389)
Charleston, West Virginia 25328

TELEPHONE:
(304) 348-3333

VERIFIED BY THIS OFFICE:
No.

WISCONSIN

NAME OF TAX:
Property Taxes.

VALUATION STANDARD:
Full Value, defined as the value "which could ordinarily be obtained thereof at private sale."

REVALUATION CYCLE:
County Assessor systems (at present, only one county is in this system) - every four years. Other tax districts - not specified by statute. State-assessed manufacturing property-every four years.

ASSESSMENT LEVEL:
100% of full value is required by law, each tax districts must access property at full value at least once in every five-year period.

HOMEOWNERS EXEMPTIONS:
1. A Wisconsin Property Tax Deferral Loan Program is available to State residents age 65 or older. The Property Tax Deferral Loan Program provides loans up to $1,800 to qualified homeowners. Principal and interest are repaid when ownership of the home is transferred or the recipient stops living in the house. The loan becomes a lien against the property.

2. The Wisconsin Homestead Credit Program reduces the burden of property taxes on low and moderate income residents through a direct payment to the individual. The amount of the benefit varies depending on the total household income and the property tax liability. Full year residency and income limits of less than $18,000 do apply. The maximum credit has been increased to $1,350 for those who qualify.

ASSESSMENT DATES:
January 1.

LEVEL OF GOVERNMENT RESPONSIBLE FOR ASSESSMENT:
County, township and municipal are responsible for residential, commercial and agricultural property. State is responsible for manufacturing property.

EQUALIZATION:
Yes.

ASSESSORS:
Elected and appointed (elected two years: townships appointed three years; city and village appointed indefinte), certification is required.

STATE ISSUED MANUALS:
Property assessment manual.

PROPERTY OWNERSHIP MAPS REQUIRED:
No.

PERMIT REAL PROPERTY TO BE VALUED IN CURRENT USE RATHER THAN IN A FINANCIALLY BETTER USE:
No, currently at highest and best use.

MEDIAN AREA ASSESSMENT TO SALES PRICE RATIOS:
1988 - 92.66%.

FREQUENCY OF STATE RATIO STUDIES:
Annual.

STATE RATIO STUDY AVAILABLE TO PUBLIC:
Yes.

ADMINISTRATION OF ASSESSMENTS AND TAX LAWS:
The Department of Revenue has the responsibility to supervise over the administration of the assessment of property taxes in the State. The department has appointed a supervisor of assessments for each property assessment district in the state. These supervisors work with the local assessors to ensure that they follow the assessor's manual and maintain equitable assessments throughout the state.

APPEALS AND PROTESTS:
The taxpayer may protest the assessed value placed on any real property owned by him and located within the State of Wisconsin.

The Department of Revenue has prepared several booklets which explain the general property tax system in Wisconsin. If you would like a copy of "A guide for Property Owners", you can contact the department at the previous address.

The procedure for appealing the assessment of non-manufacturing property commences with a discussion with the local assessor. If dissatisfied with the results by the local assessor, the taxpayer may file a written appeal to the Board of Review at any time prior to adjournment. The board commences its hearings on the second Monday in May each year and continues until all appeals have been heard. In counties where a County Assessor system has been established, a County Assessor will assume the functions otherwise performed by local assessors and the board of review will be a county board rather than a local board.

In first class cities, such as Milwaukee, the taxpayer must first appeal before the Tax Commissioner prior to the third Monday in April before appealing to the Board of Review, which will commence its hearings upon the completion of the tax rolls. The decision of the board of review may be appealed by the taxpayer within 90 days of the issuing the board's decision.

REFER TO STATE LAW IMPOSED BY:
Chapters 70 and 73 through 77 of the Wisconsin Statutes, as amended.

CHANGES:
1.   1/1/74 - Department of Revenue assumed assessment functions for manufacturing property.

2. 1986 - Provided for Department of Revenue supervision of municipalities failing to meet 90% minimum assessment level.

3. 3/10/86 - Directs appeal of local board of review decision to the Department of Revenue under Wisconsin statute 70.85 was reestablished.

ADDRESS (STATE):
State of Wisconsin
Department of Revenue
Bureau of Property Tax
Glenn Holmes, Director
P.O. Box 8933
Madison, Wisconsin 53708

TELEPHONE:
(608) 266-1187

VERIFIED BY THIS OFFICE:
Yes.

COMMENTS:
State assessment process and manuals are considered by many national authorities to be a model for other States to copy. In the Milwaukee area the assessors tend to assess properties so close to 100% that property owners can prove overassessment by current market sales.

WYOMING

NAME OF TAX:
Property Taxes (Ad Valorem Tax).

VALUATION STANDARD:
Fair Value, established "in accordance with values and procedures prescribed by the State Board of Equalization."

REVALUATION CYCLE:
Not specified by statute, other than to require that "all property shall be annually listed, valued, and assessed for taxation."

ASSESSMENT LEVEL:
100% of fair value.

HOMEOWNERS EXEMPTIONS:
1. Veterans and their unremarried widows are entitled to an exemption. The annual exemption for veterans is limited to $2,000 of assessed value and not to exceed a tax benefit of $800. Veterans receiving the $800 exemption and who have a service-connected disability are entitled to an additional exemption not to exceed $2,000 of assessed value times the ratio of the percent of disability to 100%.

2. A credit is allowed for homesteads of persons who occupy the homestead as their home and principal residence. If the dwelling and land (not to exceed two acres) is owned by the same person and if the dwelling has been occupied since the beginning of the calendar year by the applicant, the credit is $1,115 times the mill levy to be applied against the property if the dwelling and land have a combined assessed value of less than $5,600 or $560 times the mill levy to be applied against the property if the dwelling and land have a combined assessed value of at least $6,160 but less than $8,200. If the land on which the dwelling is located isn't owned by the same person owning the dwelling and if the dwelling has been occupied since the beginning of the calendar year by the applicant, the amount of the credit is $625 times the mill levy to be applied against the property if the dwelling has an assessed value of less than $10,200.

ASSESSMENT DATES:
February 1.

LEVEL OF GOVERNMENT RESPONSIBLE FOR ASSESSMENT:
County.

EQUALIZATION:
Performed both within and between counties. State Board of Equalization equalizes assessed values between counties by percentage adjustments to total values of property classes and through orders to county boards of equalization to make necessary corrections.

ASSESSORS:
Elected to four-year terms, certification is not required.

STATE ISSUED MANUALS:
Appraisal manual.

PROPERTY OWNERSHIP MAPS REQUIRED:
No.

PERMIT REAL PROPERTY TO BE VALUED IN CURRENT USE RATHER THAN IN A FINANCIALLY BETTER USE:
No.

MEDIAN AREA ASSESSMENT TO SALES PRICE RATIO:
6.60.

FREQUENCY OF STATE RATIO STUDIES:
None.

STATE RATIO STUDY AVAILABLE TO PUBLIC:
No.

ADMINISTRATION OF ASSESSMENTS AND TAX LAWS:
The County Assessor will determine the assessed value on all property that isn't assessed by the State Board of Equalization, and the county treasurer collects all property taxes. The State Board of Equalization has authority by the State Constitution to administer over the property tax and adjust any assessment determined by the County Assessor to equalize the assessments throughout the State.   The State Board also furnishes the County Assessors with guidelines for their use in determining the assessed value of property not assessed by the State.

APPEALS AND PROTESTS:
A taxpayer receiving an assessment from the County Assessor that he believes to be excessive should first send a written statement to the assessor giving the reasons for the grievance and requesting a meeting or hearing to try to resolve the difference.

If the taxpayer doesn't obtain the relief he's seeking from the assessor, he should file a formal appeal within 15 days from receipt of the notice with the County Board of Equalization. The appeal should be under oath and should specify the reasons why the taxpayer thinks the assessment is incorrect. The County Board will commence hearings on the fourth Monday in May and will continue for no more than seven days. The board will reconvene on the second Monday in June and will continue for no more than six days. The taxpayer can appeal the decision of the County Board of Equalization if he thinks the decisions aren't satisfactory by filing a written appeal with the State Board of Equalization, stating in full the reason for the appeal, within 30 days from the entry of a decision of a County Board of Equalization.

Should the taxpayer be dissatisfied with the decision of the State Board of Equalization, he can appeal to the State District Court in the county where the property is located.

REFER TO STATE LAW IMPOSED BY:
Title 39, Chapters 1 through 5, of the Wyoming Statutes 1977, am amended.

CHANGES:
None.

ADDRESS (STATE):
State of Wyoming
Department of Revenue and Taxation
Ad Valorem Tax Division
122 West 25th Street
Cheyenne, Wyoming 82002

TELEPHONE:
(307) 777-7215

VERIFIED BY THIS OFFICE:
No.

GLOSSARY

Ad Valorem	According to value.
Appeal	The act of filing a grievance against an assessment.
Appellant/Grievant	Taxpayer filing appeal or for whom the appeal is being filed.
Appraisal	An opinion of value, supported by evidence.
Arm's Length Sale	A sale between two parties, neither of whom is related to nor under abnormal pressure from any source.
Assessed Value	Market value or legally authorized fraction thereof assigned to a property for tax purposes.
Assessment	Official act of discovering, listing and appraising property for *ad valorem* tax purposes.
Assessment Level	The percentage of full value at which property is assessed.
Cash Equivalency	Indicated value after factoring sales price by the monetary value of the special financing conditions pertaining to the sale.
Depreciation	Loss from upper limit of value, from all causes, of property having a limited economic life: A. *Physical* - Normal wear and tear; B. *Functional* - Impairment of functional capacity or efficiency; C. *Economic* - Impairment of desirability arising from economic forces extraneous to property itself.
Effective Age	Number of years indicated by the building's condition.
Equalization	The process of providing uniform, aggregate assessments between townships and/or counties (see multiplier).
Equalized Assessed Value	The assessed value multiplied by the state equalization factor; gives the value of the property from which the tax rate is calculated after deducting homestead exemptions, if applicable.
Equalized Value	The assessed value multiplied by the state or local multiplier, giving the value of the property to which the tax rate is applied.

Full Value	(Market Value) The highest price estimated in terms of money which a property would bring in a sale between a willing seller and willing buyer.
Gross Rent Multiplier (GRM)	Factor expressing relationship between gross rent and property value.
Improvements	Improvements to the land, things affixed to the land (building, fences, paving, etc.)
Level of Assessments	Indicated statutory percentage of full value by which property is assessed in that jurisdiction.
Levy	The amount of money a taxing body certifies to be raised, often subject to statutory limitations.
Market Value	The money that probably will be arrived at through fair negotiations between a willing buyer and a willing seller, taking into consideration the property's use.
Multipliers or Equalization Factors (Township, County,etc)	Factors that may be applied to assessments to bring aggregate-assessed valuation for a jurisdiction to the mandated level of assessments.
Notice of Revision	A notice mailed to the property owner when a property's assessed valuation is changed by the assessing officials. Noted upon the form are the assessed valuation, property number, township, name of owner, date, and cost of the newspaper in which the assessment is published.
Parcel	A defined area of land, with or without improvements, entered as a separate item on the assessment rolls for the purpose of taxation.
Permanent Index Number (PIN) or Parcel Identifications Systems	Numbering system that defines ownership of a parcel, its location on the tax maps or tax roll entry.
Principle of Substitution	A property's market value tends to be set by the cost of acquiring an equally desirable and valuable substitute property (applies to all three traditional approaches to value: cost, market and income).

Property Record Card　The assessor's record of individual property appraisals used for assessment purposes. Recorded upon the card are size, condition, details of construction, a sketch of any improvements and other information.

Quadrennial　Four-year period often used as a measure of time for which a property may be valued before re-evaluation. **biennial** - same as quadrennial except it's a two-year period; **triennial** same as quadrennial except it's a three-year period.

Real Property　Sum of the tangible and intangible rights in land and improvements.

Real Estate　Expenses Operating expenses considered ordinary and typical to keep real property functional and rented (excluding interest).

Replacement Cost　Cost of producing building or improvement having the same utility, but using modern materials, design and workmanship.

Sales Ratio Study　An analysis of the percentage relationship of assessed value to actual market value for real property in certain categories and geographic areas.

Tax Rate　Rate by which assessed valuations are multiplied to determine the tax dollars, generally shown as dollars per hundred ($9.00 per hundred, same as .09).

Taxing Body　A governmental organization that levies a tax.

Taxing District　A territorial area under the taxing body's jurisdiction.

Units of Comparison　Common measure of value extracted from comparable sale properties and applied to property being valued ($ per square foot, $ per room, $ per acre).

BIBLIOGRAPHY

The information contained in the State-by-State Summary was researched from printed material sent to me from the various states. As well as:

Source: National Property Tax Manuals, Vertex, Inc.,
Berwyn, PA 19312
Printed with permission of Vertex, Inc.

Source: Commerce Clearing House, Inc.
Publishers of Topical Law Reports

Source: New York State Board of Equilization and
Asessment-Valuation and Assessment Statndards in
the States, May 1986

The comments in the State-by-State Summaries were provided by R. J. "Les" Arling, national real estate tax consultant/trainer and Certified Rela Estate Appraiser.

LIST OF FIGURES

INDEX

Dear Friend:

Thank you for purchasing **DIGGING FOR GOLD IN YOU OWN BACK-YARD:** *THE COMPLETE HOMEOWNERS GUIDE TO LOWERING YOUR REAL ESTATE TAXES.* Since the author plans to revise and expand this book with each new printing, we are interested in what you think of it. Please use the space below to tell us your opinion of this book: what you liked, or how much money you saved, and where you feel it could be improved. Thank you very much for your comments and suggestions.

Sincerely,
R.E.I. Press

Lynn Ongman
Editor

_____
_____
_____
_____
_____
_____
_____
_____
_____
_____
_____
_____
_____
_____
_____

( ) Check here and sign your name, if we may quote you in our National Publicity Campaign - T.V. • Cable • Radio • Print • Mail

_____   _____   _____
        Signature   Occupation   Date

ORDER BLANK

( ) I would like to order additional copies for friends and relatives of...

DIGGING FOR GOLD IN YOUR OWN BACKYARD

THE COMPLETE HOMEOWNERS GUIDE TO

LOWERING YOUR REAL ESTATE TAXES

@ $19.95 ea.

I understan͏ ... ͏or any reason,
no question

( ) I do not wi ... ͏ailing list so I will
receive any ... ͏e of a new
edition of t

Please send me __

SHIPPING:
Please add $3.05 f ... ook. Airmail is
$4.50 per book.

SALES TAX:
Please add 6.75% ... residents.

Your Name:_____

Address: _____

City:_____

Ship To (if differe

Name: _____

Address: _____

City:_____